D1247148

"A powerful story of self-discovery, survival in the wild. In its darkest passages, [*Jungle*] is a Conradian tale of men at odds with themselves and each other in the very heart of darkness. As in other classics in the literature of survival, Ghinsberg describes the blend of physical courage, practical knowledge and quiet spirituality that allows him to survive the deadliest threats of the wilderness."

The Los Angeles Times

"A thrilling book . . . one man's amazing adventure opened up the Bolivian wilderness to the world."

The Washington Post

"Simply breathtaking. Yossi's story of survival haunted me for weeks."

Bryce Courtenay, author of *The Power of One*

"A damn good read . . . it has an immediacy that puts the reader right there in the biting, clinging, rash-provoking jungle. Its close-to-the-bone experiences make Redmond O'Hanlon's *In Trouble Again* look like *The Bobbsey Twins Go to the Circus*."

Lawrence Millian, author of *Last Places*

"A gripping story set in a steamy exotic locale . . . the descriptions of the Amazon and its hardships are vivid and complete. The fantasies he shares are amongst the book's most memorable passages . . . a thing well worth reading about."

Brad Newsham, author of *All the Right Places*

"The brutal politics of rainforest exploitation provide a somber backdrop, but it's the gripping foreground action here that makes this yarn . . . A strong bet for armchair adventure."

Kirkus Reviews

"A real page-turner, with all of the elements of a great adventure saga, [*Jungle*] could prove to be the from-out-of-nowhere bestseller of the season."

Destinations Magazine

"This is an inspirational and apparently very honest book by a man who has been deeply affected by his death-cheating experiences, and is well equipped to share those experiences in a most moving way."

The Sunday Mail

"Told simply and yet with a novelist's eye for structure and drama, the story unfolds like a nightmare move. A good adventure yarn, made all the more haunting because of its basis in truth."

The Sun Herald

"A most graphic account of a struggle against both a hostile environment and other people, is well described."

The Canberra Times

"His tale represents a survival epic, being perhaps most valuable in its cautionary aspects; a guide to what not to do in the Amazon."

The Age

" . . . it provides intriguing glimpses into the way such isolation warps and distorts the human mind. A tale of triumph over adversity . . . 'real life' survival saga, it is."

The Big Issue

"[*Jungle*] should be compulsory reading for anyone who wants to know just how horrible those trekky adventure-type holidays can get when things go wrong. Your Lonely Planet guide never explains how to deal with hungry leopards."

Ralph Magazine

"It's a wild tale about a beautiful, unforgiving, enchanted land that lured him into a nightmarish hell of self-discovery."

LA Village View

"One of those amazing survival stories that almost brings you [to] a cold sweat just from reading it. Once you start it you won't put it down."

The Mercury

"Gripping as an adventure story, [*Jungle*] also has profound things to tell us about human nature. I'll be surprised if a more memorable travel book is published this year."

The Sunday Star Times

"Yossi found himself alone in the jungle for weeks where he was subjected to jaguar attacks, starvation, injury, and other horrors. These are outlined in grueling detail in this rather ripping yarn about human fortitude and survival in one of the last truly wild places on the planet."

Brisbane News

"As we follow the *mochileros* into one of the harshest terrains on the planet, we are witness to both beauty and horror on a grand scale."

Manly Daily

"Yossi's straightforward style tells a grimly compelling story of self-discovery and survival that draws you in and refuses to let go . . . A story that will stay with you long after the last page is turned."

The Geelong Advertiser

"It makes a wonderfully involving read. Fact is once again proven to be much, much stranger than fiction."

Ballarat Courier

jungle

Yossi Ghinsberg

jungle

A Harrowing True Story of Survival

BOOMERANG
NEW MEDIA

AUSTIN · LONDON · MULLUMBIMBY

Published by Boomerang New Media,
100 Congress Avenue, 22nd floor, Austin, TX 78701

First published in Hebrew in 1985 by Zmora-Bitan Publishers,
Tel Aviv, Israel. Hebrew Rights Copyright © 1985 by Zmora-Bitan Publishers,
P.O.B. 22383, Tel Aviv, Israel.

First published in English by Random House, Inc., New York, and simultaneously in
Canada by Random House of Canada Limited, Toronto. English translation by
Yael Politis and Stanley Young.

Published in Australia in 1999 by Pan Macmillan Australia Pty Limited,
Sydney, Australia.

Author photograph: Wolfgang Schuler
Jacket design: Greenleaf Book Group LP

Submit all requests for reprinting to:
Greenleaf Book Group LP
4425 Mopac South, Suite 600
Austin, TX 78735
(512) 891-6100

Library of Congress Control Number: 2005931038

ISBN-10: 0-9771719-0-6
ISBN-13: 978-0-9771719-0-3

Printed in the United States of America

10 9 8 7 6 5 4 3 2 1 08 07 06 05

For Marcus

Acknowledgments

I am filled with gratitude for life itself—if I've learned nothing else from the following story, I've learned that the gift of life is not to be taken for granted. Nothing is mundane; it is all a miracle.

With that said, it must be sweet serendipity that brought my gorgeous wife into my life. Thank you, my Bella Belinda, for beautifying my environments, for being my first mirror projecting such a loving image of myself, and for the world of beauty that is in you, the beholder. I love you.

Thank you, my two daughters, Mia and Cayam, who teach me unconditional love, unshakable trust, and total acceptance. I am constantly overwhelmed by your grace. You bring deeper meaning to my existence, and through you, evolution makes sense.

To my parents: from you I learned that being a happy old person is the purpose of life, for our last moments color it all. I pay respect to you, for my debt will never be paid.

My brother Moshe and his wife Miri are my heroes whom I look to for inspiration. Their compassion is intrinsic, and service is their way of life. Such fine specimens of humanity are indeed rare to find.

It is said that each one of us is personally assigned a guardian angel. Well mine has been exposed. He goes by the name of Ron Fremder, and a real angel he is.

"When a student is ready, the teacher will appear" was just an adage until you manifested in my life, Rohm Kest, my sensei. Your teachings have transformed me—I bow to you every day.

I am a fortunate man of many assets, and these are my friends. Like solid rocks in calm and rough waters, in them I rejoice and find respite. I love you all, though can only mention a few: Alexio and Veronica, Amir and Nirupa, Ari and Adi, Avishai and Anita, Christopher, Darren, Gall and Caroline, Jimi the shaman, Margaret, Marion, Michelle and Vince, Stanley and Janice, Tal and Maya, Tom and Pamela, and Uzi the Zadik. You are my tribe.

This book upsurges at this special time through the burning passion of Meg La Borde and her team at Greenleaf Book Group. When work is a labor of true love laced with a sense of calling, we cease to work and become purposeful. Thank you.

Finally to Bharat Mitra and Boomerang New Media—thank you for making it all possible. What goes around comes around.

Queste? Queste?—Helaqui! Helaqui!
(Where is it? Where is it?—It is here! It is here!)
—Vesty Pakos

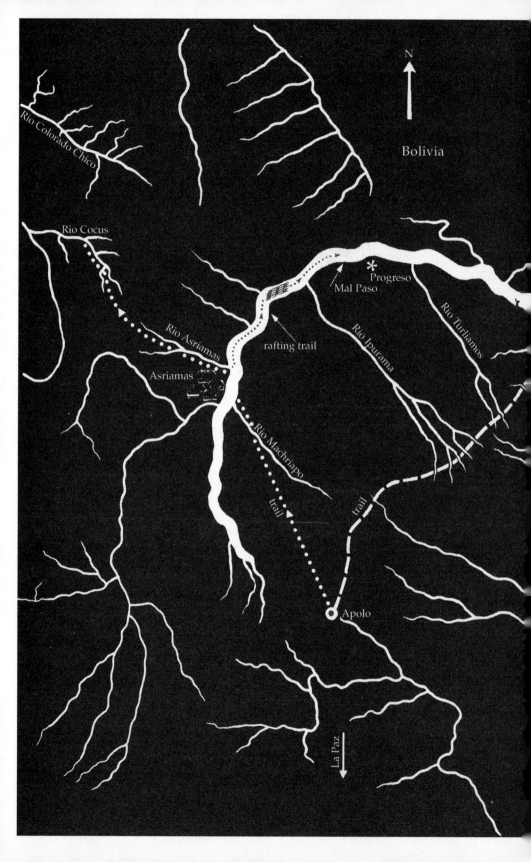

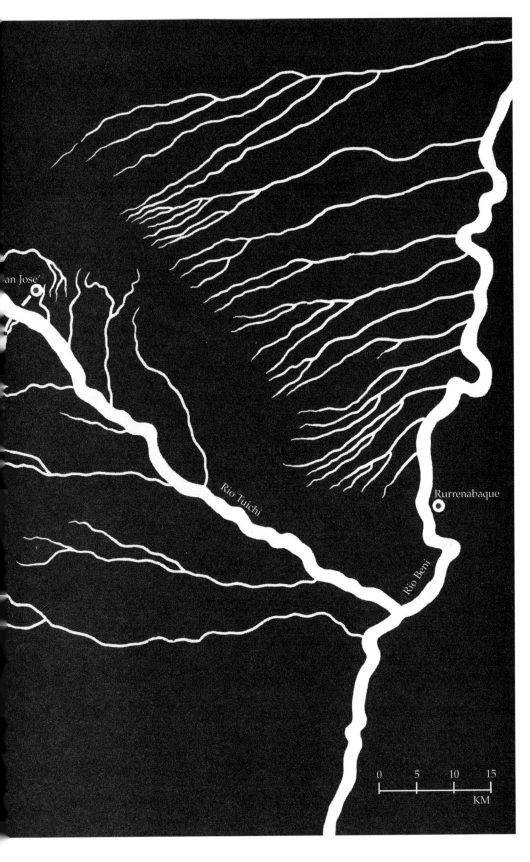

CHAPTER 1

MEETING MARCUS

If I had never fallen in with Marcus in Puno, I might never have met Kevin or crossed paths with Karl. If I hadn't met Karl that morning in La Paz, Kevin might well have spent Christmas with his family, and poor old Marcus might still be wandering South America with his girl. But that's not the way things happened.

When I arrived in the Peruvian town of Puno, my knee was hurting badly; walking was terribly painful. A French *mochilero* (backpacker) offered me coca leaves to chew.

"Have a little of this," he said. "You'll feel better."

I put a pinch of leaves in my mouth and chewed on the strange little rock, another gift from the Frenchman. The rock, made of pressed liana ashes, extracts the active alkaloids from the leaves and causes them to ferment in the mouth. Without the rock there's no fermentation, no effect, no high. All it did was put my tongue and the roof of my mouth to sleep.

I rose early the next morning feeling better nevertheless. The boat to the island of Taquile would be leaving at eight o'clock. The truth is, I could have headed straight to Cuzco, where all the mochileros start out on their trips to the legendary city of Machu Picchu, the ancient Inca capital, but I preferred to make a brief detour and visit the storied island.

Taquile rises out of Lake Titicaca, the highest navigable lake in the world. The shores of the lake were filthy, but when one looked out toward the horizon, the water was shimmering. Mountainous islands peeked through the mist that blanketed the lake. It was a beautiful sight.

I had no difficulty finding the ferry. In effect, it found me.

"Taquile or Los Uros?" a small boy asked me.

"Taquile," I answered.

He led me to a boat on which a few people were already waiting: a few young Germans and a group of French youths, who were staying at the same hotel as I was. I took a seat close to the stern and read a book.

Soon it was time to start. The pilot, an Indian, stuck out a long pole, which he used as both rudder and oar, and gestured to the boy to cast off the rope securing the nose of the boat and push us away from the dock.

"*Espera, espera* (wait)!" a mochilero running, panting, cried breathlessly, and climbed down into the boat. "I almost missed it," he said to the Indian in Spanish, "*gracias.*"

He sat beside me, and as I moved to make room for him, he smiled at me. "You're Israeli," he said in English.

I looked down at the book I was reading, Albert Camus's *A Happy Death* in an English translation. I was astonished. "How could you tell?"

"I knew right off. You Israelis have taken to the roads in droves."

"My name's Yossi," I said.

"Nice to meet you. I'm Marcus. I came here straight from the train station. Lucky for me I caught the boat. I would have had to wait a whole day for the next one."

Marcus went on talking as if we were old friends. "The train was the pits. I left Juliaca early this morning. It's impossible to get anything to eat on that train. I haven't had a bite. I hope we get to the island fast. I'm starving."

I pulled a roll, some cheese, and an orange out of my pack and offered them to him.

"Thanks," Marcus said. "I've noticed Israelis always share whatever they have. I appreciate it."

He made himself a sandwich of the roll and cheese and ate hungrily. The orange was his dessert.

"I'll pay you back when we get to the island."

"Forget it," I told him. "I've heard things are expensive in Taquile. If it's all right with you, we could stay together tonight and share our food."

"I'm in."

Marcus turned to the Germans and had a lively conversation with them in their language. Then he turned to the French group and spoke French with them. He had a compelling personality, and in no time we were all acquainted, talking and joking like him.

"Are you German?" I asked him.

"Swiss," he replied.

We were almost to the island when the boat broke down. The engine just went dead. The boatman quickly located the trouble, and before long he had the engine running again. Marcus noticed that he had injured his finger during the repair, however, and whipped a first-aid kit out of his pack. He disinfected the Indian's finger and asked me to cut a strip of adhesive tape. But, no, my efforts weren't precise enough. He took the roll himself and cut a neater strip—just so—then went back to his bandaging. The man thanked him with a wide smile.

Moments later we were in Taquile. From the dock we climbed up toward the village along a steep path cut into solid rock. The higher we went, the more my lungs fought for air. I climbed two steps and stopped. Climbed and stopped.

"Take it easy," Marcus encouraged me. "We're in no hurry."

"And what about you?" I asked.

"Ah, Swiss Alps," he said with a smile. "I was in the services over there."

We found ourselves a room in the village, with mud walls and a wooden platform for a bed. We spread our sleeping bags out and prepared a meal. Marcus made coffee on a small kerosene burner he carried; I split the rolls and carefully assembled cheese, onion, and tomato sandwiches. Although we had only just met and despite the fact that I had plans of my own, Marcus started planning a trip we might take together.

"I haven't seen Machu Picchu yet," I explained, "so I'll be heading back to Cuzco."

"No, no, come along with me to La Paz," he urged.

"Machu Picchu," I said, "and then I'm planning to cut across Brazil. I've been thinking about leaving from Puerto Maldonado, not far from Cuzco, by way of the Madre de Dios River; it cuts through Peru and runs into the Amazon."

From there my plan called for me to follow the Amazon to its mouth near Belém on the Atlantic coast. I traced the route on the map. "There are a lot of interesting little villages on the way, and anyway I love the jungle. Why don't you come along with me?"

"Thanks for offering. It sounds like a great plan, a real adventure, but I'm at the end of this trip. I'll spend some time in La Paz, maybe take a few side trips, maybe buy up some handmade vests to ship back to Switzerland, but nothing very ambitious."

We found Taquile different from other Peruvian villages, and it was easy to tell a Taquile islander from a Peruvian Indian. The island people seemed nobler, cleaner, handsomer, healthier. They dressed differently too. They all wore the same hat, the same *chaleco* (embroidered vest), and broad trousers with an embroidered belt. The embroidery of Taquile is known all over Latin America for its beauty and fine quality, and it's done exclusively by the men, though the women spin and dye the wool.

The island is a kind of commune of about fifty families managed by a community council. Life is tranquil. The men sit about doing their embroidery and gossiping, while the women toil in the fields. The rocky soil is difficult to cultivate and nothing grows there except potatoes. In the village itself are a small grocery and two or three restaurants. In one of them Marcus and I met the French group from the boat.

There were five of them, three girls—Dede, Annick, and Jacqueline—and two boys—Jacques and Michel. We drank the local *maté* (herb tea; there are many varieties served all over Latin America) and chatted. They preferred speaking French, and I didn't understand a word, but Dede smiled at me, and I smiled back. She was on the plump side with a pretty face and short hair that gave her a mischievous look. She smiled again, and I asked her to come sit by me and began speaking English with her.

The dinner was delicious: coarse bread, two eggs apiece, and fried potatoes. For dessert another cup of maté; the natives think it alleviates the effects of high altitude. Then home. A mochilero changes beds almost every night, but every place he rolls his sleeping bag open is home.

Marcus and I went back to our room. He unpacked his *charango* (a small musical instrument like a mandolin but made from armadillo shell and wood) and strummed it. Marcus was a wonderful player, and I listened, enchanted.

"Now listen to this, Yossi," he said. "It's one I wrote for a girl I was in love with. Her name was Monica. She was mine for nine years, and now she's left me."

"Far, far from my heart . . ." he started to sing sadly.

I had known Marcus only a short time, and already he was sharing his most intimate secrets with me. Monica had been the love of his life. When they met, she was fourteen; he was five years older. Almost ten years had passed since then. Marcus became a schoolteacher; Monica, an academic. She thought his horizons too narrow and challenged him to broaden himself, to travel, so he went to South America. But out of sight, out of mind. With Marcus gone, she had fallen for another. The song was so doleful, pouring out of a thoroughly broken heart, that I myself grew sad.

We spent the day in Taquile together with the Frenchwomen: me with the smiling Dede, Marcus with Annick. Then we all took the boat back to Puno.

Lake Titicaca was stormy, and we had to take cover on the Uros, drifting "islands" of *totora* reeds (Thor Heyerdahl built his vessel *Ra* from such reeds). We finally made it to Puno, soaking wet, but in high spirits.

In Puno I went back to my old hotel, and Marcus moved in with me. Again he brewed tea on his kerosene burner.

"So what do you say, Yossi? Are you really leaving for Cuzco tomorrow?" he asked.

"Yes," I said. "I've already got the schedule for the morning train."

"I don't get you," he argued. "Why not come along to La Paz, just for a week, and then you can come back to Peru?"

"I would like to come along, I really would," I said, "but I can't change my plans. I don't want to miss Machu Picchu, and I don't have enough money to do both."

Marcus wouldn't give in. "Look, Yossi. You shared food with me before you even knew me. Now let me treat you to a visit to La Paz." He stuck two fingers into the hem of his pants leg, pulled a few bills out, and held thirty dollars up to me. "Please, take the money, Yossi. It means nothing to me. It will only be worth something if you use it to come along."

"I couldn't take it, Marcus," I answered, embarrassed. "I appreciate it. I do. But you have nothing but the pack on your back, the same as me, and there's no reason in the world why I should take your money."

Marcus began reciting a poem. I don't remember the title or the poet's name, but I'll never forget its content or the way he recited it. It was about a man who never wanted to take anything from anyone and never learned how to give.

The next morning we were all on the bus to La Paz—Marcus and me and the five French mochileros.

CHAPTER 2

THE MOCHILEROS

Although La Paz lies in a valley, it is still the highest capital city in the world, almost twelve thousand feet above sea level. Despite modernization it has retained the character of a prosperous colonial city. We arrived on a bus crowded with locals. I wandered around the monumental sites: Plaza Murillo, where all the major government buildings have been located since colonial days, and San Francisco Square, where the Jesuit friars built their monastery in the seventeenth century. In the narrow alleyways that lead away from these plazas are shops selling the finest handicrafts of the continent.

Up Sagarnaga Street are the wooden booths of the bustling witchcraft market of Pachamama, the Andean goddess of the earth. The women hawk good-luck charms, healing herbs, and spell-brewing grasses, never revealing the true nature of their wares.

Peddlers swarm the sidewalks selling pastries and fruit. Bolivian music blares from record shops: the sounds of the *charango*, flute, and *samponía*, the words part Quechua, the Inca language, and part Spanish.

During the gleaming morning hours the peddler women, all wearing the same blue smock and hat, offer *api* and *tohori*, delicious beverages made of corn. The steaming drinks are served together with hot rolls or fresh donuts dipped in honey.

Along Sixteenth of July Street, which the locals call the *prado* (promenade), the high school girls dressed in white smocks linger during recess. They tease every passing gringo, whistling and calling, "*Te amo* (I love you)."

At noontime the old people, leaning against the church in their knitted hats, spit out wads of coca leaves, getting ready for lunch. After they've eaten their fill, the pouch comes out, and a pinch of fresh leaves goes into their mouths along with the extract-ing stones.

In the evenings the prado is packed. Strolling youngsters and adults fill the theaters, cinemas, and restaurants.

Marcus, Dede, and Annick were staying at the Rosario Hotel. Jacques and Jacqueline went back to Peru together, and Michel went on to Brazil. Marcus and Annick were becoming very close; I could see they were falling in love. Dede and I spent a lot of time together, but our relationship was different. She was a nice girl, and I liked her a lot. But love? That was something else altogether.

I had taken a room in the Jewish old-folks' home. A lot of Israelis were staying there, and I made new friends. I spent some nights with them, some in Dede's room, ate my meals cheaply in the market, and was enjoying myself thoroughly.

One afternoon Marcus and I were sitting in a small teahouse that I had discovered in an alleyway beside the market of Pachama-ma. Marcus was telling me about the great time he had been having lately and tried to talk me into joining him on a trip to the coun-tryside.

"I like being in Bolivia," he said happily. "Even my clairvoyant would be surprised if he knew . . ."

"What do you mean, Marcus, by your 'clairvoyant'? Don't tell me you believe in that kind of nonsense."

Marcus smiled. "I not only believe in them, I'm a bit of a clair-voyant myself."

"I don't get you," I said, amazed.

"It may sound funny to you, Yossi, but it's the truth. I'm not an ordinary person. I have some kind of special power. I don't know exactly how to put it, but sometimes I feel things in the air. Some-times things happen to me . . . strange things. When I was younger, I used to tell all my friends' futures. I told them who would get mar-ried and when, how many children each of them would have. Years went by, and what I had predicted came true. Pregnant women used to ask me whether they were carrying boys or girls. I would hold a needle suspended on a thread and concentrate. If the needle swayed to the right, it was a boy. If it moved to the left, it was a girl. I was almost never wrong."

He paused, sipped his steaming tea, and then went on.

"I have some kind of power. I'm some kind of medium. That was the way I decided to come to South America. When Monica suggested the trip, I tested the idea with the needle and thread. The answer was that I should go. I didn't want to. I kept trying, hoping that the needle would go to the left, but it kept moving to the right, ordering me, 'Go!'

"I believe in that type of thing, though I am a good Christian. I do say my prayers.

"Monica didn't believe in such things, but she loved me nevertheless. I thought I would die when she wrote that she was leaving me and asked her to come see me. I knew she would not refuse, but when she arrived in Peru, it was horrible, just horrible. I felt myself losing her. Then I heard about a *brujo* [witch doctor] in Lima and went to see him. He told me that it was all over. There was no future for us. Before I left, he warned me that he felt danger hovering over me in South America. 'You or someone close to you will die here. Be careful!' I knew he was right, but I didn't care. There was no other place for me to go. Not then. Not after I lost Monica."

Later at the old-folks' home I thought how lucky I was to have come on this trip. I had wanted so badly to avoid going along with the crowd, walking the well-worn path: from kindergarten to grade school, from high school to the army, and then on to the university, work, marriage, a child . . . Stop! Yes, I was lucky to have escaped all that after my military service.

There were hordes of mochileros like me in South America. The *mochila* (backpack) is what characterizes them. These packs are all they have. In them you'll usually find a pair of patched and faded jeans, a sweater, a raincoat, a Coleman burner, *The South American Handbook*, which the mochileros call their bible, a sleeping bag, a few toilet articles, and a small first-aid kit. That's it. They keep their money in a money belt inside their pants. Some, like Marcus, even more cautious, cut a slit across the inside hem of their pants leg and stick rolled bills inside.

The idea is to carry everything on your back, forget your troubles, and let tomorrow take care of itself. You learn from the natives to live for the moment, not to hurry. You travel to breathtaking places—the kinds of places tourists dream of seeing—but you're not a tourist. You're a mochilero, a drifter, and there's a big difference. You're in one place today, someplace else tomorrow. You may stay for a day or a month. You make your own plans, every day full of surprises.

You meet a lot of drifters like yourself. You usually find them in the cheapest hotels in town or in restaurants that could pass for soup kitchens. You get to know the local people, who are usually friendly to strangers.

South America is overrun with mochileros of many nationalities, but Israelis are particularly numerous among them. I don't know why that is. Perhaps the long, mandatory military service in Israel has created among its young people a need to break out of molds, and there is no better way to do that than packing a mochila and wandering.

Anyway, we Israelis are privileged characters: in almost every large city in South America, the Jewish community has provided some kind of hostel for backpackers. These free hostels are a welcome refuge. Friendships are formed there.

Each hostel has its "travel journal," a book to which the guests contribute notes on a recommended side trip, a place of interest, the cheapest place to stay, to eat, what play is worth taking in, the easiest way to get around. Over time these journals have grown encyclopedic, full of reliable information.

The old-folks' home where I was staying had been the Jewish community center; but a more modern center had been built, and the former one was turned into a home for the community's senior citizens. Its owner, Señor Levinstein, let the mochileros stay free and gave them use of a refrigerator, a gas burner, and mattresses. His Sabbath meals of roast chicken had become a Friday-night tradition.

There were only a few old people living in the home. Some of them weren't quite all there, but they were harmless. The one I liked best used to knock on our doors and shyly ask to enter. Once inside, his sweet expression was abruptly transformed, and from his mouth came a stream of the foulest curses you can imagine—that is, if you speak Yiddish. Then he would take his leave politely and go on his way. When he lacked the time for a proper visit, he tapped on our windows and hurled an obscene gesture or two. Another old guy was obsessed with Bolivian soccer and was always looking to regale someone about his favorite team. He once came out of his room at one in the morning, asked us to help him put on his best suit, tie his tie, and lace his shoes. Once dressed, he kindly thanked us and went back to bed.

"Grandma" was the boss of the house. She must have been about eighty years old, with frizzy white hair. She had an apartment on the ground floor and was in charge of seeing that the rules were kept. She was the one who checked your passport and papers from the Israeli embassy in La Paz and gave you permission to stay. She showed you where you'd sleep and where the bathroom was. She made sure you didn't make a lot of noise and didn't waste water or electricity. God help anyone who crossed her. She knew how to yell loud enough that no one could ignore her, but underneath her tough demeanor was a fabulous woman, adored by everyone. She spoke broken Spanish and called everyone *hijito* (my son). Flowers for Grandma were another Friday-night tradition.

The travel journal in the old-folks' home was filled with detailed information about Bolivia and its neighbors—Chile, Peru, and Brazil—and about La Paz. Several residents recommended a visit to "Canadian Pete," who was serving time in San Pedro Prison. An entire section was devoted to San Pedro cactus, the plant that contains mescal, one the strongest hallucinogens existing in natural form. Many Israelis, it seemed, had tried the drug.

I decided to try San Pedro cactus for myself. It wasn't difficult to talk Dede into joining me, so we found ourselves on our way one morning to the Valley of the Moon, where it grows.

We each carried our backpacks. We had brought along a tent, a Coleman burner, a pot, two sleeping bags, two bottles of Coca-Cola, a large jar of jam to help disguise the taste of the plant, and a loaf of bread. Dede also had a large, red waterproof poncho.

The Valley of the Moon itself was frightening, remote and desolate. The entire area was rocky, with gray-white crags jutting out of the ground forming weird, jagged shapes. Some said Neil Armstrong had named the valley. Flying overhead had reminded him of the moon. It really did look like something not of this earth. Nothing grew there except for a scattering of cacti of many species. Following the descriptions in the travel journal, it was not difficult to recognize the San Pedro cactus. Some of the stumps were carved with names and dates. I looked around for a nice, clean specimen and found one to my liking. I checked out the seven ribs and the spacing of the thorns. Everything was exactly right. I cut off about a foot and a half of the trunk with my pocket knife. Dede put it carefully in my pack, and off we marched.

We climbed a hillside covered with eucalyptus and were alone up there among the trees, the eerily beautiful valley stretched out at our feet.

"I'll get the cactus ready," I told Dede, "while you put up the tent."

I sat down to concoct the drug. I pulled the thorns out with my knife. Then I peeled the rind. There were two layers: one, very thin and green; the other, white and containing strychnine. After carefully separating them, I finally had two big cups full of green pulp. I lit the burner and put a small amount of cactus in the pot to cook. About fifteen minutes later I emptied the pot into a cloth and squeezed out all the liquid. My efforts were rewarded with hardly more than an ounce. Would it be enough? Perhaps I had misunderstood the instructions.

It was already dusk, and I decided that we had no choice: we would eat the cactus raw. We found a comfortable place to sit on the edge of the hill. The view was fantastic, otherworldly. We sat with the Coke, the jar of jam, and a large spoon. I put a small piece of cactus in my mouth. Did it taste awful! Really disgusting. I shoved a spoonful of jam into my mouth, but it couldn't disguise the horrible taste.

I was dying to spit it out but forced myself not to. I couldn't swallow the doughy wad and had to chew it some more. My whole body convulsed. I choked back the nausea and took a long drink of

Coke. Poor Dede. Now it was her turn. It seemed to me that she had an easier time swallowing the bitter plant.

We repeated the routine five times until we had eaten the whole thing. Just to be sure, I drank the tiny amount of liquid that I had wrung from the cooked cactus.

The vanishing sunset was an incredibly beautiful backdrop for the Valley of the Moon, but I was too nervous to enjoy the scenery. I was trembling all over and felt terribly nauseated. Otherwise nothing unusual was happening to me. Dede also looked perfectly normal. She wanted to fix me a cup of tea, but the pot was filthy with the mess of the cooked cactus, and we hadn't brought along enough water to clean it.

Darkness fell, but a different light reached me. I smiled to myself and gazed down into the abyss below. It beckoned me, and, terrified, I took a few steps back. The very last red rays of the sun lingered over the cliffs across the valley. I clutched tightly to a tree, resisting the alluring abyss.

Dede clung to me from behind. "I feel wonderful," she said. "I'm flying."

I grinned to myself. She pressed her pelvis up against me, and I was afire. She moved slowly back and forth. I was enraptured.

"Let's go into the tent," she whispered.

Walking was difficult, and I was frightened. It was already nighttime, and I groped my way from tree to tree. Dede took me by the hand, but I didn't trust her. I wanted to feel the trees for myself.

Once in the tent we lay down on one of the sleeping bags and covered ourselves with the other. Suddenly I was astride a galloping horse. To my right, to my left, everywhere I looked were galloping horses and soldiers in green uniforms, wearing visored caps—and I was one of them. Where was I?

Dede laughed but seemed so far away. I rode swiftly on, not knowing where I was or where I was going. We were quiet, then suddenly the sky was lit by lightning, and we heard the loud crack of thunder. It started pouring.

"Oh," Dede murmured, "it's so stormy."

The rain poured down, and the tent began to leak.

"I really love storms. I don't know why. They excite me," she said.

In no time at all we were soaking. Everything was. The sleeping bags were drenched, and a large puddle formed in the middle of the tent.

"Let's go outside," she whispered. She had taken her poncho out of her pack. It was really just a large sheet of nylon, I put it on, and she crawled underneath. We stood like that, the rain pelting down upon us. I was still wondering where I was and with whom I was galloping. I could hear Dede whisper, "I love it so much. I don't know why. It's so exciting."

She was pressing her buttocks up against my groin. Suddenly she seemed so tiny. I stroked her short hair.

"I love it so much," she repeated. "I love it so much."

The rain stopped as suddenly as it had begun. Soon the wind subsided too. I could hear a faraway flute, its strains pure and pleasing. Captivated, I listened, almost in a trance. The sound drew nearer. It was an enchanted flute from the world of legends.

"Do you hear the flute?" I whispered.

"Of course," said Dede. "Where can it be coming from?"

We were so far from the village, the night was so stormy, and it was so late. "Hey, you, come here!" I yelled, but the flute slowly faded.

Dede left my side and wandered among the trees, humming.

The abyss, I thought. *Lord, she'll fall into it!* And I shouted after her, but she didn't answer my calls, and I became hysterical. I shouted, gripping the trunk of a tree with both hands. "Don't go over there! Stay away from the cliff! Get right back here!"

At last she returned. She wasn't at all frightened or upset. "Let's go back into the tent," she said quietly.

She spread her poncho out over the sleeping bags, and we lay down, holding one another. I was conscious of being cold and yet felt curiously indifferent. The coldness didn't matter; it was alien to me. I hovered in other worlds.

"Do you want to?" she asked in a murmur.

Do I ever! I thought to myself, *but what makes me think I can?*

"I'm not sure that I can," I said.

Dede laughed. She removed my belt and stretched out on top of me. I guess I was off in another world. Everything felt different, new, unfamiliar. It was endless. When it happened, it just went on and on for I don't know how long. Afterward we just lay there. I was still trying to get Dede to tell me into what army I had been conscripted and where we were. She didn't even try to answer my questions. She only laughed. The horses galloped along with me until daybreak.

Dede pulled me outside, but my legs wouldn't do what I wanted. I stood there, watching while she took the tent down and packed our wet belongings. She wadded everything up and shoved it into the packs, and we started trudging back toward the village.

"Have you come down?" I asked her.

"I think so."

"Do you think I have?" I asked.

"I don't know. You're really funny."

I had no more hallucinations, but nothing seemed as it should. I had difficulty walking, and everything I saw—cliffs, stones, trees—looked unfamiliar.

The bus we caught was full of Indian workers; I felt they were staring at us, but then I must have dozed off. Before I knew it, we were in the middle of La Paz.

"Do you want me to help you get home?" Dede asked.

"No, I'll get a cab," I answered.

"Will you be over to see me later?"

"Yeah, sure."

I hailed a cab and gave the driver my address. I ran into my friends Eitan, Raviv, and Shukrun at the entrance of the old-folks' home. They burst out laughing at the sight of me.

"So how was it?" Raviv asked.

"I'm scared," I told them. "Really. I'm not coming out of it."

They just laughed some more.

"Come and have some breakfast with us. You'll feel better," Eitan said.

I left my pack in the hallway and joined them. It was hard to walk, and I was afraid to cross the street. Eitan helped me.

"Am I going to stay this way?" I asked in terror.

"No, no, don't worry," Eitan assured me. "It'll be all right. You get some sleep, and when you get up, everything will be all right."

"You're a happy man, Yossi," Shukrun said. "You should only stay that way. That's the whole point."

CHAPTER 3

KARL AND KEVIN

I awoke at noon and lay staring at the walls. The room's only ornament was a faded poster of La Paz bearing the caption "The Jerusalem of Bolivia." My vision was clear, not the distant blur it had been. I sighed with relief. I was my old self again.

I went downstairs, took a shower, shaved, and went out. It was a beautiful day, especially after the gloomy weather of the night before. Huge banners at the city's central soccer stadium proclaimed the imminent contest between The Strongest and Bolívar. On a nearby corner stood a hamburger stand run by a young American, where the mochileros gathered. I walked on in the direction of the amusement park. Little kids, squealing gaily, were sliding down a gigantic chute on plastic bags.

I didn't feel like seeing Dede again. It was weird. Friends had warned me that the trip could turn violent, that either one of us might come to harm, but it hadn't been like that. I had needed her and even been afraid that if something had happened to her, I would be left alone, helpless. I was glad that she had been there near me, but now I simply didn't care to see her, and I didn't think I would be able to bring myself to touch her again.

I liked La Paz but wanted to return to Peru the next day. I could already picture myself at Machu Picchu. Every nomad knows the feeling: longing for every place he must leave mingled with anticipation of a new destination, always certain that the next place will be even better, even lovelier.

I walked in the direction of the Rosario Hotel, hoping to find Marcus and tell him that I was leaving.

"The Swiss hasn't come back yet," the clerk said. Marcus and Annick had gone to Coroico in the Yungas Cloud Mountains. I asked him for paper and a pen. I was supposed to meet Lisette, a

Bolivian girl, at five-thirty at the university to attend a Brazilian jazz concert. I asked Marcus to meet me there at five.

I left the hotel with a European-looking man close behind me. I had seen him around the hotel before.

"*¡Hola!*" he greeted me. "You know the Swiss man, don't you?"

He had a German accent, was in his late thirties, tall—about five feet eleven inches—broad-shouldered, solidly built, with brown hair receding above the temples. His eyes, which were slightly crossed, were blue. His clothes, which were worn but not threadbare, gave him the air of an adventurer.

"He's supposed to be back about now. He went to the Yungas for two days," I answered, and hurried down the street.

"Are you American?" he asked, quickening his pace to keep up with me.

For some reason every foreigner on this continent, especially if he happens to be tall and blond, is assumed to be an American. The problem with that is that many of the locals aren't particularly fond of Americans.

"Israeli," I answered abruptly.

"I'm Karl Ruchprecter. I'm Austrian, but I've been living in Bolivia for ten years now."

"Yossi Ghinsberg," I said, and shook his big, firm hand.

"I'm a geologist and work mostly in the jungle. We look for gold, uranium, antiquities."

"That's certainly an unusual way to make a living." He had aroused my curiosity.

"Oh, yes, sure. It's very interesting. I have some photographs here of my last expedition, if you'd like to see them."

"Yes, I would."

We marched up Comercio Street until we came to Plaza Murillo. Some of the old people there leafed through the afternoon papers in boredom or sat warming themselves in the sun. Others tossed kernels of corn to the fat pigeons. Their grandchildren ran about trying unsuccessfully to catch the birds. An ice-cream vendor made a racket hawking his Popsicles. We chose a wooden bench. A young shoeshine boy offered to polish my canvas tennis shoes.

Karl's pictures took me by surprise. The dapper European by my side looked totally different in them. He was dressed in khakis, a wide-brimmed hat, and boots, and had a shotgun dangling from his shoulder. In one picture he was skinning a wild boar, and in another he was gutting a huge fish on the riverbank.

Karl could see that I was intrigued and explained that the following week he was leaving on a three-month expedition to an unexplored region of the jungle to look for precious metals. He would be happy to take me and perhaps one or two of my friends along. At the end of a day's work, he said, it was always nice to sit around the campfire talking. Though he had many interests in common with his native assistants, he was always glad to have a few gringos along as well.

"You can stay as long as you like," he said. "If you want to go back, I can send a guide with you to the nearest village. You'll eat the game we hunt, sleep in the great outdoors, and your only expense will be an airline ticket out and back."

He was on his way to lunch. I was tired and still had an upset stomach and preferred my bed. We arranged to meet the next afternoon, and I promised to bring a few friends along.

I went back to the old-folks' home burning with excitement. I would talk to Marcus that very afternoon. Finally a chance to explore a real jungle!

Five o'clock that afternoon I spotted Marcus crossing the road to the university. As always he wore his coarse, black-brown cotton shirt and his wire-rimmed John Lennon glasses. He was beaming as he told me about the day spent with Annick. She loved him, he declared ecstatically. He asked me about the San Pedro cactus trip. I told him what had happened, and he listened attentively. And what had I decided? Was I going to go on with him into the countryside? I started elaborating upon the reasons why I wouldn't be traveling around Bolivia with him.

"The answer is no, I take it," he cut me off, disappointed.

"Hold on a minute," I answered. "You haven't heard the best," and I told him about the Austrian geologist.

Marcus wasn't as excited as I was, but he promised to come with me to meet him the next day.

After the concert I walked back to the old-folks' home. I told my friends there about the expedition. A few were enthusiastic, but others didn't take the plan seriously. Only Itzik voiced any genuine interest in the details and asked to come along to the meeting. I was very pleased. Everyone liked Itzik. At thirty-four he was the oldest of the mochileros and was often asked to represent our collective interests. He had a terrific sense of humor and an infectious enthusiasm, and he was helpful and good-natured.

The next day he and I marched off in the direction of Plaza Murillo. On our way we met up with Marcus, who himself had a companion, Kevin Gale. It was the first time I had met Kevin, but I already knew quite a lot about him. Every traveler did. Among the mochileros he was a legend. Kevin Gale had done it all. They said that he carried the heaviest pack in South America, that he walked faster than the llamas up the sides of mountains. He was an enthusiastic naturalist and photographer, and one more thing: he was Marcus's best friend.

"Are you interested in going into the jungle?" I asked him.

"The truth is, I only came to La Paz to catch a plane home," he answered. "I've been in Latin America for almost two years, and I had decided to go home for Thanksgiving, but the idea fascinates me. I haven't really been into the jungle."

Karl was waiting for us in the square. He got out his photographs once again and told us about his past expeditions. Kevin bombarded him with questions, with Marcus translating from English to German and back again, since Kevin had difficulty understanding Karl's peculiar Spanish. Kevin was interested in a tribe of wild Indians that Karl promised we'd see. I took it all in attentively.

"Would it be possible to go partway by river?" Kevin asked.

"This is my work, not a pleasure trip," Karl answered, "but maybe when you want to come back, you could do so by river."

Karl sketched a map on a notebook he had in his pack. He charted rivers, mountains, villages, towns, and mining camps. We were impressed by his knowledge. Kevin seemed satisfied but wanted to see a published map of the region. Karl promised to get one for him.

"Okay, I'm in," Kevin declared. "I'll tell my parents that I'll be home for Christmas instead."

"I'm going too," I said, though I had never doubted that I would.

"I wanted to do some more traveling with Annick," Marcus said regretfully, "but I guess this is a once-in-a-lifetime opportunity. I'm with you too."

Only Itzik held back.

Karl smiled at the lot of us, and we arranged to meet him that evening at the Rosario. Marcus left to find Annick, and Kevin, Itzik, and I walked back from the square. On a side street we found an ice-cream vendor. A small cone cost five bolivianos; a large cone, seven. I ordered large cones for us all.

We looked around for a place to sit and chose the steps of a nearby shop, only to discover it was the entrance to a coffinmaker. There were boxes of every description, including one covered in blue vinyl and trimmed with gold buttons, and another sized for a baby. We sat on the steps and licked our ice cream.

Kevin was excited. "I have a lot of things to do," he said. "Cancel my flight and call my parents. They're going to be really disappointed, but I've been dreaming about a trip like this the whole time I've been down here. A real jungle, a real Indian village, not a tourist trap. I'll take photographs like mad. I'll take a lot of film along, even a tripod. I'll have to find some way to pack the cameras in waterproof tins or plastic, something that will keep the water out and float. I have to extend my visa. We'll be there more than a month, won't we? I'm sure it's going to be really great."

"I don't think that I'll be coming along," Itzik said.

"Why not, Itzik?" I asked in surprise. "It's going to be a fantastic trip."

"If I go off into the jungle, I won't have any time left to travel in Chile. The rainy season will start, and I'll miss the chance."

"Chile, schmili. Don't you think a trip into the jungle sounds a lot more interesting?"

Kevin didn't understand, for we were speaking Hebrew, and he went to get more ice cream. I heard him tell the vendor, "*Más grande, por favor.*"

"What's the problem?" he asked as he handed us cones.

"Itzik doesn't think that he wants to come along," I explained. "He wants to go to Chile."

"Don't worry, he'll come," Kevin smiled. "I'll see to it. Take my word."

Kevin tried to change Itzik's mind. He promised to map out a fantastic route through Chile for him. He explained that the weather now was lousy down there now, and he would be better off waiting. Itzik smiled and promised to think it over.

We kept returning to the ice-cream vendor. "I know, I know," she said, "*grande, grande.*"

The coffin dealer looked a little sad. He didn't say anything to us about blocking the steps to his store.

At five that afternoon we were waiting for Karl in Marcus's room at the Rosario. It was a new hotel with clean, spacious rooms, but the best thing about it was the price: two dollars a night. Kevin was staying there too. I had gone to his room to fetch him. Good Lord, what a mess! There were clothes everywhere, cameras, maps, cigarettes, a jackknife, half a loaf of bread, cheese, melted butter—all heaped on the floor, the sink, and the dresser. Kevin reclined contentedly on the bed; he didn't seem at all bothered by the disarray. Though I had known him only a short time, I ribbed him about it. Something about him made me feel particularly at ease.

Karl arrived at six o'clock. He didn't apologize for being late, but, then, Latin America isn't famous for punctuality. He had prepared a detailed list of things we would need to buy. It was all written down precisely in large, round letters. Spices, salt, sugar, alcohol, tea, and medicines. Cooking and eating utensils, cups, waterproof rubber sacks, and a machete to cut through the jungle. Snakebite serum and mosquito repellent were particularly important, but most important of all were nets to keep out stinging insects and large sheets of plastic for shelter at night.

As for the route, he again promised to get us a map but, for the time being, charted it out for us from memory. We would fly to Apolo and be met by his crew, four Indians who lived in a village on the Tuichi River. From there we would have a week's hike to the place where we would be working. The Indians had accompanied Karl on every expedition, equipped with digging tools and armed with shotguns and ammunition. There was no need for us to buy our own shotgun unless we felt the need for one on our trip back.

The plan sounded perfectly acceptable. Kevin tried to get as much detail as possible about the river and reminded Karl of our need for a current map. We agreed to meet the following morning to do our shopping and try to find the map. Karl shook hands with each of us before he left.

Despite our plans, the following morning Karl and I were left to ourselves. Marcus was going to ski the slopes of Illimani with Annick and Dede, and Kevin had errands to run. I suggested to Karl that we search for the map. We didn't find one in any of the bookstores. On a large wall map Karl pointed out to some salespeople the relatively small area where we would be traveling; but we left the stores empty-handed.

"Never mind. I don't need a map. I know that area better than my own backyard," Karl reassured me, "but for you a general map will be better than nothing," and having no other choice, we bought one with a scale of 1:500.

Karl knew his way around La Paz. We saw some jaguar-skin coats in one of the shop windows. They reminded Karl of a jaguar hunt he had been on, and he described how he had bagged two jaguars and how much he had gotten for the skins.

"The jaguar is a creature of habit," he explained. "If you spend any time in its territory, you'll notice that it has regular paths it always uses. All you have to do is study the trails it takes, hide yourself well, make sure that you are downwind, and wait for your chance."

"Do you think we'll be hunting any jaguars on this trip?" I asked eagerly.

"Could be. Sure, there's no reason why not," Karl said. "You can make good money from a jaguar skin."

On our way back to the hotel Karl stopped at the post office while I waited outside. He came out looking upset. He had an opened letter in his hand.

"Yossi, I'm sorry, but I have to call off the trip," he told me.

I was stunned. "Call it off! But why?"

"Look, I just got an urgent letter from my uncle. He has a big cattle ranch over in Reyes Province. He says in the letter that he bought a surplus truck from the Chilean army. It will be in La Paz at the beginning of December, and I have to bring it up to his ranch right away."

I was sorely disappointed.

"I'm sorry, I can't let my uncle down. I'm the only family he has here. Do you understand? He has some other relatives back in Austria, but he's never been in touch with them. He knows that if he dies, they would just sell the place off without even bothering to come see it. I'm the only one who could run his ranch, but he's let me know in no uncertain terms that if I want to inherit it, I had better follow his instructions. The only problem is, I can't stand him. I can't stand to be round the lonely old miser for more than a day or two. That's why I'm biding my time working in the jungle. After he kicks off, I might settle down there, get married, and run the ranch myself."

I couldn't have cared less about Karl's family problems. "Isn't there any way at all that you could still come with us, Karl?" I implored. "Maybe just for a month. There's more than a month until December."

"No, no. What could I get done in just a month?" It takes a week to get into the jungle and another week to get back out. That's ridiculous. I need at least three months in order to accomplish anything."

"So why not come with us for a month, just for fun? Not to work. You said yourself that you prefer life in the jungle to life in the city."

"No, Yossi. I'm not a tourist like you. I know the jungle well enough and have no call to just go wandering around in it for nothing. Anyway, it's expensive: airfare there and back, food, and equipment. What for? There's nothing in it for me."

He's right, I thought to myself. *Too bad.*

What would we do now? Maybe we could go into the jungle on our own. We could get along without him. I was beginning to get carried away with the idea when Karl broke into my thoughts.

"Look, Yossi, there is a way. If you really want a taste of the jungle, I could plan out your route and be your guide. I know the jungle like the palm of my hand. You'll see. But I couldn't do it for nothing."

His suggestion was a terrific letdown. Up until then I had admired him, seen him in a romantic light. I thought he was the last of the Great White Adventurers. Risking his life in the primeval rainforest, searching for treasure—gold and uranium—staving off wild beasts and savages, making his living hunting jaguars. And here he was figuring up nickels and dimes, offering package deals, guided tours.

"How much would you want?" I inquired coolly.

"Well, six thousand bolivianos would be enough. Of course, I would pay my share of all the expenses: tickets, food, and so on. It really isn't that much. What do you say?"

"I'll have to talk it over with Kevin and Marcus," I answered abruptly.

"I'll be at the hotel at six. Put my offer to them, and you'll see that you won't be disappointed."

He held out a warm hand. I shook his hand without looking him in the eye.

I met Kevin and Marcus that afternoon in the hotel.

"We'll pay him!" Kevin said before I even had a chance to bring up my own idea of going without Karl. "How much is six thousand bolivianos? One hundred and fifty dollars. Fifty bucks apiece for a guide for a month. He can be a big help to us. There's an advantage for us in it too. This way we don't have to follow along wherever he goes; we can decide on the route ourselves and go where we want. We'll plan a nice trip down a river, and he'll be our guide and take us wherever we want."

After some consideration I agreed with Kevin. Marcus also thought this could be for the best.

Karl was on time this time, and we explained to him that we wanted to take a route through the real jungle; wilderness, wild animals, birds, savage Indians, and of course rafting down one of the rivers. Karl looked at the map and made an alternate suggestion. We could fly as planned to Apolo, which was the farthest point accessible by plane. From there we would have a two-day hike to the village of Asriamas. That was, in fact, the entry to the jungle, the last settlement. From there it would be about a six-day walk to the Toromonas Indian village. That would be a real experience, for we would be passing through completely untamed jungle.

"This Indian village isn't full of souvenir shops, is it?" I asked, having heard of villages like that. The guide lets out a warning whistle before he gets there with the tourists, and the Indians scramble about hiding newspapers, turning off tape decks, and changing from jeans to loincloths, and then go out to greet the visitors whooping and dancing.

"No, of course not," Karl said. "It's a big village; about six hundred Indians live there. I've been there twice. They aren't hostile. But for myself, one other gringo, and perhaps a few missionaries, these Indians have never laid eyes on a white man. We can spend five days in the village, resting up, seeing what we like in the area. Kevin can take all the pictures he wants, we'll get our provisions ready, and then we'll head for the Tuichi, a two-day, downhill walk. There we'll come to a place called Curiplaya, a gold-mining camp. It's still in use, but when we get there, it'll be deserted because they only work it from June to October. In Curiplaya we can pan for gold," Karl went on, "and we'll stop over for five days or so. We'll build a raft and spend the rest of the time panning for gold in the river. I can guarantee you one gram of gold for each day's work; five days of work, five grams of gold apiece." He calculated the price of gold and concluded that we would make money from our adventure.

Karl apparently noticed that we were all a bit skeptical. "You know what? I'll buy your gold!" he declared. "You only have to pay me three thousand bolivianos now, and you can give me the other half in gold."

"And what if we don't find anything?" I asked.

"There isn't the slightest chance that you won't find gold," Karl answered. "I worked there for two years, and I found gold."

Kevin and Marcus smiled tolerantly, but I had gold fever. I was eager, full of expectations.

"The raft will be ready within five days," Karl said, having gone back to planning our route, "and we'll go down the Tuichi on it, about one hundred and twenty miles, until we come to the mouth of the Beni River." He pointed at his map. "There, near the mouth, is the town of Rurrenabaque. From there we can get a plane back to La Paz, or if you prefer, we could go on a little farther to the Reyes territory and visit my uncle's ranch for a few days."

All three of us gave this plan our enthusiastic endorsement. Karl added a shotgun and ammunition to the list of provisions we would need to buy. His crew wouldn't be going with us, he explained, so we would need a good shotgun for our own protection and to hunt game. "It's a big expense, but we'll be able to sell it at a profit at the end of our trip in Rurrenabaque."

"But this is a military dictatorship," I protested. "Won't it be dangerous shopping for guns?"

"You're right, it's risky, but you can't get along in the jungle without a shotgun, and out there the army doesn't hassle anyone. I have a friend in prison here in La Paz. He can tell us where to find one, and 'Canadian Pete' is always happy to have visitors, especially if they pay him well."

"Canadian Pete?" The name rang a bell. "He's mentioned in the Israelis' travel journal," I said. "Nice guy, likes visitors, especially those who bring a chicken. Karl, how about if I go visit him to get the information?"

CHAPTER 4

CANADIAN PETE

On our way to San Pedro Prison Kevin and I stopped at the marketplace and picked out a nice, fat chicken. We asked the butcher to clean it and cut it up.

A handful of officers patrolled the prison gate. "Who've you come to visit?" they demanded.

"Pete, the Canadian."

"And what's in the bag?"

"*Pollo.*"

They led us into an anteroom, and after a quick body search one of them said, "You can go in."

Prisoners flocked about us in the courtyard. "Who've you come to visit?"

"Pete, the Canadian."

"Pete again?" one of them grumbled in disbelief and then yelled, "Hey, Pete, you got company."

Pete hurried down from the second floor, waving at us energetically.

"You lucky son of a bitch, Pete," a gringo prisoner growled. "This is the third visit you've had this week. Look at the belly on you!"

"Are you Israelis?" Pete asked with a smile.

"I'm American," Kevin said. "My friend here is Israeli." We shook hands, and Pete invited us up to his den.

The prison was a strange building, two-storied and very old. Haphazard additions had been tacked onto it, made from wood, corrugated tin, cloth, or any material that had come to hand. We climbed a ladder at the end of the corridor up to Pete's room. The room itself was of no definable geometric shape. It was built of wooden beams and tin panels, asbestos, and plywood. The ceiling was low and slanted, made mostly of taut nylon sheets.

"Home sweet home," Pete said cheerfully.

The bed was on the side of the cell where the ceiling was lowest. Kevin and I sat there, hunched over slightly. Pete sat on a mat on the opposite side of the room, about four feet from us. In the corner by the door was an electric hot plate.

"Oh, this is for you," I said, and handed Pete the heavy sack.

"Chicken!" he exclaimed. "My favorite. Thanks, pals."

The room was stuffy, windowless, but the ceiling of nylon let the light filter in. Pete whipped out a wrinkled notebook and pen and asked if we would mind writing down our names and addresses.

"Someday, when I get out of this joint, I'll put a pack on my back and visit all the terrific people who visited me here."

Kevin opened the notebook. "You've got half the State of Israel listed in here," he said, looking down the long list of addresses.

"Yes, most of my visitors are Israelis," Pete said. "They have some kind of book that recommends paying me a visit. They've all been bringing me chickens."

Pete went on to tell us how he had ended up in a Bolivian prison. He had been caught smuggling a kilo of cocaine and was sentenced to eight years. After telling his story, he suggested a guided tour.

We went down to the yard. It was a weird place. Something like the Turkish prison in the movie *Midnight Express*. An outer wall and inner wall surrounded a large courtyard. The old structure was built around the inner wall. There were no cells or bars and it looked more like a market, with prisoners milling about at liberty. Vendors sold fruit, ice cream, cakes, and other sweets. There were even a restaurant, billiard hall, and movie theater.

"This all belongs to the prisoners," Pete explained. "If you've got the dough, you can open a business and live pretty well in here. One prisoner has a restaurant, another runs a vegetable stand, someone else even sells grass. Money rules. They don't even give you a cell or room. You have to buy one. When I first got thrown in here, I spent a few nights on the bathroom floor, until the money my mother sent me from Canada arrived. Then I bought that little place and made it into my room.

"You have to pay for the food here too. And they don't give you any clothes. You have to buy those. The rich prisoners have it all right here. Look over there, on the second floor. There's a wealthy political prisoner. He has a furnished apartment: a television, you name it, everything. You won't find any of the big-time pushers here 'cause they just plain don't get arrested in the first place. They only lock up the small fry like me here."

Life in the courtyard revolved around a water hole in its center. The prisoners did their laundry there and in hot weather took a dip. A shower cost money. A prisoner passed by, selling Popsicles. I offered to buy one for Pete. He refused politely.

"Come on, and I'll show you the prison's slum," he offered. At the edge of the wall huddled a few small cells made of wood and tin, dark little cubicles that looked more like pigsties than human habitats. That was where you lived if you were penniless, and it wasn't a pleasant sight.

"When I first got in here, they had a coup. The army took over. The rebels broke through the prison walls, and almost everybody escaped. Me, with my luck, I was still being held over in the wing for guys awaiting trial, and I couldn't get out."

We wrapped up our tour with visit to a few of the other rooms and the restaurant. Pete stood looking at us.

"I've sunk just about as low as a man can sink," he said. "I'm reduced to having to ask you for a handout. You saw the way things are here, and my poor mother doesn't have much money. I would appreciate whatever you could let me have."

"You can earn yourself some money, Pete," I said. "We'll pay you well if you can get something for us."

"Hmmm, I see. You want a little grass? Great stuff."

"No, we want something else. Information. Where can we buy a good hunting gun?"

Pete gave us a solemn look. "If you guys are planning another revolution, don't leave me out this time."

We laughed and told him the real reason we wanted the gun. Pete left us and came back a few minutes later with an address written on a scrap of paper.

"I don't know nothing about this. You remember that good," he warned us.

Kevin and I got out our wallets and paid Pete generously.

"Thanks, guys," the Canadian said. "I'll use this for a ticket to the movies and a little grass tonight."

We all went together to the Lebanese arms dealer whose address Pete had given us. He owned a noodle factory and sold arms on the side. He showed us a brand-new, shiny 12-gauge Winchester. Karl checked it over, spent a long time haggling over the price, and finally agreed to pay six thousand bolivianos. We bought two kinds of buckshot, the kind that makes a concentrated pattern for hunting large animals and the kind that scatters widely for hunting birds.

We stopped next at a hat shop. Karl recommended that we all buy wide-brimmed hats, then said goodbye. A very nice Bolivian woman smiled at us patiently, though we each tried on dozens of hats until Kevin came up with the idea that we should wear distinctive headgear; that would make us more photogenic.

When we finally left the store, I looked like a gangster out of the 1930s, with a stiff, light-colored felt cocked over one eye. Marcus wore a sombrero, and Kevin a broad straw that made him look like a kibbutznik.

Kevin and Marcus returned to the Rosario, and I went to inform the Israeli embassy of our planned adventure, but they were too busy to see me. I left a note detailing the route we would be taking and the exact dates that Karl had set. I wrote down Kevin's, Marcus's, and Karl's names along with their ages and addresses and ended with the request that action be taken if I hadn't returned by the fifteenth of December.

The secretary told me to leave the note in the register of Israeli tourists visiting Bolivia. The note was extremely important to me. It made me feel safe: if something were to happen to me, the embassy would come to my aid.

When I returned to the old-folks' home, there was the usual bustle: people cooking, doing laundry, doing handicrafts to make a little money, and Grandma shouting advice to everyone. I packed my things and tied them up in two bags and with a safety pin fastened a note to one of them: "Property of Yossi Ghinsberg. Will return December 15." I shoved the bags under a bed. I took my backpack. It held only the bare necessities, including Dede's red poncho. It had been in my pack since the trip.

Although I wasn't leaving for two days, I wanted to get my farewells over with. Then I would be completely free of obligations. So early that evening I went to say goodbye to Lisette and her family. They were good people, and I had become attached to them during my stay in La Paz. Their home was in the city's wealthiest neighborhood. I had spent many pleasant evenings there listening to wonderful Bolivian music, enjoying fascinating conversations, and eating delicious foods. I was on particularly cordial terms with her mother, and at the end of these evenings her father would drive me back to the old-folks' home in his fancy car, and the guys there would give me a hard time, teasing me about my good fortune.

Lisette and her parents listened to my plans for the trip and grew anxious.

"That's too dangerous, Yossi. Don't go. Stay here. Terrible things might happen to you there."

I promised to be careful. I left my documents and my remaining cash—two hundred and fifty dollars—with them.

"If I'm not back by December fifteenth, please call the Israeli embassy and inform them that you have my papers. Ask the staff to check the note that I left in the register."

The next day all of us were very busy. We did some last-minute shopping, then Marcus and Kevin went to their embassies to leave word. They packed their belongings and stored them with a Canadian friend. I added my wristwatch to Kevin's belongings. There was no need to keep track of schedules and dates in the jungle, Karl told us.

The French girls were leaving that day, and we hurried back to say goodbye to them. Dede asked that I write to her in France and tell her all about the trip. Annick's eyes were red with tears. She hadn't slept all night. She was very much in love with Marcus.

We went out for dinner but returned early. Karl came over with a large rubber sack.

"This is my backpack," he said. "It's better than yours because it is made out of rubber and is waterproof."

"That's ridiculous," Kevin said. "How do you think you're going to carry it?"

"Don't worry," Karl smiled. "I'll attach straps to it, and it will make a great pack. You'll see."

He was as excited as the rest of us. Tomorrow was the big day.

We decided to leave the final packing for morning. Kevin went up to his room to sleep. I stayed to spend the night in Marcus's room. He wrote a letter home, and I did the same, a letter to my brother telling him about the trip into the jungle.

La Paz
November 3, 1981

Hi, Moshe,

What's new, Big Brother? I know that I haven't written for quite a while and hope that you aren't angry. But the truth is that I'm more concerned about the fact that I haven't had a letter from you, or from Mom and Dad, for about three months now.

This trip has been a once-in-a-lifetime experience. It's something really special, out of the ordinary. What I'm trying to say is that I'm doing this differently than the other kids backpacking around South America, including the other Israelis. Most of them go from one tourist site to another, from one museum to the next. They seem to think they have to climb every mountain in sight and have a look at every scenic view. I've visited a few museums, seen some nice spots, and climbed a few mountains. The mountains are really something. You keep climbing and climbing, and everything is so high here in South America that you run out of oxygen and think your lungs will burst. And finally, after all that, you stand on the summit and look around, and you really feel like you're on top of the world. But I'd rather go climbing once a month or every two months, otherwise it becomes routine.

What I'm doing here in South America is looking for the extraordinary. I love the unusual. Mystical religious ceremonies, pagan rites, local Indian witchcraft. Unusual people, places that have their own special atmosphere, new friends, all those things. There are a few special things here that I just had to try. Just a short while ago I had one of the most fantastic experiences of my life. I climbed up to the top of a mountain with this French girl, took a piece of cactus, and prepared a drink from it. The girl only had a little, and it didn't affect her that much. I had a lot and was flying for seventeen hours. By the end of the trip I was scared that I would never come down.

Now the main thing I want to tell you is about another kind of trip I'm leaving on tomorrow. I don't want it to sound like I'm overdramatizing, but it could be very dangerous. I might even be risking my life. I'll be gone between four to six weeks, and I won't be writing home during that time. Think of something to tell Mom and Dad so they won't worry.

I'm taking a flight tomorrow from La Paz to Apolo with three other guys:

Kevin Gale, age twenty-nine, American.

Marcus Stamm, age twenty-eight, Swiss.

Karl Ruchprecter, age about thirty-five, Austrian.

The American and Swiss guys are very good friends of mine. The Austrian is a geologist. He has been working in Bolivia for the past nine years looking for gold and uranium and other precious metals in the jungle. He is coming with us as our paid guide. He has an uncle with a ranch in Bolivia. The uncle's name is Josef Ruchprecter, and his address is Santa Rosa Ranch, El Progreso, Reyes, Beni.

From Apolo we will walk to a village called Asria-mas on the Tuichi River . . .

I am planning to fly from Riberalta, the last place on our route, back to La Paz and take a train and buses from there to Uncle Nello in São Paulo. If I haven't called home by the first week in January, something has happened to me.

I'm sure that everything will go right, and there's nothing to worry about. I'm being somewhat melodramatic but wanted you to know all the details just in case. Tell Mom and Dad that I've gone to some little island or village up in the mountains for a month. Try to think of something that won't worry them, because I won't be writing at all. Tell them you got a letter and that I feel fine and I'll be at our uncle's soon.

Be seeing you, Brother,
Yossi

CHAPTER 5

GOLD AND PIGS

We hailed a cab on Calle Illampu and loaded our packs into the trunk and onto the roof. The taxi wove in and out of traffic, then turned toward the airport. A ten-minute drive and we were there. I had a funny feeling: this wasn't just a plan or a story to tell anymore. We were really on our way.

The flight to Apolo took less than an hour. The plane was small. The passengers were seated side by side along benches of taut canvas that ran the length of the aircraft, leaning back against taut strips of fabric. All the luggage was in a heap at the back.

Most of the passengers were residents of Apolo. The men had short, bristly hair. The women, like the men, had high cheekbones. They wore their black hair in thick braids intertwined with yarn and tied off with ornamental tassels. There was also a European, a priest in a brown soutane.

Flying over the Andes was inspiring: snow-covered peaks and breathtaking panoramas. Once in a while we flew into an air pocket, and the plane lost altitude with a quiver, then steadied itself. Whenever that happened, the women became hysterical, screaming and crossing themselves in a frenzy. One of them, her eyes dark and frightened, took hold of the priest's hand and wouldn't let go for the rest of the flight.

Then the scenery below changed drastically; suddenly we were looking down on rivers winding through vast jungle. In no time we touched down in Apolo, and I quickly realized why the women had become so hysterical during the flight. Hanging from the trees on either side of the airstrip were the broken, burnt, and rusted hulks of earlier flights.

We waited for our packs and were soon on our way into town, along with the crowd that had gathered to meet the plane.

Two officers on motorcycles stopped us to ask what we were doing there. When we told them, they said that we should go to the police station to register.

"Nonsense." Karl waved them off after they had ridden away. "Just a lot of unnecessary red tape."

We started walking, Karl in the lead with Kevin and me right behind him. Marcus brought up the rear. I could hear him softly singing,

> Freight train, freight train, going so fast,
> Freight train, freight train, going so fast,
> Please don't tell the train I'm on,
> 'Cause I don't know where I've gone.

The heat was sweltering, and we struggled up a steep incline. Karl had tied his rubber bag to his back with two crossed strips of cloth, but we could all tell that the strips were digging uncomfortably into his shoulders. Our progress was slow because we stopped to rest frequently. We didn't waste our breath talking. We weren't carrying any water with us, so we were glad when we came across a small ranch, where they gave us *chicha* (a sweetened, fermented beverage made of corn or yucca). We drank it down greedily.

By late afternoon we came to a flat, wooded area, and the going was easier. We had hoped to find a ranch where we could spend our first night, but since it had grown dark, we decided to set up camp where we were. Marcus got out the tent, but Karl preferred to improvise a shelter of nylon sheeting.

He cut down a few thick, straight bamboo stalks and chopped off their leafy tops with a swipe of the machete. He tied two stalks together in an asymmetrical X, the bottom half wider than the top. He did the same with a second pair of stalks and stuck the legs into the soft earth. He dropped a long pole between the Xs, tying it down securely. He reinforced each end with a third pole, tied at the crotch of each X, the lower end jammed into the ground. He tied everything together with *panchos*, the fibers between the bark of a tree and its wood. (Balsa trees yield good, strong panchos, though climbing vines, which are always abundant, are surprisingly resilient and can be tied into many knots without breaking.) He stretched nylon sheeting over the bamboo poles, pulling the edges taut and weighting them down with heavy rocks. He padded the floor of the tent with a thick carpet of leaves to keep us from the cold and damp.

We got a little fire going and sat around it, preparing rice and tea with spring water. The food wasn't filling, but Karl told us not to worry; there wasn't much game here because we were too close to settled areas. Once we passed Asriamas, he promised, we would have all the meat we could eat.

The noise in the jungle at night is unbelievable. There were moments it seemed as if we were in the center of some busy industrial area. Karl informed us that it was just insects and birds. We were all exhausted (poor Kevin—I couldn't even lift his sixty-pound pack full of camera equipment) and soon fell asleep on the ground.

In the middle of the night I was awakened by a horrible screech. It was Marcus. Kevin had gotten up to relieve himself, and when he passed over Marcus, Marcus woke up screaming, thinking that a wild animal was attacking him. Karl laughed, and we settled down and went back to sleep.

Before we set out the following morning, we divided the weight that had to be carried more equally among us, though Kevin insisted on carrying more than his share.

After an easy two hours' walk we came upon a ranch. The owner and his wife greeted us hospitably, seated us around a wooden table in the yard, and served us ripe papayas and a beverage made from sugar cane and lemon. We rested for a while and then set out once again after ceremoniously thanking our hosts.

We came upon another ranch as noon approached. As Karl discussed lunch arrangements with the rancher, I wandered about the yard, passing fruit trees, chickens, a pig or two, and a few skinny dogs, who languished in the shade, too lazy even to acknowledge the presence of a stranger.

Through the door of the cookhouse I could see the rancher's wife and daughter slaughtering a chicken. The poor bird lay on the floor with a broom handle pressed against its neck, fluttering helplessly. The women caught sight of me, blushed, and fled into the recesses of the cabin. The lucky chicken grabbed her chance to flee, screeching. I walked off, amused.

For lunch we were served a tasty soup and the unfortunate chicken, despite all that, cooked with rice. While we ate, the dogs gathered around begging for scraps. "¡*Que flaca* (so skinny)!" Karl marveled at a scrawny pooch that resembled a German shepherd. She was all bones with matted fur. She gazed at us, her eyes dull and lifeless.

"What would you think about buying the dog?" Karl suggested.

"What! Are you nuts?" Kevin exclaimed. "What would we want with a mangy dog?"

"Don't look at her like that," Karl said. "You don't know how important a dog can be in the jungle." Then he told us a story that he would repeat at least a dozen times. "I once hiked alone through the jungle with only a dog for company. After three days a jaguar appeared, poised to spring at me, but the dog saw it and barked a warning. The jaguar came closer, but the faithful dog lunged and tried to chase it away. I didn't see any more. I only heard barks and roars." Karl started imitating the sounds of a dog and jaguar fighting. It all ended with the dying yelps of the dog being eaten by the jaguar.

We asked if the moral of the story was that we should have a dog along as jaguar bait.

"Don't laugh," Karl said. "She can come along with us, eat a lot of the fresh game that we'll soon be hunting. She'll get stronger and turn into a beautiful, lively dog." As if anxious to demonstrate his point, he began tossing bones to "Flaca," angrily driving off any of the other dogs that tried to snatch one of the bones away, and the dog did perk up a bit.

It wasn't difficult to talk the rancher into selling her. Karl fastened a rope around her neck. "No, no, sweetheart, you aren't going to go running back home," he said to her. "I'll keep her on a leash for a few days until she gets used to me, and then she'll follow along on her own."

Kevin snapped a few profiles of the newest member of our party, and we set out again.

The damned dog slowed us down terribly. She refused to keep pace with us, and every once in a while she'd lie down and wouldn't budge. Karl tried everything. First he sweet-talked her, promising better things to come. Then he cursed her, threatened her, kicked her, and beat her with a flimsy branch.

We had a good steep climb ahead, and the dog was determined not to move an inch. Karl dragged her cruelly over every root, dry branch, or rock in her path until Kevin took pity on the poor animal. He untied her, picked her up, and draped her across his shoulders, two legs hanging down on each side of his neck, like a lamb. This was in addition to the heavy gear that he was already carrying.

The way down was just as steep as the way up had been. We had to be careful not to slip and go tumbling down with our bulky packs. Only Karl hurried ahead, dragging Flaca after him and talking to her out loud. Suddenly Kevin, Marcus, and I lost sight of them. Marcus grew anxious. He wanted us to call out in unison so that Karl would hear us and wait.

"What's the difference?" Kevin asked. "We all have to go in the same direction anyway. We'll catch up with him sooner or later."

Marcus didn't say anything, but he couldn't conceal how worried he was. About half an hour later we came to a fork in the path. One direction seemed to be a continuation of the path we had been traveling, and the other cut off to the side. Kevin went striding resolutely along the main track.

"Wait!" Marcus cried. "How do you know that this is the right way? He could have gone the other way."

"Don't be so uptight, Marcus. This is obviously the way. If Karl had turned off, he would have waited to tell us. Come on, let's get going."

"No," Marcus insisted tremulously, "let's wait here and call out until he comes back for us. It could be really dangerous if we lose him. We could get lost all alone in this jungle."

"Marcus, why don't you just turn around and go back?" Kevin asked testily.

"What do you mean?" Marcus demanded. "Go back where?"

"You're not going to enjoy this. You're not cut out for it. Why don't you just forget it and go back to town? It's not too late. There are a lot of ranches back there on the way. You could even rent a donkey and make it back to Apolo by tomorrow."

"Bullshit!" Marcus fumed. "Of course I'm enjoying myself. Who are you to decide if I'm going to enjoy myself or not?"

"Okay, forget it. Just forget it," Kevin closed the subject and walked on.

We trailed behind him in silence, the mood tense. After a while we spotted Karl and Flaca; they were sitting, resting next to a little stream.

"Look what I found!" Karl called, waving to us.

He was holding a large frog. I would never have believed that frogs could get that big. It must have weighed at least four pounds.

"They taste like chicken," Karl said. "I sometimes eat them, but for now I'll let Flaca have the pleasure."

He skinned the frog and tossed Flaca a piece. To our amazement the dog wouldn't have anything to do with it. Karl's cooing and pleading did no good. Flaca just wasn't interested.

After a few hours of arduous walking we came to a wide river.

"Great," Karl said happily, "this is the Machariapo River. We don't have far to go now."

The river was deep; its waters came up to my chest. We hung our shoes around our necks. Karl cut some sturdy branches from the trees and demonstrated how to ford the stream, sticking the poles into the rocky bottom to brace ourselves against the current. Kevin went first, and Karl followed behind him, his pole in one hand and Flaca's leash in the other. The dog treaded water weakly, trying to keep its head above the current. Marcus and I were last to cross. We tottered from side to side and almost lost our balance but finally reached the other side.

Karl suggested that we set up camp. We were tired enough to agree readily. Once again we erected a tent of bamboo poles and nylon sheeting. Karl started making dinner, and the rest of us stripped and raced back to the river.

We splashed around in the cool water, swimming with the current and then against it. Marcus had brought some soap, and we passed it around.

In the morning our packs were on our backs, and our spirits were high. We have just started out when we ran into two campesinos leading a huge, white bull by a rope tied to its horns. We tried to learn from them how much farther it was to Asriamas but couldn't understand a word of their Spanish. A while later we emerged from the jungle into a wide, grassy field fenced with barbed wire. A little bit of paradise. The river cut through the field, and cows grazed contentedly. On the other side of the fence I could see papaya trees. Without a second thought I crawled under the fence, gave one of the trees a good shake, and came back with four ripe pieces. For the past two days we had had barely one square meal a day. The juicy fruit was a pleasure.

Soon we found the gate to the ranch and went in. The settlement consisted of several mud huts and one two-story stone building. The people we saw completely ignored us. When we drew nearer, however, the women pulled their children into the huts. Curious eyes peeked out at us. One lone man approached us with a smile. He was drooling and held out one hand, gesturing that he wanted a cigarette. He wore a tattered black hat, and his clothes were a mass of patches over patches. His fingers were encrusted with dirt. He was a dwarf, and his features made it clear that he was retarded.

"*Esclavos* (slaves)," Karl muttered darkly.

A young woman came out of the stone building. She was dressed simply, but not in rags.

"¡Hola! gringos," she said in greeting. "Looking for gold?"

She listened, shaking her head doubtfully while Karl told her where we were headed. She poured us some chicha and told us that she was married to the ranch's foreman. Her husband had gone to Apolo for a few days, leaving her here alone.

Karl inquired as to the whereabouts of Don Cuanca's ranch, and she replied that it wasn't far. She called out a name, and a young boy materialized.

"He will show you the way," she said, and gave him an order in Quechua.

The boy kept his eyes on the ground and led us out of the ranch. We marched along behind him on a path that ran alongside the river.

"What's the story here, Karl?" Kevin asked.

"Hard as it is to believe, these people are slaves," Karl explained.

"Slaves?" I asked skeptically.

"Well, you might not call them that, but they are virtual slaves. They don't receive any pay. They are dealt with harshly. They don't have anywhere else to go."

"What about the government? Don't they help?" Marcus asked.

"The government?" Karl laughed. "The government, my eye! Those generals stay in power several years, make a bundle smuggling drugs, and once they're millionaires, they retire. Some other lousy generals take over from them, and history repeats itself. You think they give a shit what happens to a few lousy Indians?"

We came to level ground and a herd of at least thirty horses. A man stood nearby. The boy walked over to him. Karl shouted to the boy, asking which way we should go, while pointing in what he thought was the right direction. The boy nodded, without looking back at us. We left him and went on.

After walking for another two hours, nudging Flaca along, we came to a ranch. More mud huts and another stone building, just like the earlier ranch. More grassy pastures and grazing cows. It was all so similar and yet different.

We hadn't even entered the yard when we met a little man dressed in tatters holding out his hand and asking for a cigarette. He was drooling. Hell! It was the same dwarf. Could he have left after we did and still gotten here ahead of us?

The young woman once again came out of the two-storey building. We glared at Karl. We had been huffing along for more than two hours for nothing, walking in a circle and coming back to the same ranch through a different gate.

The señora laughed in amusement. She said we would be welcome to spend the night at the ranch and even invited us to supper. She showed us to a room with two rickety beds. One would be for Karl, we all agreed, since he was the oldest. We drew lots for the other. Marcus won.

We ate chicken, rice, and fried plantains by candlelight in the dark cookhouse. The cursed boy, our guide, kept peeking through the window all the while we were eating. He didn't crack a smile, just looked.

When we came out of the cookhouse, we found the boy's father, the man who had been grazing the horses in the pasture, waiting for us. He wanted someone to tell his troubles to. He looked about guardedly, afraid the señora might overhear him.

"Take a look at me," he said. "I don't even know how old I am. When I was young, the señor brought me here. He promised to pay me and give me a plot of my own. Look at my clothes," he said, pointing to the patches covering his body. "I can't remember how many years I've been wearing them. I have no others. I live in that mud hut with my wife and sons. They all work for the señor, like me. They don't go to school. They don't know how to read or write; they don't even speak Spanish. We work for the master, raise his cattle, and work his fields. We only get rice and plantains to eat. Nobody takes care of us when we are sick. The women here have their babies in these filthy huts."

"Why don't you eat beef or at least milk the cows?" I asked.

"We aren't allowed to slaughter a cow. And the milk goes to the calves. We can't even have chicken or pork—only if an animal gets sick and dies. Once I raised a pig in my yard," he went on. "She had a litter of three. When the señor came back, he told the foreman to shoot them. That's the only time we ever had good meat. I don't mind working for the señor, but I want him to keep his promise. I want a piece of land of my own so I can grow rice and yucca and raise a few chickens and pigs. That's all."

"Doesn't he pay you anything?" Kevin asked.

"He says he pays us, but he uses our money to buy our food. We never get any cash. Kind sirs, maybe you could help me to persuade the master. Just one little plot is all I want. The master has land, much land."

We were shocked by his tale. Marcus took out a notebook and pen.

"What's his name?" He wrote down the name. The man didn't know the address. He only knew that the señor lived in La Paz.

Marcus was infuriated. "When I find the owner of the ranch, I'll spit right in his eye. What a lousy bastard! I mean, it's really incredible."

"That's just the way things are," Karl said. "It's sad, but there's nothing we can do about it."

"I'll get the owner's address from the señora," Marcus said.

"Don't, she won't like it. Anyway she'll never give you the address."

"You know," said Karl, "when I got my degree in agronomy—"

"Agronomy?" I was startled. "I thought you said you studied geology."

"Well, not exactly. I majored in agronomy, but I spent years working here with a famous geologist. I learned geology from him. But it doesn't matter." And Karl was off reminiscing. "I was quite a radical as a student, a Communist. The party sent me on a two-month visit to Russia, which was a big disappointment, and I gave up Communism. I went over to another movement, even more radical. It sounded good—very idealistic and high-minded— but my friends became terrorists. Some of them are wanted now internationally. That wasn't for me. That isn't the way to achieve your ideals. Fortunately I got out in time.

"I got a scholarship to finish my degree in a tropical climate and was sent to Brazil. That's how I got to South America, and I've been living in jungles ever since. I've covered every inch of this continent," Karl went on. "I've seen the poverty, the injustice, the corruption, and the exploitative regimes. I've wondered how the world could be changed. Communism isn't the answer. Neither is violent revolution. I've given the matter a lot of thought and arrived at a new social theory. The only way to solve the world's problems is mathematical cosmopolitics!"

"What's that supposed to mean, Karl?" Marcus asked.

"Just look at the world. All of its problems would vanish overnight if it wasn't for politicians. There's enough food to go around, enough land, enough resources. Why do people fight one another? It's all because of the politicians. They don't care about the people. They're only after money and power.

"The world is very advanced technologically. Why should egotistical politicians have control, make all the major decisions? Let's put a computer in charge. Then government ministers would be nothing but computer programmers, processing data, with no ego trips, no stupid pride, greed, or chauvinism. It'll all be for the common good."

We hid our tolerant smiles as he unfurled his naive theory, but Karl himself was terribly enthusiastic.

"Of course it's a difficult plan to carry out, so it's advisable that one nation be first to revolutionize itself, and then its neighbors will follow suit until the entire world has adopted the new system. One central computer will control the whole world, and that will be mathematical cosmopolitics."

Soon Marcus and Karl went to sleep on their soft "feather-beds" like nice little bourgeois. Kevin and I stayed up talking.

We left the ranch the next morning after we had bid the señora farewell with mixed feelings. We could see people working in the fields at a distance. Again we passed the herd of skittish horses. We were determined not to walk around in circles again. Karl took a different path.

Flaca kept up a reasonable pace all morning. The night before, she had received all the chicken bones and a healthy serving of rice. "What did I tell you?" Karl beamed proudly.

We reached Don Cuanca's ranch a few hours later, another two-storied building of bricks and wood, but this one had only two mud cabins near it. A sow and her young lay wallowing in a puddle of mud. Once again we were greeted by a retarded-looking dwarf. At first we were stunned, but, no, it wasn't the same one.

Don Cuanca himself came out to welcome us. He and Karl were friends. They shook each other's hand warmly, and Karl introduced us.

We all sat around a coarse wooden table. The dwarf served us coffee, a large bowl of boiled yucca, and a dish of salt. We dipped the yucca in the salt and ate hungrily. After a short rest Don Cuanca took us on a tour of his ranch. The place was sadly neglected. Most of the land was overgrown with weeds and brambles, and the fields were uncultivated.

"I'm too old. I don't have the energy to run a ranch anymore," he said. "If one of you would care to stay on here, I would make you a full partner if you help me. Mark my words, this place could blossom like heaven on earth."

He led us to the gate on the opposite side of the ranch. "You'll be in Asriamas by evening. Think it over. Maybe by the time you're back from your trip, one of you will want to settle down here with me. Goodbye for now."

This was our fourth day of hiking, and our heavy packs seemed to have found their proper repose on our backs. Though we were by now inured to the burden, we were nevertheless weary and anxious to reach Asriamas.

We made our way up and down a few steep hills in the jungle and heard the faint rush of flowing water.

"Listen," Karl exclaimed happily, "that's the Tuichi."

We hastened forward until we came to the riverbank. It was a stunning sight. The river was wide, at least a hundred yards across. Its waters were clear and calm. The current was mild. On the other side we could see thatched roofs. At long last we were there.

"How do we get across the river, Karl?" I asked.

"You see those wooden platforms on the other side? Those are balsa rafts. We'll soon catch sight of someone and holler for him to bring us over."

We waited for about half an hour.

"Maybe we should fire a shot." Karl suggested. "Somebody's bound to hear it."

The shotgun was slung over my shoulder. I fired lazily, the butt of the shotgun resting on my hip. The blast was incredible, the sound deafening. It was the first time that I had ever fired a shotgun. I held on to my side where it hurt from the powerful kick of the gun.

Karl laughed. "You just blew your image as a big, tough Israeli," he said.

Since no one seemed to have heard the shot, Kevin lost patience and decided to swim across the river. He swam with powerful strokes. The undertow was strong, and he couldn't make it straight across but came up on the other side quite a way downstream. He vanished in the direction of the straw huts and returned a few minutes later surrounded by black heads. From a distance it was a funny sight: a fair-headed giant encircled by droves of short, dark-skinned people.

In no time they rowed across and transported us, together with our gear and our dog, to the other side, where a large, curious crowd awaited our arrival. Their appearance was entirely different from that of the people we had met on the ranches. Their dress was modest, neat, and clean. They looked healthy, strong, and robust.

A narrow brook carried water into the village. All four of us removed our shoes to cross it. When we got to the other side, all the people watching us burst out laughing.

What was so funny? They were staring at the other side of the brook. I turned around and looked back. The shotgun was lying there on the pebbles. I had put it down when I took off my shoes and forgotten it.

"What kind of a soldier are you, anyway, Yossi?" Karl teased me again. He turned to a group of boys and said, "Five pesos for whoever brings the shotgun." One small boy beat the rest of them to it, came back with the shotgun, and collected his coin.

The people were very friendly. They came up and talked to us. The women and children watched us curiously but without fear in their eyes. They had no doubt that we had come to prospect for gold.

After they had offered us sweet bananas and ripe papayas, Karl asked if his friend Don Jorge was in the village. The man's brother was among the crowd, and he led us straight down the bank of the Tuichi to Don Jorge's home.

Asriamas is a small, relatively new village. About ten years earlier the government had allotted the land to the campesinos from the altiplano (high plains). They had gone into the jungle, put in an enormous amount of work, cut paths through the foliage, cleared trees from their fields, built huts, and planted banana groves. They had brought in cattle, sheep, and horses and raised vegetables and large quantities of rice. They sold their rice to wholesalers in Apolo.

Don Jorge's was the oldest and wealthiest of the families in Asriamas. His family enjoyed the status of founders.

After walking alongside the Tuichi for an hour, we came to an enormous clearing in the jungle, carpeted with green grass. Papaya trees, heavy with fruit, were planted here and there, and huts of bamboo and clay stood about the clearing. Karl had known Don Jorge for quite a while, but this was his first visit to the man's home.

Don Jorge came out to greet us. He was very friendly, led us to a spacious room, and asked his wife to prepare us a feast. He showed us the trail to the Asriamas River, from which the village had taken its name. It was a small, shallow river that emptied into the Tuichi. Deciding to bathe, we lathered ourselves, shampooed our hair, and dove under to rinse off. We ran in a frenzy on the way back, emitting shouts of rage as mosquitoes swarmed over us and bit our bare skin.

Don Jorge's wife was determined to demonstrate the full range of her culinary skills, and we ate like kings. Delicious soup, well-seasoned salad, chicken, roasted yucca. We thanked her profusely, and she blushed shyly.

We awoke early to a rooster crowing, ushering in a bright, sunny day. Outside was a pastoral scene. Ten or more sinewy horses grazed amid the huts, lazy sheep dozed under the fruit trees, and a flock of chickens competed with two pigs for the grains of corn the señora scattered about the yard.

After we had breakfasted on fried eggs, rice, and hot *caña* (sugar-cane juice), Don Jorge came to us. He was extremely worried. His oldest son had injured his big toe the week before, and the wound wasn't healing. He was suffering terrible pain and hadn't slept at all the past few nights.

Marcus took out the first-aid kit.

"Let's go have a look at the kid," he said to me.

The boy was barefoot. His toe was swollen and had turned completely black. Pus oozed from the wound, and the infection had begun to spread. It looked horrible. Marcus asked for a pan of hot water. He gently dipped the foot into the water and then took cotton soaked in alcohol and swabbed away the dried pus. He spoke kindly to the boy to take his mind off the pain. Then he spread the toe with disinfectant and bandaged it properly. He gave the boy antibiotic tablets.

The news spread fast: there was a doctor in the village. People converged on the little hut from all directions. They recited a litany of aches and pains, injuries, and diseases. Marcus asked to have a look at the wounds, so as to be of more help, but none of them would show him. They just wanted medicines.

We laughed. The campesinos are wild about medicine and don't hesitate to make up all kinds of ailments in order to get their hands on some. Kindhearted Marcus took out a tin of hand cream and gave a little to everyone who wanted it.

Karl was talking business with Don Jorge. He bought a large quantity of rice and pork. The prices were ridiculously low. I was a little put out with Karl. "Why does it have to be pork and not lamb?" I demanded.

"Pork keeps better. We'll smoke it to take along with us. Lamb tastes good but spoils quickly."

We slaughtered the pig ourselves. Karl jumped over the fence into the pen, where a large sow and four fat shoats ran about. He picked one out and began an entertaining pursuit. The squeals of the pigs were deafening. Finally he caught one, lifted it up by its hind legs, and handed it over to Kevin. Karl climbed back out of the pen and drew out a sharp knife. "You all hold its legs, and I'll slit its throat."

"How can you do it right here, in front of its mother and brothers?" Marcus protested.

"Bullcrap," Karl replied. "Their turn will come soon enough."

Marcus refused to have any part in it. He wouldn't even watch. Kevin and I firmly gripped the fluttering legs. Karl grabbed hold of the pig by its ears and skillfully slit its throat. A pool of blood gathered on the ground near the fence. Karl carried the pig over to the oven, which stood under a thatched roof in the center of the clearing. He tied its front legs to one of the pilings. I looked back at the surviving members of the pig family. Two of them had gone over to the pool of blood and were slurping it up thirstily. Inside the pen a fat little piglet was attempting to mount its mother.

What a world, I thought to myself.

Kevin went to get some wood for the oven, and I helped Karl butcher the pig. We laid the loins in large roasting pans. The oven was made of clay, shaped like a little igloo. Within half an hour aromas from the roasting pork wafted through the entire village, and when it was ready, we had to share it with all of Don Jorge's family and the neighbors.

We laid out a banquet of fresh salad, hot sauce, roast bananas, and yucca. The pork was served with rice and beans. We drank hot caña and had sweet bananas and papayas for dessert.

After dinner, we gathered around on the grass with Don Jorge and a few other men. Karl was feeling mellow and broke out the liquor that we had bought for the Indians. He poked a hole in the tin and generously spiked the pitcher of caña. Drinks were served all around. We drank and enjoyed every moment. Don Jorge rose, went into his house, and came back a moment later carrying what looked like a prayer book.

"Now he'll offer a prayer of thanks." Marcus smiled and then added, "Who would have thought that they knew how to read?"

Don Jorge took a wad of tobacco out of his pocket. He cut a plug with his pocketknife, tore a page out of the book, and rolled a cigarette. Kevin and I burst out laughing, but Marcus's feelings were hurt.

The next morning we got ready to leave. Karl bought some freshly ground coffee from Don Jorge's wife. Marcus and I went to have another look at the son with the infected toe. His mother said that he had slept soundly all night, and she was extremely grateful to Marcus. Marcus removed the bandage and saw that there hadn't been any improvement. The toe was black and oozing pus.

"I'm afraid that the infection will spread to his whole foot," he warned Don Jorge. "He has to see a doctor. Otherwise he could lose his foot."

Don Jorge listened while Marcus explained in detail. Marcus showed him how to clean the toe with alcohol and warned him not to drink any of the alcohol that we were leaving with him. He gave him some antibiotic cream as well, along with bandages and antibiotic tablets.

"If it doesn't get any better in a couple of days, you have to take your son to Apolo," Marcus warned him again.

"I will do as you say," Don Jorge promised.

"And don't let him go barefoot. He has to wear a sock at least. He can't let the bandage get dirty."

Kevin returned from a short picture-taking stroll through the village. We put our packs on our backs. They had grown heavier because we were now carrying the rice, five pounds of coffee, smoked pork, bananas that Don Jorge's father-in-law had given us, and some *chancaca* (a lump of brown sugar derived from sugarcane).

I was sorry to say goodbye to Don Jorge, his wife, and his neighbors. They were all good, pleasant people, and I hoped that I would see them again.

Flaca had mistakenly thought that she would be left to loll about the village, but Karl let her know in no uncertain terms that wherever we went, she went too. The dog's displeasure was obvious, and Kevin tried to talk Karl into leaving her behind.

"She's got it made in the shade here," he said, "and she's just a nuisance to us."

"You don't know what you're talking about," Karl replied angrily. "Just look at how she's perked up now that she's got her strength up. Once we get going, you'll see that I won't have to drag her."

Our plan was to follow the Asriamas River upstream, then to cross a range of mountains to the Cocus River. We would descend the Cocus and then continue crossing mountains until we came to the Colorado-Chico. From there it would be only a short distance to the Indian village.

The Asriamas River isn't particularly wide or deep, but its current is very strong. On both its banks the jungle encroaches right to its edge. There is hardly any shore. Neither is there any kind of a trail, so instead of cutting our way through the jungle, we waded in the river, crisscrossing from time to time. The going was slow at first. Each time we wanted to cross the river, we took off our socks and shoes. Kevin was the first to lose patience and begin crossing with his shoes on. Soon we were all following his example. It had been difficult wading across the river barefoot anyway. The water was very cold, and smooth, sharp stones cut into the soles of our feet. It was more comfortable to cross with shoes on, but we soon had blisters from walking in wet socks.

It was a hard day for all of us. An irritating rain had been falling since morning, and we shivered with cold. Flaca was the most pitiful. Now and then she stopped in her tracks, wet, cold, and miserable, and refused to go on. Karl had to kick her to get her going. Once, while we were crossing the river, she had gotten caught in the current and was swept almost out of sight. I went after her, letting the water carry me along too. I found her perched on a small rise on the riverbank. I went over to her, but she tried desperately to get away from me. She didn't want any help. She just wanted to be left alone. I dragged her quite a way and then picked her up and walked back against the current to rejoin the others.

It was getting late. Karl decided it was time to stop for the night. We quickly set up camp a short distance from the riverbank. Fortunately, the rain had stopped, and we got a fire going. Karl made a big pot of soup from rice and bits of smoked pork.

Marcus and Kevin, who had both brought a change of clothes, hung their wet clothes to dry by the campfire, but Karl and I had to dry our clothing while wearing it.

"Don't put your clothes too close to the fire," Karl said. "The threads wear out that way, and they'll start falling apart at the seams."

Before we fell asleep, Karl promised, "Tomorrow I'll find some kind of game, for sure."

"That's good, Poppa," Marcus laughed. "You have to provide for your hungry children."

I awoke very early in the morning and found Karl already up and outside. He was whittling chips of wood from a broken branch with the machete. He placed the chips over the ashes from last night's fire, bent over, and blew on one of the still-red logs. The fire rekindled. Karl added dry twigs and soon had a good blaze going. I crawled out of the tent and warmed myself against the morning chill. Kevin had also arisen and was breaking up a large branch. I took the pot and utensils down to the river to clean them.

The weather was better than it had been the day before. It had stopped raining, our clothing was dry, and we were soon on our way, wading in the icy water of the river.

At noon Karl noticed a gathering of dark clouds on the horizon. Before long a heavy rain was pouring down on us. Determined, we marched on, drenched to the bone.

Flaca, who was being dragged by the rope around her neck, rebelled. Her legs went out from under her, and she lay down. Karl's shouting and kicking did no good. He dragged her a long way over the muddy ground. She didn't let out a whimper. Finally he got really mad, took the rope from around her neck, and shouted, "You don't want to come? Fine, have it your way. Just stay here!"

We went on, looking back sadly at the poor dog, sure we would never see her again. What a bum deal she had gotten, I thought to myself. We had bought her from her poor owners, thinking she'd be better off with us, but had brought her nothing but hardship. Now we were abandoning her to her fate. Alone in the jungle she would die of cold and hunger. I looked back again. Flaca was stretched out in the mud, watching us apathetically, as if resigned to the end that would soon be hers.

"Look, cattle!" Karl cried. "They belong to the people of Asriamas. They let them wander freely about the jungle to graze and breed."

About twenty head stood on the narrow riverbank. The calves frolicked between their mothers' legs. One, all soft and white, nuzzled its mother's udder.

"She's giving milk," I said. "Maybe we could catch her and get a little milk for ourselves."

"Why bother?" Karl said. "Better we should take a young calf and roast it over the campfire. It's even legal," he added. "There's an unwritten law that a hungry man traveling through the pampas can slaughter a whole cow in order to have something to eat."

We were all starving, and it didn't take much effort on Karl's part to convince us that there wouldn't be anything immoral about killing a calf belonging to the people who had sheltered us in Asriamas. So the hunt was on. Karl and Kevin sneaked up on the herd holding ropes. The cattle got wind of them and fled.

"I have a great idea," Karl proclaimed. "We'll keep spooking them in the direction we're going until it's time to set up camp. Then we'll shoot one of them. We won't even have to carry it that way."

We carried on enthusiastically, driving the cattle forward with loud shouts. They tried to give us the slip, but we managed to keep them together; only one or two got away. All of the others were ahead of us, and the moment of truth had arrived.

I suddenly spotted a black bird gliding about fifty yards ahead of us.

"Shhh," I said to quiet everyone, "look."

Karl moved forward cautiously, and while still a considerable distance from the bird, took aim with the shotgun and fired, decapitating the bird. He rushed to the river and drew it out of the water. It was a fat, black wild goose. Karl was grinning from ear to ear. I was just as proud as he was of his admirable marksmanship.

Marcus suddenly cried out, "It's alive! It's still alive!" and indeed the goose was still fluttering with life in Karl's grip. I looked at Marcus suspiciously, half expecting him to break out the first-aid kit, but Karl thought nothing of it. He grasped the goose by it neck and twisted it to set Marcus's mind at ease. Marcus let out a painful groan and covered his eyes.

"Way to go, Karl." I slapped him on the back, while he tied the goose to my backpack. "Now we won't have to shoot a calf."

"The calf isn't out of it yet," he replied. "One lousy goose isn't going to make a meal for the four of us, and the calf will give us enough for tomorrow too."

None of us objected. Karl took aim at the white calf. I put my hands over my ears, and Marcus squeezed his eyes shut. Kevin watched attentively. The calf's salvation arrived from different quarters. The bolt stuck, and Karl couldn't get it unjammed. While he was fiddling with the shotgun, the entire herd made a break for it, back to the riverbank.

There is a God in heaven, I thought to myself with relief.

Karl wasn't upset. "So they got away," he shrugged. "We'll have plenty of game tomorrow. Look at the fat goose we got today."

We set up camp quickly. Karl cleaned the goose, put a pot of rice on to boil, and set the goose in it. We sat down to warm ourselves around the fire. We each held a deep bowl and concentrated on the delicious stew.

"Poor Flaca," I said.

"Stupid, pigheaded dog," Karl cursed.

"Tell us about the Indian village," Kevin said, changing the subject.

Karl liked nothing better than to be asked to tell a story.

"We were panning for gold in Curiplaya," he began, "the camp we'll be coming to later on. There were villagers from San José there, and a Swiss friend of mine, Don Matías, who owns a ranch farther down the Tuichi. The campesinos, together with Don Matías, had already visited the village once. They said that the Indians were supposed to know where there was a large treasure of gold in the area. It got me curious, and I asked to go there."

It was a difficult journey, three days' hike up a mountainside. There wasn't any water on the way, and they had to carry water with them, but they finally made it. It was a big village: six hundred inhabitants. The women wore short grass skirts and went barefoot and bare-breasted. They were solidly built, with high cheekbones and somewhat slanted eyes. All in all, Karl declared, they weren't bad-looking. The men wore loincloths, and most of them also wore belts from which the shrunken heads of their enemies dangled. Each man had two or three wives. Besides cooking and cleaning, the women also worked the fields. They tended banana groves and raised yucca and corn. They carried long knives, made of a very hard wood called *chonta*. Their bows, spears, and blowguns were made of the same wood. The men made the weapons and spent most of their time hunting or playing games. Jungle boys.

Not far from the village—about three days' walk, almost on the Peruvian border—lived another tribe, known for its ferocity. This tribe would attack the village, carrying off its women. The villagers protected their women, and when they killed one of their enemies, they cut off his head and shrank it. This was done by burying the head in the sand by the river. Over the place where the head was buried a hot fire was lit. After a few hours the head was dug up and the skull bones pulled out through the jagged neck. The head was buried again under a fire for many hours, until it shrank to the size of a clenched fist. The shrunken head looked just like the man when he was alive: all the features—the lips, eyelids, lashes, eyebrows, everything—just the same. Finally the head was filled with sand to make it solid and hung as an ornament from a belt. According to Indian lore, the strength of the dead enemy passed to the warrior who killed him, and the warrior became twice as strong. The more heads an Indian has on his belt, the stronger he is assumed to be.

When one of the members of the tribe dies, the village has a big cremation rite. Karl had been present at one of them and recalled it with great enthusiasm. The deceased was an old man who had died a natural death. Average life expectancy for the tribe was about forty-five years. The men built a big bonfire in the center of the village. The women brought urns of chicha and sang mourning songs. The deceased, with his belt of five shrunken heads, was tossed into the bonfire.

"The smell of the burning body made me nauseous," Karl said with a grimace, "but I managed to keep a straight face. I didn't want them to see how disgusted I was."

The women wailed some incomprehensible lamentation, while the men danced about to the beat of drums and roared sounds like animal calls. Now and then they added more wood to the fire. Then the women brought millstones. A few men smothered the fire with broad leaves and removed the red-hot bones from it. They divided the bones among the women, who ground them on their millstones. The resulting powder was poured into urns of chicha. Afterward all the participants received gourd bowls into which the yellow chicha was poured.

"*I'm not drinking any of that!* I said to myself, but Don Matías, knowing what I must be thinking, said to me, 'Drink it, Karl, if you want to get out of here alive. Just be careful to keep your teeth clamped shut.' I soon found out what he had meant. Unground bits of flesh still clung to the bones.

"The men sat around smoking something. I don't know what it was. It was wrapped in dry leaves and had a sharp scent. They invited me to have a smoke. Of course I couldn't refuse. Don Matías warned me that the drug was very dangerous and that its influence could be permanent. He told me to smoke as he did, holding the smoke in my mouth without inhaling any of it.

"The smoke burned my mouth, and my eyes started watering. I coughed loudly, but none of them laughed or showed any interest in me at all. They looked about gazing into space. They didn't say a thing except when one of them cried out from time to time. Don Matías and I got out of there after about half an hour, and none of them reacted when we left."

By the time that Karl had finished this story, I was covered with goose bumps but eager to have and savor similar experiences of my own. I was amazed to discover that both Kevin and Marcus had fallen asleep without hearing the ending.

When I opened my eyes in the morning, I saw Karl, as he had each morning before, bringing last night's fire back to life and putting on a pot of coffee. Karl never woke us to help him. He looked after us as if we were his children. There was good reason for Marcus's having started to call him Poppa.

Within a few minutes we were all up and out. We had our by-now traditional breakfast, sweet rice porridge. Kevin complained that he hated this glop, but that didn't stop him from having a second helping or licking the pot clean. He knew that we wouldn't have anything else but a cup of cold tea until evening and that he had better fill his belly as best he could now.

We were off. Karl led the way at a rapid pace. I admired how tough he was. He was wearing cowboy boots, which weren't suited to long-distance trekking. In fact, they were disintegrating from repeated immersion in the river. That day the sole fell off one, and he had to tie it on with a piece of rope. I'm sure that walking in those boots was agonizing, but he never complained and never slowed down.

Without consciously deciding to do so, we had broken up into pairs. Karl and Marcus walked together in the lead with Kevin and me close behind them. Our marching arrangement affected our social relations as well. Karl and Marcus spoke German to each other. Kevin and I spoke English. Besides that, I was happy to be in Kevin's company and was feeling less friendly toward Marcus. Somehow he had changed. He was too kind, overly sensitive, and polite enough to drive one to distraction. We were in the jungle, carrying heavy packs, hiking through rugged terrain for no less that ten hours each day. We were wading through the river, plodding through mud, and fighting through the foliage. It was natural that we would all become tougher. Except Marcus. When he saw a bramble bush, he would stop and hold its branches aside until we had all gone past, or he would call out, "Watch it, there's a thorny bush here," or "Be careful that that branch sticking out doesn't scratch you." It got to be ridiculous. If he happened to be walking behind us and got hit by a branch or scratched, he was insulted that we hadn't warned him. Kevin and I couldn't help deriding him privately. Among ourselves we called him Girl Scout.

I had felt a gulf opening between Marcus and me ever since the beginning of the trip. We couldn't bridge the widening gap, and our conversations centered around purely practical matters. Neither one of us felt comfortable with this change in our relationship.

Kevin, who after all had known Marcus even longer than I had, had also become concerned.

"Marcus seems different," I said to him one morning. "He's sad all of the time. Don't you think so?"

"I noticed it, too, but it isn't just recently. He's been like that for months. He must have told you about Monica."

"Yes, he told me about her. He must have really loved her."

"I was with him when she was here, and when she left him, he went to pieces. It was as if he had lost the desire to go on living.

"Marcus and I used to be like brothers. I loved him, and I still do, but he's changed. I thought at first it was because of Monica, but I'm not so sure anymore. Marcus is a special person. He wants to save the whole world. He wants to help every needy person he runs into, and he lets people walk all over him. I feel bad for him. He should never have come into the jungle. He's not comfortable here in the wilderness. It's too savage for him. Look at the way he acts. He's scared, insecure. He's really miserable. It hurts just to look at him."

"Have you tried talking to him about it?" I asked.

"A couple of days after we left Apolo, when Karl had gone off to see if there was a ranch nearby and you were with Flaca, Marcus and I were left alone. I told him how I was feeling, that his friendship was very important to me, and that I was afraid of losing it. I felt weird, I said, almost like he couldn't stand being around me. I told him I thought maybe we should keep a little space between us, that that might save our friendship. I suggested maybe we should try just talking about things having to do with the trip, but it didn't do any good, except for keeping up appearances.

"I see that with you, too, Yossi. It's getting worse every day. I know he gets on your nerves. He behaves like a child, hanging on Karl all day long. He stepped on my foot the other day and spent half an hour apologizing. He wanted to check to make sure I wasn't injured."

"Maybe you should try talking to him."

Later that morning, when Karl stopped to attend to his disintegrating boot and told us to carry on, he'd catch up, I found myself walking alongside Marcus and was surprised when he revealed that he, too, felt and regretted the chasm that had opened up between us.

"Yossi, don't you think that our relationship has changed since we started on this trip," he asked suddenly, "like we aren't such good friends as we used to be? Haven't you noticed?" He spoke quietly, his voice sad.

I didn't know what to say. "I don't think anything has changed, Marcus," I answered him. "You just seem very unhappy, like something is bothering you. I don't know. Maybe you can't get Monica out of your mind. Maybe you miss Annick. You keep everything to yourself, bottled up inside. But I'm sure that things between us are just the same," I said, even though I knew he was right.

As we walked along that day, the Asriamas became narrower and narrower. By the time we approached some hilly terrain, it was little more than a stream. It was a hot, sunny day. Thousands of brightly colored butterflies—yellow, orange, blue, green, purple—rested on the sand or hovered above it, their wings fluttering. At Kevin's request Karl strode directly into their midst, while Kevin snapped pictures of each step that he took. The butterflies took flight, and Karl was engulfed in a cloud of colors. It was a stunningly beautiful sight. Marcus discovered a single butterfly warming itself on a rock. Kevin bent over quietly and took a closeup. Its wings were transparent with yellow stripes.

Karl stooped over as he walked, his eyes glued to the ground. I thought he was looking for butterflies, but he said, "Look, tapir tracks, a mother and a calf. That explains the butterflies. The cow and calf must have come down to drink from the stream. Then they peed in the sand. The butterflies go after the minerals in urine."

Pointing out what he thought our approximate location to be on our poor excuse for a map, Karl decided to turn away from the stream and cross the mountain chain. "The Cocus River is on the other side," he explained. "Once we're over the first ridge, any trickle of water that we stumble across will lead us there. That's why we don't need an exact map."

We started our ascent, and soon our bodies were pouring sweat. When I spotted a large, green fruit near my foot, I called out to Karl. He was pleased with the find—he called it *manzana de monte* (mountain apple)—showed me how it broke evenly into four pieces, and handed them around.

"Let's look for the tree," Kevin suggested, and in a few moments, when we'd found it and discovered the fruit too high above our heads and the trunk too smooth to climb, he said decisively,

"Let's chop it down."

Marcus immediately took the opposite view. It wasn't right, he argued, to kill a tree just to get at its fruit. "And what about other people who might pass by here and need food?"

"We're here now," Kevin retorted, "and we're hungry."

We took turns striking at the trunk with the machete. Kevin worked at it longer than the rest of us, and in no time the tree toppled with a crash, breaking branches off neighboring trees on its way down. We pounced on the fruit and gathered up a good deal of it only to find that not a single one was edible. They were all green and hard inside. I thought we could take them along and eat them when they'd ripened, but the others disagreed; the burden wasn't worth the reward.

It took five long, exhausting hours to climb the steep mountainside. Karl showed us how to extract water from the bamboo shoots that grew in abundance on the mountain. Little reserves of potable water build up between the joints on the stalks. He chopped off one of the shoots with the machete, and, sure enough, water poured out.

We needed a rest before going on. I leaned my weary back against one of the stalks, but it offered no support, and I fell over backward. Long, thick thorns stuck up among the stalks, and when I fell, my hand struck one of them, piercing my wrist more than half an inch deep.

Marcus had begun laughing at my fall, but when he saw the look on my face, he grew frightened and silent. I was in severe pain. I pulled the thorn out, and, surprisingly, there wasn't much bleeding. Marcus disinfected the wound, and Kevin bound it with a large bandanna. My hand was paralyzed from the wrist to the fingertips.

We descended the mountain rapidly, the way down as steep as the ascent had been. Karl seemed to know what he was talking about; when we reached level ground, we did find a narrow brook. We waded along in it, and its current gradually quickened. The scenery was magnificent, and Kevin couldn't stop taking pictures.

When we came around a bend in the stream, we took a lazy little sloth by surprise. It was drinking from the stream and was too slow to run away from us. Karl was the first to spot it. He ran toward it shouting happily, "*A la olla! A la olla!* Into the pot with you!" He fearlessly grabbed the sloth by the scruff of its neck and picked it up. The animal batted at Karl's hands clumsily but struck only thin air.

"It would be a shame to waste a shell on it," Karl said, while Kevin photographed the cub for posterity.

Karl threw the animal down on the ground, pulled the machete from his belt, and raised it over his head. Marcus looked away, horrified. Karl brought the machete down on the back of the sloth's neck, and it sighed its last breath.

"We finally got some game," Karl observed proudly, tying the carcass to my pack.

Before another hour had passed, we heard sharp cries.

"Shhh, shhh." Karl waved us back. "There are monkeys coming this way."

A family of black monkeys appeared in the treetops. They swung from branch to branch like acrobats. *Boom, boom.* Karl fired the gun, and a monkey plummeted to the ground. Karl ran to it and fired another shot from close range. The monkey let out a gurgle, and Karl smashed the butt of the shotgun into its head until it was still. "A wounded monkey can be very vicious," he explained. The monkey was quite small, weighing about twenty pounds.

Karl suggested that we make camp. It wasn't yet growing dark, but we had a lot or work to do. We had to clean the animals and prepare them for cooking. We chose high, dry ground, as Karl instructed, and set about our usual preparations. I couldn't work with my wounded hand and just sat watching Karl and Kevin set up camp, while Marcus ground spices together with stones that he found lying about. After the tent was up, Karl began skinning the sloth. It was a difficult task, because he didn't have a sharp enough knife. The monkey was easier. Karl tossed the whole thing into the fire, and its fur burned right off. It was a disgusting sight: its face was all shriveled up, its teeth and nose bone were stark white, the eye sockets were creepy, and the hands and feet looked human. I could hardly stand to watch. Karl was soon crouched over the stream cleaning out the innards and thoroughly washing the entire carcass. I helped him cut the animals to pieces. He stuck the sloth meat on green, skewerlike branches and set them down near the fire.

"That's our dinner. We'll smoke the monkey to take along with us," he said.

Besides the sloth meat, which was seasoned with the spices Marcus had prepared, Karl made rice in place of our usual soup.

After dinner Karl rigged a small domed structure of green branches over the fire and set the cuts of monkey meat inside: legs, arms, body, head, and tail.

"We'll let it smoke all night. By morning it will be good and dry."

For breakfast we had rice soup and monkey meat. It was the first time the three of us had tasted monkey. I was nauseated by it, but my hunger overcame my disgust. Marcus and I tried to choose nondescript pieces of meat from the breast and loins. Kevin was less squeamish and sat there smacking his lips.

"I'll be damned, it's really good."

Karl savored every bite. He grasped a thigh and tore the flesh from it with his teeth.

We shortly came to the Cocus River. Traveling along it was astoundingly beautiful. The Cocus was different from the Asriamas. The farther downriver we went, the more streams ran into it, and the wider, deeper, and more powerful it became. Walking in the river was very difficult, more so for me because the wound on my hand was still painful. We chose each step carefully. Progress was slow. We came upon deep pools and waterfalls and had no choice but to climb up into the jungle and hack our way through the foliage until we came to a place where the river was shallow again.

Karl's boots were now entirely shapeless, yawning with wide holes. He wrapped them in nylon bags and used rope to secure them to his ankles. His feet were covered with blisters, but he didn't complain. He only paused now and then to tighten the ropes. Once in a while he stopped to examine the rocks at the water's edge, looking for traces of gold and other minerals.

By afternoon we were exhausted. We stopped to rest, and Karl gave us each a slab of monkey meat. This time Marcus and I devoured it hungrily. For second helpings Karl pulled out the monkey's tail and cut it into pieces. Marcus and I declined, but Kevin and Karl munched around the tail the way you would corn on the cob, leaving only the bare, white cartilage.

We sat a little longer studying the map.

"We have to keep traveling down the Cocus to here," Karl said, pointing. "Then we'll cross back over the mountains and come down to the Colorado-Chico. I've been told that there's a lot of gold to be found in that river," he added. "If we find any traces, maybe we'll change plans and set up camp there instead of Curiplaya. I think we should be able to pan a good few hundred dollars' worth."

Kevin and Marcus weren't particularly impressed. They didn't really take him seriously, but I was intoxicated by Karl's enthusiasm and wanted to believe that we might go home rich.

After a few more hours' walking over rugged terrain, we set up camp. Karl added the last of the monkey meat to the rice soup. He broke open the shriveled skull and tossed in the brains. Marcus was absolutely disgusted and wouldn't take a bite of the soup. I was reluctant at first but overcame my aversion and dug in with the others.

Another day of arduous walking in the river, the fifth since we had left Asriamas. According to Karl, this was the day we would find that Indian village. I had almost full use of my hand by then. Kevin never stopped snapping pictures. The scenery was really splendid; the wilderness was without a trace of civilization—no rusty tin cans or cigarette butts. No one had been here before us. Everything was clean, natural.

A goose flew overhead. Karl shot at it but missed. We were all disappointed. For the first time since we had started out, Marcus held back to walk with Kevin and me. He confided that he was worried and didn't want to rely on Karl. He was afraid to go on.

"We don't have enough food," he protested.

Kevin tried to reassure him. "This evening we'll check just how much rice we have left." he suggested reassuringly, and yet I noticed he seemed less than friendly to Marcus.

That evening we sat around the campfire. The clouds that had gathered overhead all day broke up, and the moonlight shimmered on the Cocus River. The current glittered a silvery reflection. Nor was the jungle dark. Hundreds of fireflies danced about. It was a magnificent evening, but Marcus was anxiety-ridden.

"Look, we've been going for five days, and who knows how far we've really gone, how close to our plan," he said. "In the meanwhile we're running out of food. Maybe we'd better go back. We can't know for sure that we'll even find the Indian village. We don't even have a decent map."

"There's nothing to get uptight about," Karl said. "We're not about to get lost in the jungle. No way. I know the jungle too well, and I have a great sense of direction. It might take another day or two, but we'll get there."

We studied the map. Karl had marked the approximate location of the village. We seemed to have covered only about half the distance, and our progress was now slower because of the painful blisters on our feet. Marcus was also weak and had lost a great deal of weight.

Kevin and Marcus measured out cupfuls of the rice. Considering that we ate it for both breakfast and supper, the amount that we had left would last barely four days.

"There's no point in going on any farther," Marcus decreed. "Let's turn around and go back."

Karl tried to change his mind. "We aren't far away. By the day after tomorrow, at the very latest, we'll be at the Colorado-Chico River. There we'll fire some shots into the air. The villagers out hunting will certainly hear them. They don't like anyone firing guns in their territory because the noise scares the animals away. They'll come to see who's shooting. When they do, we'll give them the presents and liquor. That works like a charm on them. They'll probably carry our packs for us and help us make the climb up the mountain to the village. There we'll be able to rest up. Kevin can take his pictures. Marcus can get his strength back. Before we set out again, we'll stock up on yucca, corn, fruit, and plenty of meat. The provisions will last us the rest of the trip. I'll be able to find out if they know where gold can be found in the Colorado-Chico. We should keep on. We aren't going to follow our own tracks back to Asriamas, are we?"

I was convinced. "Onward," I shouted. "Where's your spirit of adventure, Marcus? Whatever happens, we'll make it. If we run out of rice, we'll hunt game."

"That's the spirit," Karl went on. "No one ever dies of starvation in the jungle. We'll find food."

But Marcus wasn't at all convinced. "I want to turn back," he said stubbornly.

Kevin looked thoughtful. He bent over the map a long while. "Maybe we should follow the Cocus down to the mouth of the Lansa River," he suggested. "It's on the Peruvian border. There are villages marked on the map there. We could stock up on provisions there and then go on."

"No, I don't want to go that far out of the way," I objected. "If we go all that way, I'm sure that we'll never turn back to the Indian village. Either we go on as planned or we turn back. I'm not about to walk all the way to Peru."

We decided not to decide at least until morning.

CHAPTER 6

BACK TO ASRIAMAS

You could set your watch by Karl. I awoke in the morning to find him once again up and about. When he saw that I was up, he beckoned to me urgently. He pointed to fresh tracks on the riverbank, just fifteen yards from the tent. "It's a jaguar. A big one. Look at the size of those paws. He was this close to our camp. It's a good thing the fire didn't go out during the night."

A great deal remained to be settled, and over breakfast the four of us discussed our alternatives.

Karl said, "Just look at my boots. They certainly are ready to head back to Asriamas, but I'm willing to keep on going, no matter what, barefoot if I have to, to get to the Indian village. Trust me."

But Karl's opinion didn't really count. He was merely our guide. He had to do as we chose.

Marcus was adamant. "We're going back!"

I objected just as stubbornly, "We're going on!"

Kevin would cast the deciding vote, and I was sure that he would side with me. It surprised me when he took a long time weighing the options, making up his mind. Finally he cast his vote. "We're going back."

Karl accepted the outcome gracefully. We climbed back up the mountainside, following the same path we had taken the previous day. Kevin was in a rotten mood. It was the first day of the trip that he didn't take any pictures. He wore a sour expression and wasn't at all friendly toward me. Marcus and Karl walked ahead of us, talking. Their disagreement hadn't adversely affected their friendship.

I spotted a fig tree growing right on the edge of the river. How could I have missed it yesterday? Kevin and I picked the fruit together, but it turned out to be unripe and sour. Only a few were edible. Kevin took some coca leaves out of his pack. He chewed a lot of them during the day, as they calm the stomach and dull the appetite, but I found their taste sickening. Karl munched on cinnamon sticks as he walked along, but they were so strong that I passed on them as well.

Suddenly we heard excited cries up ahead. Karl and Marcus had almost stepped on a large snake.

"It got away." Karl shook his head in regret. "Too bad. They're delicious. Taste just like fish."

"Isn't it poisonous?" Kevin asked.

"No, that one wasn't particularly dangerous. There are two species of venomous snakes in the jungle," Karl started lecturing, "the pucarara and the lora. The pucarara has yellow and black stripes. Its bite causes almost immediate death, but the lora is even worse. It's the same shade of green as the leaves and usually lives up in the trees. It's likely to strike right at the head, and if it isn't within striking distance, it can spray its venom, spit it right into your eyes. I know a guy who went blind. But other than those two, the snakes aren't dangerous, except for the boa, of course, which can crush you to death. So can the anaconda; they live in the rivers. They get to be a few yards long, and they're very thick around.

"I'll tell you something though. The most dangerous animals—worse than snakes and even worse than jaguars—are the wild boars. They have brains. They run in herds, following a leader. Once I was on an expedition, and when we stopped to rest, we were attacked by a pack of boars. There must have been twenty of them. They have vicious tusks and razor-sharp teeth. They caught us off guard. We all ran away, scrambled like hell up the trees. Then those fucking pigs started rooting around the trunks. They were trying to uproot the trees, determined to make a meal of us." Karl enjoyed elaborating. "We fired a lot of shots at them from up in the trees and finally scared them off after we had killed eight of them. We didn't have to do any more hunting the entire expedition; we had plenty of smoked meat. Wild boar meat is a real delicacy."

But we didn't run into many wild animals other than monkeys, which we frequently saw and even more frequently heard; they made a terrible commotion at night. We did come across tapir and deer tracks every day, but the vast majority of our contact with the animal kingdom was unfortunately with various species of insects, who inflicted much pain upon us. The most bothersome were the fire ants: small, brown ants that climb trees. If one of us inadvertently brushed against a branch of fire ants, he quickly regretted it. Masses of them swarmed over us, under our collars, up our sleeves, and down our pants. Their sting burned like fire. Whenever one of us was attacked, he danced about in a frenzy. Kevin would strip off his clothes and try to shake them out. Marcus would scream, "Those son-of-a-bitching ants, those lousy son-of-a-bitching ants! Come help me!" He would point to those parts of his body that he couldn't reach, and we would pluck the merciless ants from him. When I fell victim to them, I would rush to the river and leap in, hoping to drown them, but the pain was horrible. Karl told us that fire ants can always be found on the *palo santo* (holy wood) trees. The missionaries used to tie recalcitrant Indians to the palo santo, and while the fire ants attacked them, they had the opportunity to rethink their resistance to Christianity.

In addition to the fire ants the bees also pestered us, mainly when we were trying to eat, and the mosquitoes were a constant plague, stinging every patch of bare skin. We had malaria pills and conscientiously swallowed one each day. If these scourges didn't inflict sufficient misery upon us, we also fell victim to the leeches. They clung to our bodies, digging their heads under the skin and sucking our blood. If you don't get leeches off in time, they bloat up, and then you have to be careful how you pull them out. You have to dig the head out from under the skin with a pin or risk getting an infection.

Our progress was rapid, as we knew the way and were marching over trails that we had cut only the day before. At night we slept in camps that we ourselves had set up only recently. We walked without enthusiasm, however, barely speaking. Both Kevin's and Marcus's shoes looked as if they had had it. Karl's boots were completely useless, and he was wearing Kevin's sandals. Walking over a rugged trail and wading through streams in sandals couldn't have been very pleasant, but Karl, as I've said, was a very tough guy.

There was an unspoken enmity between Marcus and me. We didn't speak to each other at all, and even in practical matters we communicated through Kevin. It bothered me, but I felt secure, sure of Kevin's friendship.

In the evening, after dinner, Kevin would take out a spool of dental floss and break off a piece for each of us before we brushed our teeth. Kevin's father was a dentist, and he didn't let his dental hygiene lapse, even in the jungle. Marcus was returning from washing the dishes in the river one evening and offered us some of the water remaining in the clean pan to rinse the toothpaste from our mouths. I took a mouthful, sloshed it around, and spat it out. There hadn't been much water, and I used it all. Kevin was angry.

"You should have shared it with me," he complained.

"I know," I replied, "but there was so little water in there, I used it all without even noticing."

"Still, you should have shared. You always have to share."

Kevin was ticked off and went to the tent, where Karl was already snoring.

Marcus and I were left alone by the fire. Neither of us spoke a word. I was ill at ease and felt lonely after having quarreled with Kevin. I needed him. If Kevin got mad at me, he might befriend Marcus again, and then I would be left out. Marcus peeked over at me, but I wouldn't meet his eyes. I sat there thinking for another moment and then rose and said good night.

Kevin wasn't yet asleep in the tent.

"What's Marcus doing out there all by himself?" he asked.

"I don't know," I answered.

Kevin didn't seem at all upset with me. On the contrary, he put a warm hand on my shoulder when he said good night. Kevin and I were reunited. Marcus's defeat was complete now. I looked out at his fragile figure, and a chill crept along my spine. What was becoming of me? Where was all this darkness coming from? Why did I mock him? Why did I enjoy his pain? Suddenly I was afraid, afraid of myself. I wanted to rush out, hug him, and ask his forgiveness but couldn't move.

Marcus stayed out there for a long while, staring sadly into the embers.

In the morning Marcus discovered red splotches on his feet and complained that they were very painful. Karl looked worried.

"It's not good, not good at all," he said. "Those splotches are liable to spread all over your feet. That happened once to a friend of mine. It got so bad, he couldn't walk, and we had to carry him over our shoulders. I hope you haven't got the same thing."

Marcus was frightened by what Karl said and rubbed petroleum jelly all over his feet.

We tramped briskly on that day, and Marcus managed to keep up with our pace. Kevin's mood improved.

"At least we can still go down the river," he said.

At noon Karl spotted a *pavo*, a wild fowl something like a turkey. It was sitting on one of the branches of a tall tree. Karl hushed us, crept forward stealthily, and took careful aim. The shot and cry rang out together.

"I hit it! I got it!" he shouted gleefully, and ran between the trees to retrieve the bird.

Then we heard cries of fright and pain.

"Ay! Ach!"

He burst through the foliage and ran like crazy for the river, jumped into the water, got back out, and came quickly over to us, rubbing himself all over.

"Bees, fucking bees!" he yelled angrily. "They stung me all over."

He removed his shirt, and Marcus counted the stings he had on his back. Nine. His left ear was already red and swollen, and the back of his neck was inflamed as well.

"They attacked me, the sons of bitches!" Karl hadn't calmed down yet. "The pavo fell right into a beehive. The little mothers can have it, for all I care."

Kevin and I had a hard time stifling our laughter.

"You don't mean that, Karl," Kevin said. "We're not going to leave that turkey just lying there while we go hungry."

"You want it so bad?" Karl said, fuming. "Go get it yourself."

"Yossi, are you going to help me?" Kevin asked.

I joined him reluctantly. First we sprayed ourselves all over with repellent, both our bare skin and our clothes. Karl watched us with a smug grin. We crept up on the spot, approaching from opposite directions, and soon saw the buzzing swarm over the fowl. Kevin crept forward, and I did the same.

"Don't worry," Kevin said, "The smell of the repellent will surely keep them off us."

I was standing about six feet from them and hadn't been stung. Kevin took one more step, and the bees swarmed over him in one thick cloud. "Oooh, ohhh," he yelled, and started running blindly. He crashed into boughs, stumbled, and didn't stop for anything until he jumped into the river. I ran like hell, too, but wasn't stung.

Karl chuckled with satisfaction. "Hey, Kevin, so where's the turkey?"

Kevin rubbed his aching body. "At least twenty bees stung me, the bastards. I hope they choke on the damn turkey! I'm not going back in there."

The next morning Marcus's feet were in terrible shape. The splotches had spread out, and he was in agony. He smeared them with petroleum jelly again before he put his shoes on and covered them with plastic bags. He wanted to try to keep them dry, an impossibility when wading in a river. Fortunately by afternoon we were back in Asriamas.

Don Jorge's children were the first to see us coming and ran back to the village, calling out joyfully that we had returned. A few women came out to welcome us. Don Jorge's wife was among them, along with her mother and neighbors. They were genuinely happy to see us again. And someone else was happy to see us as well.

She rose from where she had been lying in the shade of the cookhouse, yawned widely, and came to greet us, wagging her tail. Flaca! Karl was amazed to find her alive and well. He tried to hide how happy he was and gave her a swift kick in the backside, as if to say, "We've had it with you, you traitor."

A boy was sent to call Don Jorge from the fields. His wife fed us in the meantime: lamb broth, rice, beans, and roast meat. A pitcher of juice was also brought to the table as we savored the delicious food for which we had hungered.

Don Jorge came in from the fields, his machete over his shoulder. He gave us each a warm handshake. We told him about our journey into the jungle and back, about the trouble and Marcus's disease. Marcus wanted to return to La Paz now, while we developed new plans. We weren't going to make it to the Indian village, but at least we could carry on with the second part of our plan. We wanted to stay in Asriamas to build a raft and float down the Tuichi River to the place where it runs into the Beni, near Rurrenabaque, and from there fly back to La Paz.

Don Jorge suggested we put Marcus on a mule and that he personally would lead him all the way to Apolo. He also offered to build the raft for us. Karl explained that it had to be wide enough and sturdy enough to carry four men, our packs, and a large quantity of food. Don Jorge replied that he wouldn't be able to do it on his own but that he would see if his neighbors would be willing to lend a hand. Marcus decided to see us off on the river and then go on the trail to Apolo.

We had time to kill and took a dip in the river. We washed our hair, and except for Karl, we all shaved off the stubble that had sprouted on our cheeks during our trek. We got out of the water and dressed hastily because the mosquitoes were swarming about us. I was in such a hurry that my wallet fell out of my pants pocket. I bent down and quickly snatched it up. It was a red cloth wallet, waterproof, but I had wrapped it in a plastic bag anyway.

"Yossi, I've been wanting to ask you what you keep in that wallet," Kevin said. "I know where your passport, money, and watch are. So what do you have in that wallet that you never let it out of your sight? What are you hiding in there?"

"It's a long story," I said with a grin.

"I'm listening," Kevin said.

We seated ourselves in the shade. "Have you ever heard of the Kabbalah?" I began.

"It's some kind of Jewish mysticism, isn't it?" Kevin said.

"Exactly," I replied, "but the truth is, I don't know any more than that about it myself. I had an uncle named Nissim, which in Hebrew means "miracles." He was born in Turkey and studied at the yeshiva in Tiberias. Then he wandered about Europe making his living as a cantor, ritual slaughterer, and performing circumcisions. Eventually he settled in Israel and opened a small toy store in Rehovot.

"My uncle was always reading old religious books. I didn't know it then, but he was studying the Kabbalah. He had his own special way of life and particular eating habits. He never visited a doctor and refused to take any medicines. Whenever he didn't feel well, he would fast for a day or two until he was better.

"Nissim never had any kids, but I was as close to him as a son. When I turned eighteen and was about to go into the army, he asked me to come see him. He sat up tall, with his full head of white hair and piercing blue eyes. He was eighty-three years old then. He took a little book out of his wallet. It was very tiny, very thin, its pages yellow with age.

"'I've carried this book in my pocket my entire life,' he said to me. 'It has special powers. It has taken care of me. I'm an old man now, and you will soon be a soldier. You need its protection more than I do. Take it and care for it well. Don't ever part with it, because it will watch over you.'

"I thanked him, gave him a kiss, and went home, thinking that it was all a lot of nonsense. When I got home, I found my mother in tears.

"'Uncle Nissim has had a heart attack.'

"I rushed to the hospital. My uncle was unconscious. I gave the little book to my aunt, and she slipped it under his pillow. When he regained consciousness, he asked her to return it to me since he wouldn't be needing it any longer. He died in the hospital."

"God, what a story!" Kevin exclaimed.

"Maybe it was just circumstance, or maybe he sensed that his time had come, but just in case I always carry the book with me. A year ago I was mountain climbing in Alaska. I had strayed from the trail and came to a dangerous overhang. The stone I was bracing myself on gave way, and I fell, but my jeans snagged miraculously on a jagged rock, and I was saved. I had the book in my pants pocket. Maybe that was just chance too. Who knows? Still, it makes me feel safe. Sometimes I think that I'm indestructible as long as I have it with me. When my own son gets drafted, I'm not so sure that I'll want to give it to him."

"Give it to him when you're eighty-three," Kevin suggested.

Kevin had just as many stories to tell about himself. One year he had returned from a trip to Nepal, arriving home on Christmas Eve. His family wasn't expecting him, as he had called only his sister to tell her he was on his way and made her promise to keep his arrival a secret. He went directly from the airport to her house, where she outfitted him in a Santa Claus costume. Then, all dressed up, with a sack of brightly wrapped presents slung over his shoulder, his face covered with a thick, woolly beard, he knocked on his parents' door. His father answered, and Kevin went into a Santa Claus routine. He asked his father and brother if they had been good little children, if they had behaved themselves and thought they deserved a present. They answered that they had, never suspecting who was hiding behind the beard.

Finally Kevin couldn't take it any longer and, choked with tears, cried out, "It's me, Dad! Kevin!"

Marcus's feet were still hurting since the rash had not cleared up. Karl told him that he should dry his feet thoroughly and keep off them. Marcus rubbed on more petroleum jelly and stretched out in the sun, but the flies and mosquitoes swarmed about his bare feet, and he was forced to cover them with a mosquito net.

Marcus wanted to have a look at Don Jorge's son's injured foot. The boy was called and came running over with only a rag wrapped around his foot. He took it off, and we could see that the swelling had gone down. There were no more signs of infection, and the wound was almost completely healed. The boy's recovery made Marcus happy and proud.

That evening Don Jorge told us that his neighbors were willing to help build the raft. Tomorrow they would cut some balsa trees and float them down the river to the village. Don Jorge said that the raft would be ready within three or four days, depending on the weather. The balsa logs had to be thoroughly dry before they could be used. It was the end of November, and the rainy season would soon be upon us, but we hoped for a few sunny days to dry the logs. The amount of money—twenty dollars—that Don Jorge and his neighbors were asking for the work was ridiculously low, and we agreed among ourselves that we would give them more than that.

We wanted to buy foodstuffs from Don Jorge—rice, meat, fruits, and vegetables—for our stay in the village. If his wife was willing, we also wanted to hire her to prepare our meals and would pay her for both the food and her work. Don Jorge was amenable.

"So now you've got a hotel with full board," Karl teased us.

We prayed for good weather because Karl kept reminding us that he had to be back in La Paz by the beginning of December in order to pick up his uncle's truck. He planned on our spending about a week on the Tuichi, so we had to start out as soon as possible.

"Maybe," Karl added, "If we got to Rurrenabaque soon enough, we'll be able to visit my uncle's ranch. It's not far from there. We could stay for a day or two."

We all liked the idea. Kevin and Marcus both wanted to fly home before Christmas. I was in no hurry to go anywhere.

How good it was to sleep on a luxurious straw mat that night. How peaceful the village was. The villagers were all fast asleep. The horses grazed among the mud huts, casting long shadows over the dewy grass. The sheep dozed under the papaya trees. The pigs wallowed in their mud, looking like they were dreaming, wiggling restlessly in their sleep. The dogs were too lazy to bark.

Karl went out at dawn to help the villagers search for balsa trees. That afternoon he came back to the hut to find the rest of us lying on our mats. Kevin and Marcus were reading. I was doing nothing. He told us that they had already selected seven thick trees, and Don Jorge and his friends were busy chopping them down at that very moment.

It was hot outside, so we were enjoying lying in the cool, dark room. Karl, never content to remain idle—a talent Kevin and I were cultivating to a fine art—looked around restlessly for something to do. He gathered up Marcus's and Kevin's shoes, the soles of which had fallen almost completely off. He took up a hammer and nails and with great diligence pounded holes through the leather uppers and the rubber soles. He wove wire through the holes, pulling it good and tight, just like sewing. Then he looked over his own boots. The soles had been lost long before in the jungle. He went out into the village to scare up a piece of leather that he could use to make new soles. He haggled a while over the price and finally traded one of the small pocketknives that we had brought along to give to the Indians for some deerskin. He cut the skin precisely to the shape of the boot, made holes all around its edge, and finally stitched it to the boot with fishing line.

"There's hardly anything that these two hands of mine can't do," he boasted. "You never can tell when you might need to call on a certain skill."

Karl spent the afternoon with Don Jorge's father-in-law, questioning him closely about gold in the region. The old man answered his questions patiently. Karl learned that Don Jorge's younger brother, Pablo, had stumbled upon a large gold nugget on the riverbank. Following his discovery the villagers had gone out to pan the area, but the results had been disappointing.

Karl came back to the hut all wound up and raring to go. He told us what he had learned and was already making plans.

"The villagers don't use very sophisticated mining techniques. They can't really judge the potential this area might have. I'm going to have a look for myself tomorrow. If there is any gold to speak of, I'll return with a machine that does the panning automatically. I can buy everything I need in Apolo and bring it here on pack mules. I'll fly in the fuel for the machine in a Piper that can land on the river. It's a big advantage having a village right here. I can live here, buy my food here. It will be good for the village too. Bring a little prosperity. I'll be able to hire a few men. Peddlers will start coming, bringing their goods to the village. The villagers will be able to sell their produce to them . . ."

Within five minutes Karl was a millionaire and had transformed Asriamas into a bustling metropolis. Throughout his recitation Kevin and Marcus had gone on with their reading. I was the only one who took him seriously, and we formed a partnership. He was glad to find a sympathetic ear.

The next morning at the crack of dawn we left Marcus and Kevin in the hut and set off for Don Pablo's house. He lived on the other side of the village, an hour's walk from our hut. We had a pack filled with presents we had brought for the Indians. On our way we traded a few hooks, fishing line, a whistle, or a pocketknife for coffee, fresh eggs, and hot peppers. Little houses were strung along the river, and we stopped at each of them. Karl left a standing order for four eggs each day at one house. He also arranged for an *aroba* (about twenty-five pounds) of yucca, hot peppers, dried onions, chancaca, sweet bananas and plantains—a stalk of each—all to take along on the journey we were planning. He promised to pay well for the provisions in money or in gifts.

We found only two little girls at home at Don Pablo's. One of them went to the banana grove to call her father while we sat down to rest in the shade. Karl started fooling around, making faces and gestures at the turkey that was wandering around the yard. When it would come over curiously, Karl tried to spit on its head. Then he grew silent and solemn. I had the feeling that there was something he wanted to say but didn't know how. Finally he spoke.

"I don't know how to put this, but I have to tell you. I've already spoken with Marcus about it. You remember I invited you all to visit my uncle's ranch after we've finished rafting down the river? Well, I don't think that I can take *you* there. You see, my uncle is Austrian. I mean, not just any old Austrian. He left Austria and came to live here. The truth is, he had to leave. He was a fugitive. I guess he had collaborated with the Nazis. I'm not exactly sure. Anyway he fled to Bolivia. He's a very primitive person. I can't stand him or his opinions. Only an idiot would discriminate against someone because of the color of his skin or his religion. My uncle goes around cursing the Jews and making derogatory remarks about them. At first I thought I would ask you to pretend that you aren't Jewish. You could say you were American instead of Israeli, like Kevin. Who needs to go looking for problems? That's what I told Marcus that we should do, but I know you better by now. If my uncle makes some stupid anti-Semitic remark, you're likely to blow your top."

"And provide you a shortcut to your inheritance," I joked to ease the tension. Still I was uncomfortable, not so much with the idea of Karl's uncle having been a Nazi, but with Karl himself and the way his stories kept changing.

Don Pablo came up while Karl was talking. He was a pleasant fellow. We had already made his acquaintance when we first came to Asriamas. Karl put a lot of detailed questions to him, and he answered obligingly. He even showed Karl a few gold nuggets that he himself had found, though the large nugget had been sold to a dealer in Apolo. He got a hoe, a pickax, and *batea* (pan), gave us a pitcher of caña, and took us to the dig. Then he left us to go back to work.

On the side of the hill that sloped up from the riverbank, we saw a tunnel chipped away in the rock.

"Here we go, off to work," Karl said.

He rolled up his sleeves, went into the tunnel, and studied the rocks. Then he swung the pickax against the stone wall, chipping off a few chunks. He piled them into the batea and headed for the river. He seated himself on a rock and dipped the batea into the water, holding the chunks of rock under water and crumbling them apart as well as he could. Then he moved the batea in slow, circular motions. Water poured off with each turn, carrying with it the sand and stones. He went on until the batea was almost empty. He stopped occasionally and tried to crumble the small chunks that remained in the batea and then resumed.

"You see," he explained to me, "the gold is mixed in with sand and rock. I'm trying to separate them. Gold is much heavier than water, sand, or rock. That's why it stays in the batea, while the sand and rocks get washed away. You just have to make rhythmic, circular motions."

Karl completed the process, and there really were two minute gold nuggets left in the bottom of the batea. Karl showed them to me.

"They aren't worth anything," he declared. "Too small. But we won't give up. Come on, let's give it another try."

Karl's remarks barely registered. I was aflame with gold fever.

"We found gold! We found gold!" I kept repeating to myself.

I took up the pickax and started slinging away at the rock, giving the chunks to Karl. He carried them to the river and did the panning. We worked until noon.

By the time we returned to the village, the flame of gold fever had been extinguished. Karl declared that the quantity of gold we had found was negligible, virtually worthless.

"For each ton of rock there's hardly any gold at all."

He made some calculations and decided that the vein was bogus.

"But don't give up hope, Yossi. You'll see, in Curiplaya we'll come up with at least five grams."

Don Jorge reported that the raft was coming along. The logs had been planed, their bark removed. The next day they would be fastened with sturdy wooden pegs. The rest depended on the weather. If it were hot and dry, we would be able to set out in another two days; but if it rained, we would have to wait a few more days.

It did rain, only a drizzle, but it lasted several hours. We had already spent eight days in Asriamas. Kevin had spent most of that time reading. Karl, as usual, kept himself busy. He went to see how the raft was coming along, went out hunting, haggled with the villagers, and told stories to anyone willing to listen.

Marcus's feet were better, but he was in a really lousy mood. He kept his distance from Kevin and me. With nothing else to do, he took to tagging along with Karl. "Just like a little Brownie following her troop leader around," Kevin remarked contemptuously.

The next morning Karl and Marcus went to try their luck fishing down where the Asriamas fed into the Tuichi, Karl bragging that he would be back in no time with a huge fish. Toward noon I went to see if they had had any success. On the way I noticed a large waterfowl perched on a rock, poised to dive into the Asriamas. It was so involved watching its prey that it didn't notice me. I backed stealthily into the reeds and recalled what Karl had told us: "All birds that feed on fish are good to eat." I would give everyone a surprise today, I thought, and catch this bird. I ran quickly back to the hut for the shotgun, praying that the bird would not fly off.

When I returned, it was still perched on the rock. I crept through the reeds, trying to get as close as possible. I took aim but couldn't bring myself to pull the trigger. The bird was so beautiful, and we had enough food here in the village. It would be wrong to kill it. But masculine pride and the need to be admired by my peers won out. I took a shot. The bird fell silently into the river. The current was strong, and as the bird began drifting away, I noticed that it was still alive, trying to fight the current. I was dismayed that it might simply vanish in the water. It would be a shame to have killed it for nothing. I took off my clothes and dove in. The bird saw me and sensed that I was coming after it. It ceased struggling and gave itself up to the current as if it preferred drowning to the ignominy of death at human hands. I swam after it in the swift waters. I was nearing the point where the Asriamas emptied into the Tuichi when I caught the bird by one wing. It pecked fiercely at my hand and let out a strangled screech, but I didn't let go. I kicked my feet and used my free hand to make it back to the riverbank. I climbed out of the water and dropped the bird on the shore. It lay there bleeding profusely. I ran back to get the shotgun and bashed its head with the butt. The soft ground cushioned the blow, and the bird writhed in pain. I put a rock under its head and brought the butt down again. This time the bird was still.

Don Jorge's children met me outside the village. They had heard the shot and came running to look the bird over. Don Jorge's wife also came to greet me, and I asked her to prepare the bird for our supper, but first I just had to show it to Kevin, who was properly impressed by my marksmanship.

Karl and Marcus came back empty-handed that afternoon. Before I even got the chance to give them a good ribbing, Karl asked me, "What's the story, Yossi? What kind of weird bird did you shoot? I saw it in the kitchen. We can't eat it."

"Why not?" I demanded to know.

"It eats all kind of carrion, snakes. It isn't fit for humans."

"Yuck!" Marcus exclaimed in disgust.

"But Karl," I protested desperately, "that bird eats fish. I saw it with my own eyes, trying to catch a fish."

"You were mistaken," Karl waved me off. "It's not fit to eat."

I felt humiliated. Karl was only saying that because I was the one who had shot it. I knew that if he had killed it, he would be telling us what a delicacy it would be. Marcus bugged me more than anything; he was so happy to see me put down.

The bird was served for our dinner, but no one took a bite. I thought sadly of the graceful bird whose life I had taken for nothing. A huge lump of frustration caught in my throat, and I felt tears gathering in my eyes.

A strange thing happened a couple of days later. Marcus, feeling somewhat better and encouraged by Karl, surprisingly had changed his mind and decided to join us on the raft.

"But how come?" exclaimed Kevin. "You should go out on a mule, meet us in La Paz. You don't feel good, your feet are inflamed."

But Marcus insisted on it; he wanted to join us. "We started up together," he said. "We should finish it together."

"What the hell are you trying to prove? I don't understand you, not at all." Kevin was very upset and Marcus adamant.

The tension didn't cease. On the next day another unpleasant incident took place. Marcus and Karl had gone to check on the progress of the raft, and a short while later Lázaro, Don Jorge's young brother-in-law, came to our hut.

"The gentlemen want you to come see the raft," he informed us.

"What for?" I asked. "We've already seen it."

"It's ready now. They said you should come see."

"Tell them we have complete and absolute faith in their judgment," Kevin said irritably, never taking his eyes off his book.

I explained to the boy that since we had already seen the raft, if Karl and Marcus weren't in need of help, if they just wanted us to come take a look, we would rather stay where we were and rest.

"Forget it, Yossi," Kevin interrupted me suddenly. "Let's send them a message."

Kevin dictated a silly letter, and I wrote it down:

Dearest Karl and Marcus,

As you are already only too aware, we are lazy slobs and goof-offs, and are quite content lying here in the shade. We have complete, total, and absolute confidence in your inspection of the raft, but if you should be in need of our assistance, you have only to take off your boots, Karl. The smell of your socks will come wafting our way, and we'll be there like a shot.

Yours truly,
Kevin and Yossi,
the good-for-nothings

I handed the note to the boy and asked him to deliver it to the two gentlemen.

Half an hour later Karl appeared. "What's with you guys? Why the hell didn't you come down to the river?"

"What for?" Kevin asked.

"We have to check the raft's buoyancy with all four of us on it. Besides us, we'll still need another two Indians to represent the weight of our provisions and equipment," Karl explained.

Kevin apologized. "We didn't understand the kid. He didn't tell us that you needed us."

"Well, no big deal." Karl smiled congenially.

We walked to the river with him and boarded the raft. The logs were a bit paler than they had been but still green. The raft was heavy. It sat too low in the water and was clumsy to handle.

"No good," Don Jorge said. "You have to wait longer."

"I don't have a lot of time," Karl said with evident concern. "We may not have any choice but to walk back to Apolo."

"There is another alternative." Don Jorge said. "On the other side of the village my brother's neighbor has four strong, dry balsa logs. Go see him. If he'll sell them to you, we can add on the dry logs, two on each side, and they'll make a big difference."

We all went back to the cabin. I hurried in ahead of Kevin to get dibs on the bed. Kevin accepted defeat and sank down on the straw mat. Karl went off sniffing around the cookhouse. Marcus stood restlessly in the center of the room, obviously upset.

"Yossi," he said suddenly.

I looked up at him. He looked strange.

"Yossi, you can have your shitty note!"

He took the crumpled note out of his pocket and threw it in my face. It landed on the floor. The room was silent. Kevin looked on without a word.

"Pick up your shitty note, do you hear me?" Marcus was hysterical. "You should be ashamed of yourself! It was contemptuous of you to have written it, an insult to the Indian. He isn't your servant. He went to the trouble to come and give you a message, and you shouldn't have made fun of him.

"For the past week Karl and I have been making all the arrangements, waiting on you hand and foot. All you do is sleep. When we finally ask you to do one thing, you screw around and weasel out of it. It's an insult to Karl, after all he's done for us."

It all came pouring out in a shrill voice. When he had finished, he stood there, glaring reprovingly at me. He probably had taken a long time building up his nerve for the outburst.

I floundered awkwardly, not knowing what to say. Marcus had recognized my handwriting and blamed the note on me alone.

"I was only kidding around, Marcus," I said in a low voice. "I didn't know exactly what the boy wanted and had no intention of insulting anyone. If I did, then I apologize. But if you can't take a joke, that's your problem."

Kevin intervened. "Hey, you two," he said, "how about knocking off this crap? Can't you behave like adults? Come on, let's all sit down and talk it over. There's no point in keeping this up. We can't let our personal relationships ruin the whole trip. We'll get everything off our chests, once and for all, out in the open."

Kevin looked at us, awaiting our response. Marcus said nothing.

"It's okay by me," I said, "but I think it's between me and Marcus. So maybe we should do it, just the two of us. Do you agree, Marcus?"

"Yes," Marcus answered meekly.

After dinner I suggested that Marcus and I take a walk outside the village. There was a large, grassy clearing where the horses grazed. I loved to sit there on a fallen log and watch them. I had noticed one particular horse, strong and sinewy, noble and unbroken. I went there alone every evening and hadn't shared this spot even with Kevin. I would sit on the log and enjoy the solitude, singing aloud in Hebrew.

Marcus and I seated ourselves on the log. It was difficult to begin, but Marcus finally did.

"I didn't think we'd ever speak to each other again," he said. "There were so many times when I've wanted to talk with you, but you always avoided me. Whenever I tried to get near you on the trail, you hurried over to Kevin. You were always with him. Talking to him. Telling him stories. I would try to join in, but you just ignored me.

"I'm stuck hanging around Karl all day, listening to his idiotic stories. I don't have anyone else. You're always talking to Kevin, and I'm left out. I wanted to talk it over with you, to ask you what happened, but you always avoided me.

"Do you remember one night just the two of us were left sitting by the fire? I wanted to talk with you, but you just went into the tent. I stayed there outside, hoping you would understand, that you would come back out to talk with me, but I was wrong.

"This whole trip is one big disaster for me. I'm miserable. I'm not enjoying it at all."

"I think you're right, Marcus," I said. "Something has changed, but I don't know exactly what. Nothing in particular happened. We just drifted apart. We don't have the same relationship we did before. Maybe I'm coarse, not cultivated enough, and you, you just don't feel at home in the wilderness."

"That's a lie! A lie! Just a cheap excuse!" Marcus burst out angrily. "Don't try to hand me that again. It's not true. I know that's what Kevin says. He's already told me that, and do you know when he told me? After two days on the trail. He had already made up his mind that I don't feel at ease in the wilderness. He said that he didn't get along with me and felt some hostility toward me, so it would be better if we kept our distance, if we spoke less with each other. Two lousy days after we started out he said that to me. That was a painful blow for me. I left Annick behind in La Paz to go off with two close friends, and after two days one of them abandoned me like that. And then, Yossi, you were all I had left. I needed a friend, I needed you. But you, you never noticed anything. You just wanted to be around Kevin. Why, why, did you shut me out like that?"

He went on crying quietly, his whole body shaking. For the first time since we had set out on our journey, I felt sorry for my friend. I was no longer happy for his loss, that I had Kevin all to myself. I understood how important I had been to Marcus. I tried to console him.

"Look, Marcus," I said, "let's go back to being friends like we used to be. I don't know what's come over us in this jungle. We'll go back to La Paz, and everything will be all right. It's not true. I didn't abandon you just because of Kevin. We were all together for a whole week in La Paz, and Kevin didn't come between us. Let's try to pick up the pieces. Let's be friends again."

Words, words. Maybe I succeeded in cheering Marcus up a little bit, but we never were close friends again. We did talk to each other after that day, but it was forced, unnatural.

We bought the four dried balsa logs. Kevin and Marcus went across the village to fetch them, floating them down the river. They were soaking wet when they got back. Marcus was in a better mood.

Karl and I went out to cut more balsa bark panchos. We wove them into long ropes with which to fasten the additional logs to the raft. We went about our task with great energy. The new logs were dry and amazingly light. We attached them, two to each side, and the raft was now wider and far more buoyant.

Don Jorge told us the raft would be safe. We decided to set out the next day.

We kept on working that afternoon. Karl built a sort of raised platform in the middle of the raft. We would tie our food supply and the rest of our equipment down onto it the next morning and cover it all with nylon sheeting. That way everything would stay dry.

Our last evening in Asriamas we gathered up all our gear and provisions. We had ten pounds of rice. We hadn't been able to buy more, as the village had run low. We bought about seven or eight pounds of dried beans. We also had a large bunch of green plantains and the rest of the supplies we'd been assembling in recent days: yucca, cucumbers, onions, and a lot of hot peppers, a little "honey" derived from sugarcane, salt, and spices. Salt was measured out like gold dust in Asriamas. We had paid for all these goods with a variety of gifts, according to the preference of the recipient. Karl was in charge of our finances, and he made a lot of mistakes. He traded off almost all our spools of fishing line, leaving us with only a few yards. He did the same with the fishhooks; he gave all but three away. We had had ten cigarette lighters with us when we got to Asriamas. We had only one when we left, and it was only half full. Even the insect-repellent spray, which was so essential, he left with Don Jorge, and we had only a small amount.

That evening we had a festive going-away meal. Don Jorge had borrowed the shotgun and succeeded in killing an enormous boar. We wanted to pay him for the raft, our purchases, and his wife's wages. He asked for only 1,450 pesos (less than 50 dollars): 800 for the sheep, 600 for the raft, and 50 for the rice. He didn't want any remuneration for the food we had eaten in his home, for the chickens that had been slaughtered especially for us, for the fresh vegetables we had received each day, for the game he and his family had hunted, and for the enormous quantities of caña we had drunk. He also refused payment for the dozens of papayas we had eaten. We were his guests, he insisted, and he wouldn't take money for his hospitality or for his wife's work. After a quick huddle we decided not to take anything from him for the things he had bought from us. And we added 800 pesos to the amount he had quoted. Don Jorge was satisfied.

CHAPTER 7

SHOOTING WHITE WATER

"**O**kay," Karl said, getting organized, "who's the captain? Me or Kevin?"

"You, Karl, you're the captain," Kevin said.

"Okay, then I'll be in the bow with an oar. Marcus and Kevin, you will each take a corner in the stern, holding a long pole. You'll push us along with the poles. Lower them down to the river bottom and give a push. Yossi, you sit here by me holding a pole. Whenever we come too close to a rock or the bank, you use the pole to push us off and keep us from colliding. Understood?"

"Captain," Marcus piped up. "The poles are too long and heavy. They're hard to handle."

Karl picked up one of the long poles that the villagers had prepared and agreed, "Yes, you're right. They made them too long." He took out the machete and hacked off the ends, leaving the poles shorter by about a yard. Then he put on my small backpack and tightened the straps. He had spent the day before cutting chips of dried balsa, filling the pack with them. He was the only one of us who couldn't swim and was afraid of falling into the river and being carried away, so he had made himself a life preserver.

Another shove, and heave-ho! We were caught up in the Tuichi's current. The river, which had appeared fairly calm from the bank, did not feel calm at all. The current was extremely swift. Karl pulled hard at the water with his oar, trying to keep the bow pointed straight forward. He yelled instructions back to Kevin and Marcus.

"If she pulls to the left, Kevin has to push her back from the right, and if to the right, then Marcus pushes."

That quickly proved to be impossible. The poles were now too short to reach the bottom of the deep river. Marcus had turned ghostly white, Kevin wasn't displaying any emotion, and I was very excited. Karl was uptight.

"If you can't reach the bottom, row, row, pull hard!"

"This is a round pole, not an oar. You can't row with it," Kevin said.

"Do as I say. Is that clear? Do as I say!" Karl yelled.

Kevin rowed indifferently, not making much effort, and it did seem to be pointless. The Tuichi was straight and smooth, and so far we were cruising along without any problems.

After about an hour we came to shallow waters where large rocks jutted out.

"Watch out! Now pull to the left, Kevin, to the left!" Karl pulled at the oar with all his might. "Yossi, get ready to push us off that rock with the pole," he said to me, as we rapidly approached a boulder. We all rowed. Marcus tried to push off from the rocks on the bottom. His pole snagged on one of them and was torn from his hands.

"I've lost my pole!" he cried. "I lost it!"

"*Mierda*," Karl swore.

"Here, take this pole."

I handed our only spare pole to Marcus.

"Get ready, Yossi . . . push!" Karl cried.

I stuck the long pole out toward the rock that the raft was approaching. I pushed but didn't have enough strength to prevent the collision. The raft took a severe blow and tilted up on its side for a moment, but then straightened out.

We were moving along again but no longer passing through smooth waters. Every few minutes we approached another rock, and Karl was on the verge of hysteria. We somehow managed to smash into every one of them but suffered no serious damage. I lost a pole, and Marcus lost his second one. Things weren't looking so good. We finally managed to pull over to the shore.

"We can't go on like this," Karl said. "It's terrifying. Not one of you has the vaguest idea how to handle a raft."

"Take it easy, Karl, take it easy," Kevin said. "Nobody learns how to do it in an hour. We'll get more practice. We'll catch on. Everything will be all right."

"This isn't child's play, Kevin," Karl retorted angrily. "We don't have time for lessons. I could be killed. You have to follow my instructions quickly, without hesitation."

"All right, Karl," Marcus said. "We'll do just as you say. Tell him that you'll do what he says, Kevin, please. Say it."

"All right. I'll follow your instructions," Kevin conceded reluctantly.

Karl took the machete and went into the jungle. He swiftly lopped off a few long branches and made four new poles. Then he sketched a raft in the sand and explained how we should deal with various situations. He showed us how to paddle with the pole, and how to use it to push off from the river bottom without letting the river take it away. He showed me how to hold the end of the pole under my arm when absorbing a blow so as not to risk breaking a rib from the impact.

Back on the river there were fewer rocks, and we were getting used to it.

"Right!" Karl yelled, and we all rowed, the raft nudging over to the right. "Good. Now left."

We practiced until we thought we had the hang of it, but whenever we came to a difficult pass or a bend in the river, Karl started yelling like a maniac, Marcus turned white, Kevin got angry, and I hid my fears under a mask of absolute indifference. Fortunately none of us was hurt or slipped into the river.

"Yossi, come trade places with me," Marcus said. "You should get some practice back here in the stern."

Good for you, Marcus, good thinking, I thought sarcastically. *Any minute now and Poppa will give you a nice pat on the head.* But I did as he said. He took up my position near Karl, and I went aft.

"He doesn't know the first thing about white-water rafting," Kevin said to me. "Believe me, we're doing everything ass backward.

Whoever heard of trying to row with a round pole? Is he putting us on?"

I suspected Kevin of holding a grudge against Karl for having yelled at him. I still believed that Karl knew what he was talking about.

That afternoon the river was serenely beautiful. We grew accustomed to the pace. Karl had calmed down somewhat. "It's so magnificent," he said with a sigh. A family of monkeys was leaping from one treetop to another, and Karl imitated their cries. "There'll be plenty of game downriver," he promised. "No one has ever hunted that area before. This river is loaded with fish, too, huge fish. They can weigh over a hundred pounds."

We came to a slight turn in the river. Karl ordered us to row in the opposite direction, to keep away from the bend.

"That's all wrong," Kevin said to me. "We should just let the current carry us along."

We made it safely around the bend, and Karl began yelling excitedly, "To the left! Hard! Everyone, row left, fast! We're liable to go into the Eslabon Pass."

About two hundred yards downriver we could see a profusion of jagged rocks jutting out of the river. We lost two more poles trying desperately to row but finally made it safely to the riverbank. It had been raining lightly, and now it started coming down harder. Drenched and shivering, we decided to look for some kind of shelter. Karl made a little clearing, and we helped him set up camp.

Kevin and I returned to the raft to tie it securely to the shore, unloaded the equipment, and took it all to the camp. The rain let up and finally stopped. Karl took a wet log, cut it in half lengthwise, and used the machete to chop off chips of the inner wood, which was still dry. We were soon warming ourselves around a fire. Kevin called me to help him carry more firewood, and I was again amazed at his strength. He lifted entire tree trunks and carried them on his back. We had chosen a lovely campsite on a hillside in the jungle. At the foot on the hill was a nice little beach.

As usual Karl prepared our dinner. We were having rice, some yucca tossed into the embers, and a little meat from the slab of wild boar that the Don Jorge had given us. Marcus got up and went over to Kevin, who was concentrating on eating. Marcus nimbly flipped his little portion of meat onto Kevin's plate.

"Happy holiday, Kevin," he said. "Today is Thanksgiving Day in America. I thought you might like a little surprise."

"Thanks a lot, Marcus," Kevin said, obviously moved, "but I can't take the only piece of meat you're going to get."

With a stubborn smile Marcus refused to take it back.

Karl started lecturing on rafts. "This is a really unpleasant surprise. I'm the only one here who knows how to handle a raft. I can't do it on my own. We'll all be risking our lives unless we learn to handle it together, quickly. I think it was a big mistake for me to have taken this upon myself. We would have been better off walking back—"

"Don't rush it, Karl," Kevin interrupted him. "It will take some time, but we'll soon be doing it like pros."

"But time is what we don't have, Kevin," Karl replied vehemently. "Don't you understand? We don't have the time. There are treacherous rapids in the pass where the Eslabon empties into the Tuichi. The Eslabon is right here. It takes a team of skilled raftsmen to cross it. I have no intention of attempting it with the three of you. Instead we'll have to secure long vines to the raft and haul it down the river."

"Good idea," Kevin agreed.

"Yeah, it is a good idea," Karl went on, "but we won't always have that option. A day or two down the river we'll come to San Pedro Canyon. They call it the Mal Paso San Pedro; it's an unnavigable pass. Waterfalls, white-water rapids, rocks sticking out everywhere. No one has ever made it through the canyon, and neither will we. Even before that canyon there are other treacherous passes, and you have to know how to control the raft, how to stop it when necessary. The risk is tremendous otherwise—we could get swept into the canyon. If that happens, we've had it. Just the thought of it scares the shit out of me. We have pulled over twice today, but both times it was only by dumb luck that we managed to stop the raft."

"What do you mean, Karl, we can't go through the canyon?" I asked. "You said that you've already rafted the length of the Tuichi more than once."

"I never said that. I've gone down the Tuichi many times to a point a little farther on, to property belonging to Don Matías, the Swiss. From there I went by foot to Curiplaya, which is on the other side of the canyon. I've rafted from Curiplaya on down to Rurren-abaque many times too. It's smooth, easy going from there, but no one has ever gone through the mal paso."

"Then how are we going to go on?" Marcus wanted to know.

"That's the point. We have to get as close to the opening to the canyon as we can and stop. There we'll take the raft apart. Two of us will bypass the canyon on foot, while the other two wait. At an agreed-upon time the two who stay behind will set the logs of the raft adrift in the current. Beyond the canyon, at Curiplaya, the river widens, and the current is very mild. The two who've gone ahead will swim into the river to retrieve the logs. By the time the other two get there, the raft will have been reassembled with panchos. From there it's a breeze, but before we reach that point, the dangers are great. You don't know how to use the poles. A real *balsero* can make excellent use of a pole, just like a paddle."

"So why don't we just make some more oars?" Marcus asked.

"An excellent idea," Karl agreed. "Tomorrow we'll look for some balsa trees and cut a few oars."

Later that evening Kevin and I sat together talking quietly.

"Believe me," Kevin insisted, "Karl doesn't know what he's talking about. It's obvious that he knows nothing about rivers. He's making such a big deal out of this bad pass, like it's so dangerous. You wait and see, we'll take the raft through tomorrow with no sweat. If you're willing, the two of us could take it through. No problem. Besides, I don't trust him. Why did he only now suddenly remember to tell us about this San Pedro Canyon? There's something fishy about the whole thing. Karl is a strange guy."

Right after breakfast Karl and Kevin went to look for balsa trees to cut oars and soon found some a little way upriver. Balsa trees are very tall with lots of branches, but their trunks are so brittle that it only takes a few machete chops to fell them.

"We'll cut each one down the middle lengthwise and get an oar out of each half," Karl said after they'd returned to camp and set about measuring the branches.

"I'd like to know how he thinks he's going to cut them right down the middle," Kevin whispered to me skeptically, but Karl proved his skills. He fashioned a wedge from the branch of a hardwood tree, made a small slit in the middle of the balsa log, fit the wedge into it, and pounded on it with a heavy rock. The log fell into two pieces like a charm.

Karl was a genius with the machete. He rapidly cut the split logs into the shape of oars and then carved them to the desired width and length. He formed concavities in the lower section of each one and whittled out comfortable grips for our hands. Kevin and I worked on the other pieces, cutting them down to the basic shape, and Karl finished them. Now we had to let them get thoroughly dry so that they would be light and resilient.

I proposed spreading them around the fire. "Otherwise we'll be stuck here for eight days waiting like we did with the raft."

"It's not good to dry them by the fire," Karl said, "but we don't really have any other choice, short of time as we are. We'll sleep here today and go on tomorrow."

Since it was still early, Karl decided to go hunting.

"What do you think, Karl?" Kevin asked before he could go. "Maybe we should move the raft down a little closer to the Eslabon Pass, so that tomorrow we'll have an earlier start, pass it by, and be on our way."

"Good idea," Karl conceded. "Maybe I'd better forget about hunting."

"No, that isn't necessary," Kevin said. "Yossi and I will just pull it along by the rope."

"Okay, if you think you can manage without me."

Karl took up the shotgun and a few shells and marched off into the jungle.

Marcus insisted on accompanying us, though he was suffering again from the painful rash on his feet.

"I think I just have to keep my feet dry," he said. "They hurt like hell."

"So maybe you should wait here," Kevin said.

"Oh, no, that wasn't what I meant at all. I'm coming to help you."

We untied the raft and started dragging it by a rope fastened to its bow. The closer we got to the pass, the rockier the riverbank became and the harder it was to haul the raft.

"We'd better get aboard and take it down out to the middle of the river," Kevin proposed. "You don't intend to try going through the pass on your own?" Marcus exclaimed in fright.

"And why not?" Kevin demanded. "It looks to me like it would be easy. We'll stay in the middle and let the current carry us right between the rocks. We might take a few knocks, but that's nothing to get excited about."

"We can't do it without Karl," Marcus protested. "It wouldn't be right. We promised that we were only taking the raft up to the pass. Anyway, Karl knows what he's doing. He could show us the best—"

Kevin interrupted him impatiently. "Karl doesn't know the first thing about rafts."

"Well, four is still better than three. Please, Kevin, let's wait for Karl."

"All right, Marcus, if you want, you can go back. Yossi and I can do it ourselves."

Marcus was terrified, but he joined us. He and I boarded the raft, while Kevin remained in the water, gently pushing the raft toward the center of the river. The water was already up to his neck before he hiked himself aboard. From there the current had its way. We started gaining speed. The center of the river was far less rocky than it had been close to the bank, but Kevin had been wrong. We took more than a few knocks. We crashed into one rock after another, the raft tilting on its side. Both Marcus and I fell into the water and clutched the raft, afraid of being swept away. Somehow we managed to pull ourselves back aboard. Marcus was beside himself, pale, too rattled to speak. The original raft stood up well to the beating it was taking, but the logs we had added, using ropes instead of pegs, were beginning to come loose.

We made it safely across the Eslabon Pass, but we were without poles or oars and couldn't row for shore. Kevin jumped into the water again, holding on to the rope that was tied to the bow. He managed to brace himself against a boulder and from there used all of his strength to pull the raft toward the shore. Together we hauled it up on a tiny beachhead and secured it.

Kevin regarded me smugly. "You see? A bad pass isn't such a big deal."

"We did it!" Marcus was exultant. "We made it on our own! Way to go, Kevin! You, too, Yossi!"

We walked back toward camp through the jungle. We were soaking wet. Marcus found walking difficult and complained of pain in his feet, which had gotten wet again. Suddenly a shot rang out. Karl must have bagged something. I raced forward, in the direction of the sounding. There was no trail, and I broke off branches, jumped over fallen logs, and crawled under low-hanging boughs. I was making a terrible commotion, when a horrible thought struck me: Karl was likely to think that I was some kind of wild animal charging through the brush.

"Karl, Karl," I called out, "where are you?"

"Here, Yossi, I'm over here," he roared.

I found him carefully studying a wide tree. "What were you shooting at?" I asked. "Did you get anything?"

"Ah, that was a mountain lion. It was too high up a tree. I missed it. But, look, Yossi, a rubber tree."

Karl struck the tree with the machete, and thick white drops, like glue, came oozing out of the gash. "I can use it to fix my boots."

The nylon thread with which he had sewn his boots together had already frayed.

We went back to the tent and got an empty tin can for the glue. We met up with Kevin and Marcus on our way back to the tree.

"We bypassed the Eslabon," Marcus informed him excitedly.

"Hey, that's terrific, really. Was it hard?" he asked nonchalantly.

"Piece of cake," Kevin replied.

"Terrific," Karl said, without the slightest trace of spite in his tone, "we'll get an early start tomorrow."

Within half an hour Karl had enough glue to fix his boots, and we went back to camp.

Marcus was lying in the tent. Kevin was turning the oars over to dry on the back side. Karl set the tin of glue down near the fire.

"It has to harden a bit before I can use it," he explained.

Restless as always, he got out the fishing line and hooks. He rooted around in the loose earth of the jungle with the machete until he found what he was looking for, a nice fat worm. He baited a small hook with half of it and started fishing.

"They're nibbling, the little bastards, they're nibbling," he said to me happily, and in a short while he had hooked a minnow. He cut the minnow in two and baited a large hook with half of it, using thick fishing line.

"Yossi, have a go," he urged, and went back to his cobbling.

I swung the baited hook over my head and cast the line into the river. I hadn't even had the time to roll in the line when it went taut and straight. I had a large fish on the line; I could feel how hard it was pulling.

Take it easy, pal, I thought, *you're not going anywhere.*

I gently drew the fish toward me. From time to time I let out a little slack and then drew it in again. After a few minutes the fish tired and was easier to pull in. It was a catfish that weighed about ten pounds.

Karl was stooped over the fire and turned around to look at me.

"Oh, ho," he called out, "what a beaut! You're really something, *pescador valiente* (gallant fisherman)."

"Don't get so excited," I boasted. "I just started out with the small fry, now I'll go catch a real fish."

I removed the hook from the fish's mouth and baited it with the remaining half of the minnow. Marcus went down to the riverbank with me to watch me fish.

The line was thick, but too short, only about thirty yards long. I tied one end to a tree branch. Again I swung the baited hook over my head, cast it into the water, and waited. The line was taut in my hand, and I could feel the steady tug of the current. Then something pulled hard. In an instant the line was pulled tight, humming like a guitar string. I had it wrapped around my finger, and it sliced through the flesh. Luckily I managed to free my hand. The branch was quivering, shaking, and then suddenly the line snapped and went slack. The fish got away with the bait and the hook.

I was stunned. I had done a lot of fishing in my time, but I had never felt that kind of pull on the end of a line. The fish must have weighed at least seventy pounds.

Marcus, too, was awed. "God, what a fish that must have been!" he cried out.

I showed him my injured finger, and he hobbled over to the first-aid kit and carefully bandaged it.

Karl laughed when we told him about the big one that got away. "Just wait," he reassured us, "you'll catch one of those yet."

"Yeah, and how will we go about that, Karl?" I asked, "with twenty yards of line and two hooks? How could you have given and traded away all our fishing gear without leaving enough for us?"

"Don't worry, we'll have enough," Karl waved me off.

I cleaned the fish I'd caught, and when it was ready, Karl skewered it on a green stalk of bamboo and tied it in place. He arranged two forked branches over the fire and hung the stalk between them. We slowly turned the fish, its fat dripping down and crackling in the flames. The flesh was tender and delicious. We could barely stand to leave a little for the next day.

Then Karl repaired the soles of his boots with the glue he had collected from the tree. When he finished, he lay down by the fire and fell asleep. From inside the tent I stared out at him: Karl, the jungle dweller, so at home in the wilderness.

In the morning Karl decreed the oars "ready to go," and we carried our provisions on our backs to the place where the raft was tied.

Rafting was heavenly. The Tuichi was placid, the day was lovely and warm, and the raft was easily controlled with the oars. We could maneuver it any way we wanted with little difficulty. After a while Karl pointed over at the left bank.

"This was Don Matías's property, but he doesn't live here anymore," he said.

We went on. I called Karl's attention to the fact that the panchos were very loose, and we were liable to lose the additional logs.

"We'll stop to look for another balsa tree and make some more panchos," he agreed.

We soon came upon a wide beach where it was easy to secure the raft. Kevin and I went with Karl. Marcus stayed aboard the raft. Karl strode into the jungle, looked up at the treetops, and picked out the distinctive large, clover-shaped green and yellow leaves of a balsa tree. He cut it down with two swift chops of the machete, but the tree was too young, its trunk too narrow. We wouldn't get many panchos from its bark.

"Take it to the raft and then come back," he instructed us. "I'll look for another tree in the meantime."

Kevin and I each picked up an end of the log but quickly threw it down as if it were a viper. It was covered with fire ants. We tried to shake them off the tree, but there were too many of them.

"Make for the water!" Kevin shouted. "Fast! Run! The sons of bitches!"

We ran, carrying the log, screaming and cursing, straight into the river. Marcus watched in bewilderment as we ran past him.

"Fire ants!" I called out to him by way of explanation.

The ants were still biting, even in the water, as we picked them off each other's bodies. The swift current washed the rest of them from the log. Once we were rid of the ants, we laid the log down next to the raft.

"You might as well go back alone," I said to Kevin. "I'll stay here with Marcus and make panchos from this log until you come back with another."

Kevin headed back, and Marcus and I set to work. With two sharp knives we peeled the bark away in strips, carefully removing the fibers that lay beneath.

"I've been waiting for a chance to talk to you alone, Yossi," Marcus suddenly said. "Yesterday Karl told me he's thinking of calling off the rafting and turning back. He claims that it's too dangerous and that Kevin doesn't know anything about rivers. He said that he'll wait and see how it goes today and then decide whether to turn back or go on."

"In that case there's no problem. We did beautifully with the oars today," I said.

"Yes, that's true," Marcus agreed, "but if Karl should decide to go back"—he paused for a moment before going on—"let's the three of us go on by ourselves. We can do it without him. If he wants to go back, I won't be able to go with him because I can't walk. My feet are getting worse every day. We're wet all the time, my feet never dry off, and the rash has already spread all over them. We have to go on whether he's with us or not."

What Marcus said took me by surprise.

"Don't let it worry you, Marcus. We'll all go on together one way or another. I don't think Karl will call it off, but if he does decide to go back, we'll have to go along with him. He's the one with the most experience, and we would have a hard time getting along without him."

Just then Kevin came out of the jungle by himself. "I can't find him," he said.

"So wait here with us," I said.

"No!" Marcus burst out. "One or the other of you has to go and help him. He's not our servant. You have to help him. If my feet weren't in such bad shape, I would be more than willing to go look."

"Okay, okay, don't get yourself all worked up," I said. "I'll go."

I found Karl dragging a young balsa log through the sand. Marcus was right; Karl was ticked off.

"Why the hell didn't you come back? Am I your slave? I'm always willing to do everything, but I can't do it without help."

"Kevin came to look for you, but he couldn't find you."

"Don't give me that. The whole jungle heard me hitting that tree with the machete. How could he not find me?"

But Karl was a good-natured guy. He never stayed angry for more than a few minutes and was always easily appeased.

We prepared the fibers from the second log and rapidly tightened the loose balsa logs to the main body of the raft. Then we were on our way again. The raft was in good shape, but the river was no longer calm. It became narrower, and the terrain around us grew mountainous. The river wound around numerous bends and scarcely had a bank. Karl soon grew tense. The current carried us up against the rocks and onto the sloping banks. In many places the rapids were white and frothy.

I was in the stern, holding the left oar. Kevin was on the right. Marcus stood next to Karl in the bow. We were rapidly approaching a bend in the river a few hundred yards ahead. Farther on we could see white water and a scattering of jagged rock half-submerged in the middle of the river. The current was very strong, and there was no way that we could stop.

"Left! Quick, to the left! Row as hard as you can!" Karl shouted. "Everyone together, hard!"

"Right!" Kevin shouted. "If we go to the left, we'll end up *on* the rocks."

"Shut up, Kevin," Karl almost went to pieces. "You don't know what you're talking about. This isn't a kayak, and you're not in Oregon. Do what I tell you."

I had no idea which way to row. I stood there holding the pole. Marcus turned to me.

"Row, row fast!" he screamed. "Watch me and do like me. Deep, like this. Put the oar in the water just like this." He was hysterical. His voice was shrill.

The rocks loomed nearer, and there was no way that we could avoid them. Our frantic rowing did no good at all. The raft was taking a terrible pummeling. It tilted on its side and then flopped down, rising up and down, up and down. I squeezed my eyes shut and gripped the ropes holding the raft together. I could hear Karl's frightened cries but couldn't make out what he was saying. Kevin made some reply, but I couldn't understand him either. A minute or two later everything was calm again, the river had become smooth as glass, and we heaved a collective sigh of relief. The raft hadn't suffered any serious damage, only the outer logs had become somewhat loosened.

"I don't want any more arguments out of you, Kevin," Karl said breathlessly. "Either you're going to do as I say, or I'm calling the whole thing off. Do I make myself clear?"

"Yeah, all right. I'll do as you say," Kevin replied, but only to calm Karl down.

Marcus drew to my side.

"I'm sorry for yelling at you, Yossi," he apologized, "but it's just that I'm pretty good at rowing. I used to row the Rhine.

I've had a lot of experience, and I just wanted to show you how it's done."

"It's okay, Marcus. You were right to do it. Anyway, you didn't yell at me."

"Then you're not mad at me?"

"No, I'm not mad at you," I said softly.

Up ahead we could see a broad river emptying into the Tuichi.

"That's the Ipurama," Karl said. "Let's stop."

The water was placid at the junction of the two rivers. It required scant effort to pull the raft over onto the sandy bank. The Tuichi was very wide, about a hundred yards across. It was silvery blue, while the Ipurama was dark green; they mingled in an exquisite blend of colors.

Karl took the map out of his pack. He pointed to the Ipurama.

"The Mal Paso San Pedro isn't far now, maybe half a dozen miles, but the San Pedro Canyon begins before that. We mustn't enter it, no matter what. It is a real *cajón* (box). There is no shore at all there, just sheer rock cliffs on both sides of the river. What we'll have to do from now on is stop at regular intervals and walk ahead a few hundred yards to check out the river to make sure there's another stopping place up ahead where we can pull up before we reach the mouth of the canyon. There we'll stop, and two of us will go around it on foot to Curiplaya."

Karl's plan made sense to all of us.

"Okay, then," he continued, "let's scout our first stopping point. We'll go through the jungle around the next bend and see if it's possible to pull over somewhere. Who wants to come with me?"

"Not me," Kevin whispered so only I could hear. "I hardly ever agree with Karl about anything. I'd better not go."

"Not me," I said. "I don't know the first thing about river rafting."

"One of you has to go," Marcus insisted. "I can't walk on my feet in the shape they're in."

"I'm not going," Kevin said stubbornly.

"Me neither," I repeated.

I don't know if we intended to torment poor Marcus, but that's what we were doing.

Karl butted in. "What's with you guys? You don't expect me to go by myself, do you? I'm only here because you were so hot to go on this trip."

I relented. "I'll go with you, Karl."

We entered the jungle and kept the river on our left. The terrain was level and the foliage less dense than in other places we had been. Karl didn't have to use the machete as we were able to work our way around and under branches.

What actually happened next, however, was unclear, though it must have been the turning point of the entire trip. As I recall, Karl turned suddenly and said something like, "What the hell are we going on for anyway?" He muttered as though he were thinking aloud. "I must be out of my mind to risk going into the canyon. No one has ever done it. And what if we miss our stopping place and are swept into it? We'll all be killed. That's what.

"What's the point? There's nothing for me there. Nobody's going to award me any prizes for doing it. So why should I?"

He seemed to catch sight of me then for the first time.

"Give me one good reason," he said, this time aloud and straight to my face. "I don't have the time. It could take three or four days to reach the mouth of the canyon. I won't make it back to La Paz on time. Why should I louse things up with my uncle? I told you in the first place that I only had one month. That month will be up in exactly four days."

He stopped and stared at me.

"That's it, Yossi. I've made up my mind. I'm heading straight back from here. I'm not going any farther. If you want, come along with me. If not, go on without me. I'm going back in any case."

Apparently I offered no objections, and Karl continued.

"Look, what did you want out of this trip anyway? To spend some time in the jungle? Terrific, we did that. We walked from Asriamas to Río Cocus and back. You wanted to raft down the river. We've done enough of that. You've seen what it's like. Why should we go on? It's just more of the same. If we turn back, we can have a few days' rest, put a camp on the riverbank, do some hunting and fishing. Marcus will have the chance to rest and take care of his feet. We'll eat well, bathe in the river. That's the life.

That's the real pleasure. Not a crazy trip down the river, risking our lives for nothing."

The truth is, I was convinced.

"I'm with you, Karl."

We headed back without scouting the river at all.

"I'm sure that Marcus will want to go back with us," Karl continued. "I don't know about Kevin. He's stubborn, but he won't have any choice. He can't very well go on alone."

When we came back to the raft, Marcus was sitting, warming his red feet in the sun.

Karl repeated his reasoning and summed up, saying, "So what do you think? Yossi has already agreed. Marcus?"

"I agree," Marcus replied.

"Kevin?"

"Okay. We'll go back," he answered softly.

Karl got the map out.

"We're here, at the juncture of the Ipurama and Tuichi rivers. It's almost impossible to return to Asriamas; it's at least a week's walk. The most logical alternative is to follow the Ipurama upstream. There is a village called Ipurama at the head of the river. It only makes sense that if we follow the river, don't lose it, we'll come straight to the village. We can put up a good, sturdy camp and spend three or four days right here. We'll use up the heavy food: the bananas and the yucca. I'm sure we'll find game here. When Marcus is able to walk, we'll start hiking. Within two days at the most we'll be in Ipurama. There's a trail from Ipurama to Apolo. We'll rest up in the village and rent a few donkeys. We'll ride to Apolo, and from there, no sweat, we'll catch a plane to La Paz. We'll be back in less than a week after we leave here."

"Are you sure we'll make it to Ipurama so easily? Has anyone ever taken this route before?" Kevin asked.

"Perhaps the villagers have come down here to fish. I don't know, but even if no one has ever done it before, it couldn't be simpler. The river will lead us straight to the village—"

"Take a good look at the map," Kevin interrupted him. "The river branches out in three different directions. How can you know which one of them the village is on?"

"Once we're that close," Karl answered, "we'll surely find a trail. Look. All three branches of the river intersect the trail to Apolo. It's a very wide path. You can't miss it. It's only a two-day walk from there to Apolo."

Kevin studied the map carefully and raised no further objections.

We started setting up camp. Karl was extremely thorough this time. He assiduously sought a dry, level area, slightly higher than the river, and diligently cleared away every rock, weed, and root. Then he took me with him to look for strong, straight stalks of bamboo and branches. He wanted to remove the panchos from the raft and use them to tie the tent poles together, but Kevin wouldn't let him.

"You aren't thinking of going on by yourself, are you, Kevin?" he asked warily.

"No, of course not," Kevin answered, "It's just a shame to wreck the raft. For sentimental reasons."

Karl laughed. "All right. I'll find some vines in the jungle."

Once the tent was up, we set the pack with the food in a dry corner, got a fire going, and rigged a pot over it. Everything was splendidly arranged, and we got down to some serious rest and relaxation.

I decided to have another go at fishing. I found a tree growing right out of the Ipurama, near the place where it met the Tuichi. I sat there under the tree trying to catch a minnow. They nibbled but didn't bite.

I decided I should take my shoes off to give my feet some fresh air. Once I had my shoes and socks off, I could see countless tiny red dots all over my feet up to my ankles. I knew that this was how it had started with Marcus and that I had to treat it right away before it spread. The mosquitoes buzzed around my bare feet. I put my socks back on and went on fishing. Kevin found me there.

"Where'd you disappear to? I've been looking for you," he said. "I've got an idea: let's you and me go alone."

I couldn't believe he was serious.

"I'm sure that we could do it," he continued. "The current does all the work anyway. Listen, I'm no idiot. I have no intention of getting myself killed.

"Think about it, Yossi. Why did we come on this trip anyway? Karl promised us an Indian village, which was supposed to be the highlight of the whole thing, but we never made it there. Do you remember how he blathered about all the wild animals along the river? Alligators in lagoons. Gold-mining camps. The village of San José, where he lived. What didn't he tell us? All we have left is rafting down the river. Now he's calling that off as well. How long have we been on the river? Less than two whole days. For that I came on this trip? Gave up going home for Thanksgiving?

"I thought that this was going to be a once-in-a-lifetime experience. And what do I find? That it was all for nothing."

I hesitated. I had already resigned myself to going back, but Kevin rekindled my spirit of adventure.

"We can do it," Kevin said. "We can go on alone."

As Karl had promised, our holiday at the river junction was the best part of the trip so far. We enjoyed surprisingly clear weather. It was the end of November, and by the beginning of December the rainy season is usually in full force.

"That's another good reason for going back," he had insisted. "Try to imagine what it's like getting caught in a rainstorm. Apart from being unpleasant, it's dangerous. The river floods its banks, and the current gets even stronger. I'm amazed that we're having such good weather."

On the second morning at our makeshift resort Karl and I took up the shotgun and machete and went hunting.

"We'll walk a little way up the Ipurama," Karl proposed. "It looks as good a place as any, and we can look around for a trail to take when we start walking."

We walked upstream for about an hour, plodding through the jungle. We saw neither machete marks nor broken branches and could only surmise that no other human beings had passed that way.

Unexpectedly we heard a loud roar.

"A jaguar! A jaguar!" Karl shouted.

I looked about, scared out of my wits. I couldn't see anything, but the roaring grew louder, and other, no less ferocious voices joined in a chorus of snarls.

"No, that isn't a jaguar," Karl changed his mind. "It's a big howler monkey, a *maneche*. Their cries are deceptively similar. Look, up in the tree."

I looked up. A family of enormous brown-colored monkeys was watching us curiously and calling down to us.

"They don't taste as good as the marimono, the black one, but they're okay," Karl said. "Let's get one."

He took aim and fired but missed his shot. From where I stood, it was an easy target. I had a clear view of the monkey.

"Give me the shotgun," I said.

I took it from him, aimed, and fired. The monkey fell, grabbed at branches on its way down, plunged again, and then one of the lower boughs arrested its fall. Karl grabbed the shotgun from me and ran toward it.

"It's the size of a gorilla," he called out as he helped the monkey to a quick and merciful death with another shot fired at close range. The animal dropped to the ground. Karl gutted it right there on the spot to make it lighter. We carried it back to the camp together.

We found Kevin in a great mood. He had been snapping dozens of photos. We had our picture taken with our prey, holding our weapons.

Marcus tried to avoid acknowledging the monkey's presence, though the smell of its scorched flesh, once we'd pitched it into the fire, was pervasive and unpleasant. Marcus had been fishing all morning and devoted all his attention to his task.

"Yossi, come here, quick!" he screamed excitedly.

The line was quivering; he had hooked a big fish, powerful and quick. I grabbed the line but didn't have enough to give the fish any slack. I gently tried to slow it to a standstill. Now the battle was on. I took in a little line, and he took it back. I knew that the fish was strong enough to break a line of this thickness. I reeled it in a few yards; it pulled back with a fantastic burst of energy. The line resounded with a shrill hum. I gripped it tightly. The fish let up a little, and I took in a few more yards of line, and then the fish tried a new tack: it swam quickly toward me, making the line go slack, and then suddenly sprang out of the water with a tremendous leap.

It was beautiful, covered with golden scales, about a yard long. We let out cries of admiration.

"Dorado!" Karl called out. "It's a dorado, the best fish in the river."

"That's my fish. I caught it. Give me back the line. Yossi, give it to me now," Marcus whined.

"It's not your fish," I yelled furiously. "It's food for all four of us. Get out of my way now."

Karl tried to calm Marcus down. Kevin was taking pictures; he caught every move I made.

After about fifteen minutes the fish got tired. I reeled it in, almost to the shore. Finally, when it was about six feet from the bank, Karl jumped into the water, grabbed hold of it, and tossed it up onto the sand. It was enormous, glinting golden in the sun.

"Nice going, Yossi," Karl crowed, and slapped me on the back.

Karl took good care of us as usual. He wanted us to enjoy our dinner and made a cucumber salad with garlic and lemon. He had collected the fat from the fish and melted it in the pan to fry slices of plantain.

Dinner was served. We all held our bowls in our laps and busied ourselves eating. The fish was delicious, white, tender, and boneless. Marcus sat on a log at a distance from the rest of us. He looked depressed. I went over and sat next to him.

"I'm sorry I acted like a baby," he said, "but I've never caught a fish before, and I wanted to land it myself. I know it was stupid of me. I apologize."

"Forget it, Marcus," I replied. "I owe you an apology, too. I didn't mean to hurt your feelings. I wasn't just trying to show off. It's just that I knew we needed the food. I mean, all of us would rather eat fish than monkey."

"You're right, Yossi. I'm glad that we can talk. I don't know what to do. Kevin is so hostile to me."

"He's just in a rotten mood because we aren't going to be going on down the river. It's hard for him to accept the fact that we're giving up and going back."

"To tell you the truth," Marcus said, "I would just as soon go on, too, even if it is dangerous. At least we wouldn't have to walk. I don't know if I can take a long walk."

"Don't worry about it. Karl says it will only take two days. Then we can get mules to go on."

"Maybe so, but Karl also claimed that the Indian village would only be a five-day walk, and he was wrong."

Later, Karl and I remained alone by the fire.

"So, what did I tell you?" he asked contentedly. "Rest, good fishing, good hunting, good talk under a moonlit sky. As far as I'm concerned, you can't beat it." He paused. "Weird, isn't it, how the three of you ended up here with me? Three characters: Kevin— *fuerte como tres hombres* (with the strength of three men); you—*adventurero*; and Marcus—*turista, tipico profesor*."

The next day Kevin systematically pumped Karl for every last detail about the mal paso and canyon. Karl was happy to answer his questions in order to prove how reasonable and logical his decision to turn back had been. He marked the approximate location of the canyon and the dangerous pass on the map.

Marcus harbored suspicions that Kevin wasn't asking all those questions out of idle curiosity. He asked me about it privately and said that if we were planning to go on by raft, he would seriously consider joining us.

"If you two are going on together," he said, "it could be very risky. Three pairs of hands are better than two."

"I don't know, Marcus," I said. "I don't know what Kevin has in mind."

Later, when I told Kevin that Marcus wanted to join us, he objected vehemently.

"He can't come. He would ruin everything. There's no getting around it, we'll just have to tell him that we don't want him along."

"We can't do that. He gets his feelings hurt so easily. We'll have to find some other way."

Dissuading Marcus turned out to be rather simple. Marcus hadn't given up on catching a fish. He sat on the bank of the Ipurama trying to hook a minnow. I went over to him.

"You were right, Marcus," I told him, "Kevin really does intend to go on with the raft. It would be too big of a disappointment for him to just turn around and go back to La Paz. He told me just now."

"Does he intend to do it alone?" Marcus asked, marveling.

"Yes," I answered, "and I think it's crazy, a good way to get killed, but he's just plain stubborn, and nothing will change his mind. If he tries to do it alone, he doesn't stand a chance. He'll never make it alive. So one of us has to go along to help him."

"Only one of us?" Marcus asked. "Why not both of us?"

"Well, I'd just as soon go back with Karl. I've had enough walking in the jungle and enough of this river. I'm ready to head back, but if I have no other choice, I'll go on with Kevin. Two together could make it, and I'm not about to let him commit suicide. The truth is, however, I'd rather you go. Your feet hurt, and you'd be better off on the raft than walking anyway. Why don't you go on with Kevin, and I'll go back with Karl?"

"No way," Marcus protested. "I'm not going anywhere with Kevin by myself. You've seen the way he treats me. I'm really sorry, Yossi, but there's not a chance. I'll go with Karl."

"In that case I guess I'll have to go with Kevin."

Everything was settled.

I hurried off to find Kevin and proudly tell him how I had conned Marcus into doing as we had planned. Kevin looked thoughtful.

"So," he said, "now we can lay our cards on the table."

We went over to Karl and told him that we were planning on going on alone.

Karl was more than fair. He wasn't angry and didn't try to change our minds. He was just worried and warned us of the dangers we might encounter.

Kevin asked him for a straight yes or no. "Is it possible to make it through the canyon?"

"I've already told you about the cajón. There are two rock faces rising straight up on either side of the river. Once you're in there, there's no way that you can stop. The current will take you straight to the dangerous pass."

"What's so dangerous about it? Can we make it through?" I asked.

Karl scoffed at the idea. "Not a chance. Four skilled balseros wouldn't even consider attempting it. And there's only two of you. It would be suicidal. It's called Mal Paso San Pedro for good reason. Do you know who San Pedro is? He's the guy that stands at the Pearly Gates. And that's just what they meant when they named the pass after him. Anyone who enters the mal paso can expect a personal encounter with San Pedro."

"How is it that you know so much about it?" I asked curiously.

"I've bypassed it over the mountains by foot and seen it from above. When I did it three or four years ago, there was a trail already cut, so it was pretty easy going. The trail was a year old, but I could still use it. By now it'll be all grown over, and I doubt that you'll find any trace of it."

"Is there any way to tell where we should even look for the trail and how far we can go by raft?" Kevin asked.

Our original plan had been to come to the mouth of the canyon, dismantle the raft, and put it back together on the other side.

"Just the two of you won't be able to do that by yourselves. The only thing you can do is to stop before the canyon and just leave the raft there. If you make it past the pass, you'll come to Curiplaya. There won't be a living soul there this time of year. The miners go home at the end of the dry season by raft. Every year before they leave, however, they chop down balsa trees and leave them to dry and be ready for the following year. Once you make it to Curiplaya, all you'll have to do is find some panchos and put together a small raft from the dry logs. From there on, the river is nice and smooth, and you shouldn't have any problems.

"If you do build a raft in Curiplaya, don't forget to cut down balsa trees to replace the ones you take. It isn't hard work, and it's only fair to the villagers. If you like, you can even pan for a little gold in Curiplaya. If you have a good look around, you'll find digging tools and bateas. The miners leave everything there. And there's also a banana grove there and good fishing."

Kevin had little patience. "Karl, stick to the point. How will we know for sure where to stop before entering the canyon, and where should we look for the trail?"

"Take it easy, Kevin," Karl laughed. "Yossi, you'll have to watch that he doesn't go over the speed limit on the river."

He marked our position on the map he had drawn and drew a line representing the Tuichi.

"This is the river. From here on it's rough going, but if you're willing to risk going by raft, it will save you two days of walking. You can't miss the mouth of the canyon. You'll see a big island covered with tall trees right in the middle of the river. On your left you'll see a narrow shore. That's where you have to stop. Don't forget. When you see the island up ahead, start pulling over. If you have any trouble, dive into the water and swim for it. Don't, under any circumstances, go into the cajón."

"Okay, Karl. Don't worry, we won't," Kevin said, clearly exasperated. "So that means we raft down till we come to the big island. There's a shore on the left bank. Is that where the trail will be?"

"Exactly."

"How long will it take us to get around the canyon?"

"It all depends. About two days if you find the trail. If it's completely overgrown, it could take you a lot longer."

Kevin thought for a moment, then turned to me and asked, "How does it sound to you, Yossi?"

"My grandmother could do it." Karl and Kevin began dividing up our equipment.

"You obviously will need the machete," Karl said. "Otherwise you won't be able to build a new raft. We will probably have a hard time getting through the jungle without it, but we can make do with the knife. As for the shotgun, you need—"

"We won't be needing the shotgun," Kevin broke in, "but we'll take the fishing line and hooks. You take the shotgun and ammunition. We won't have any time for hunting, and anyway the ammunition is likely to get wet in the river."

"Okay, fine," Karl agreed. "If we're taking the shotgun, then you can take most of the food. I'm sure that Marcus and I will find plenty of game. You can take the nylon sheeting too. It'll help keep your equipment dry. We won't be able to set up camp without a machete anyway. We'll take the pup tent," Karl concluded.

Karl and Kevin went over each item together in this way. We hadn't yet touched the monkey meat. Karl gave us that except for two small slabs. The lighter presented a problem, for we had only one left. Kevin and I retained possession of it, but we left them ten of the twenty matches we still had and half the paper for striking them. Kevin gave Marcus those of his possessions that he had decided not to take with him. He gave him his precious rolls of exposed negatives with the hundreds of pictures he had taken during the past month along with the accessories to his camera and the tripod.

"They'll be safer with you," he said to Marcus.

That afternoon Kevin went out to get the feel of the river. He swam downstream and came back on foot through the jungle.

"It's not so good," he told me. "Just a quarter of a mile downstream there's already a dangerous pass. I hope we won't have any problems getting past it."

"No sweat," I said. "If we're going to have an adventure, let's do it right."

"Don't be silly," Kevin scolded me. "I don't intend to take any unnecessary risks on this trip. I know just how dangerous a river can be. While we're on the raft, you have to listen to me and do just as I tell you."

I've replaced one tyrant with another, I thought to myself, though I knew he was right. I had been silly, but it was only to hide my fear.

Karl was up first as usual and roused the rest of us. He wanted to get an early start.

The atmosphere was fraught with tension. Marcus fussed with his backpack. Karl joked around a bit, trying to get his spirits up, without a great deal of success. Finally they were ready, each with his pack on his back. Karl had the shotgun, and a knife dangled from his belt in place of the machete he had left with us.

"Well, that's that. Time we were going," he said. "I'd rather walk on the opposite bank, since Yossi and I have already been a ways upriver on this side without coming across any traces of a trail. We might find one on the far side. So now would you be good enough to take us across the river on the raft so that Marcus won't get his feet wet."

"That's my only hope," Marcus said. "As long as my feet stay dry, I'll be able to walk. If they get wet again, all of the skin will peel off."

Once we had taken Karl and Marcus to the opposite bank of the Ipurama, we all shook hands. Karl commented jokingly that he hoped we wouldn't be fishbait by this time tomorrow. Then he gave us a final warning: "Stay together, no matter what, even if one of you is hurt and can't walk. Don't ever leave the other behind in order to go for help. If one of you gets hurt, do anything you can to make it to the riverbank and wait there. Whoever is uninjured will take care of the other and get food for him until help arrives. As long as you stay on the riverbank there's always the chance of help arriving." Karl promised that if we didn't arrive in Rurrenabaque by the fifteenth of December, he would notify the authorities and make sure that they came looking for us.

"We're still good friends," Marcus said to me in parting. "I'll be waiting for you in La Paz. Do you remember that little teahouse where we used to sit talking? I'll take you there. We'll sit and be friends like we used to be."

"That's right, Marcus," I answered. "We'll get out of this jungle. Back in the city we'll be friends just like before."

"I'll be praying for you. I promise that if you're not back on time, I'll go to the Israeli embassy. I'll do everything to make sure that they come looking for you."

"Thanks," I said. "Remind them that I left a note there describing our route."

"Don't be so worried," Kevin reassured him. "We're planning on surprising you and making it back to La Paz before you do."

Karl burst out laughing. "You're full of shit, Kevin," he said.

We once again shook hands, and Marcus said, "See you in La Paz. God be with you. I'll be praying for you. Goodbye."

They turned their backs on us and marched away. Karl confidently led the way. Marcus trudged after him but turned around for one last glance at us before he vanished from sight entirely.

CHAPTER 8

THE ACCIDENT

K evin broke the silence. "Get a move on, Yossi. We still have a lot to do."

We crossed back to the other side of the Ipurama and set to work. Kevin uncoupled the four logs we had added to the raft in Asriamas. Then, using panchos the way Karl had taught us, we tied the logs to one another to make a smaller raft.

"This," Kevin explained, "will serve as our life raft. We'll fasten all of our equipment down to it."

We bound the small raft tightly to the center of the larger one using the ropes and leather strips that Marcus had left us.

"The main raft will take all the knocks from the rocks, and if anything happens to it, all we'll have to do is to chop the straps with the machete, and the life raft will be set free. We just jump onto it and use it to get ashore."

It sounded reasonable to me.

Kevin emptied the backpacks and rearranged our possessions. In the larger of the two packs he put the bulk of our equipment: the pot and utensils, the sheets of nylon that served as tenting, his extra clothes and sandals, the large stalk of bananas, and the smoked monkey meat. He lined the smaller pack, which he called the life pack, with a waterproof rubber bag. Then he filled the bag with the first-aid kit, the map of Bolivia, the two green mosquito nets, Dede's red poncho, the flashlight, the lighter and matches, and his camera along with an extra lens and film. He placed our documents and what money we had into a watertight metal box. I reluctantly took my wallet with my uncle's tiny book from my pocket. Kevin was watching me. He carefully, wordlessly placed the wallet into the metal box. Finally we fitted the rice and beans into additional waterproof bags. Kevin cinched the mouth of the rubber bag tightly shut and closed the pack over it. To the top of the pack he tied two large, sealed tin cans to keep it afloat if it should fall from the raft. He placed the entire pack into a nylon bag, which he filled with balsa chips to make it buoyant. The packs were tied firmly to the life raft, and we were ready to go.

We combed the camp area one last time, but we hadn't forgotten anything. Kevin was very thorough. He kicked through the blanket of leaves that had served as our ground cover and poked through the charred remains of the fire. Nothing was overlooked.

Excited, my stomach fluttering, I boarded the raft. Kevin stood in the water, gave the raft a good shove, and then jumped up beside me.

"Everything's going to be just fine," he assured me. "Just remember what you said yourself: your grandmother could do it. And one other thing: keep alert and pay attention to my instructions."

"You're the captain," I answered.

I wanted to believe that Kevin knew what he was talking about, but at that moment I was pretty nervous. The current seized the raft, and Kevin instructed me to change the pole for an oar.

"All we have to do is to keep the front of the raft pointed straight ahead," he said. "We'll let the current carry us along. We should make the bank Karl was talking about sometime today."

We were rapidly coming upon the first difficult pass. I could see jagged rocks jutting out of white-water rapids.

"To the right, Yossi! Pull hard!"

We ran into a rock, and the raft climbed partway up, the logs shuddering under our feet. Then we were back in the current and about to ram another rock. I made no attempt at rowing but held on to the leather straps for dear life. Kevin was doing the same in the bow. The raft, tossed from to rock to rock, descended churning falls, most of the time tilted to one side.

"Hold on tight, Yossi! Don't let go!"

My eyes were squeezed shut.

Just as suddenly we found ourselves drifting once again on a placid river. Looking behind me, I could see the white waters that we had just come through.

"Hey, we made it!" I shouted joyously.

Kevin smiled back at me and gave me a thumbs-up. Now we both realized how dangerous this journey was. We had discovered how little we could control the raft. While we were being carried along by the powerful current, we hadn't even been able to keep the front of the raft pointed straight ahead. No, my grandmother wouldn't have come along on this trip. Now that there was no one else along with us sniveling, I no longer felt the need to act the tough guy.

We spent the next two hours drifting easily, convinced that we would reach our destination. The scenery was breathtaking. Evergreen-covered mountains towered over reddish cliffs along the shore. Occasionally we passed a narrow waterfall, cascading from the heights to the river. From time to time a family of monkeys accompanied us downstream, jumping from tree to tree. Kevin considered taking the camera out but decided it would be too risky and gave up on the idea.

Around noon we ran into trouble. A large rock jutted out from the shore, and the water pounding against it formed a treacherous whirlpool. The current carried us into its center. We tried for two hours to get out of it without success. Finally seeing no other way, Kevin swam to shore, climbed onto the rock, and tried to use the rope that was tied to the front of the raft to pull it out of the whirlpool. Twice he slipped, fell into the water, and was swept away by the current, but quickly recovered. On his third try the rope broke off in his hands, and he fell once again into the water, but this time he didn't return so quickly. I was left whirling with the raft, fear churning in my stomach. What if Kevin had drowned? What would become of me? I sat on the raft, craning my neck, trying desperately to catch a glimpse of him. When I saw his straw hat carried downstream, I froze.

Kevin returned about fifteen minutes later, bleeding from a deep wound on his knee.

"The undertow here is incredible," he said. "I thought I was drowning. My air was gone, but just in time the current threw me to the surface, and I made it to shore."

"What about your leg?"

"Oh, I didn't even notice. I guess I must have hit it against a rock. Shit, I lost my straw hat."

Instead of attempting to navigate out of the whirlpool, we moored the raft to the riverbank. It was a great relief to have solid ground under my feet.

The next time we tried something else. We pulled the raft upriver, jumped aboard, and rowing with all our strength, tried to get past the whirlpool and back into the middle of the river. We succeeded on the third try. After our cries of joy had died down, Kevin remarked thoughtfully, "Maybe we should have just stayed back there. It wouldn't have been such a bad place to camp."

"But we've still got a while before dark," I said. "Anyway, it's better that we should get all the way to the mouth of the cajón and camp on the bank that Karl showed us on the map. It would be nice to know that we start walking tomorrow."

"Maybe you're right," Kevin agreed.

The reddish cliffs encroached upon the riverbank. It was as if suddenly the river had no banks at all.

"This must be it," Kevin declared. "Get ready. We should sight the island any minute now. When we do, you start rowing to the left as hard as you can. If we run into any serious trouble, jump overboard and swim for shore. This is starting to look like it must be the canyon."

We were both on edge, alert. The current grew stronger. Where in hell was the island?

There was a large rock near the right-hand bank. We were swiftly being drawn toward it. To its left the riverbed dropped sharply, though it was impossible to see just how far. Nevertheless the water cascaded over the edge with a mighty roar. Maybe we could pass to the right of the rock, between it and the riverbank.

"To the right, to the right! Harder, faster!"

I was rowing desperately with all my strength. I closed my eyes, and we rammed into the rock with tremendous force.

"Are you all right, Yossi?"

Like me, Kevin was in the river, hanging on to the ropes of the raft. The water rushed past us on both sides, but the raft wasn't moving. It was protruding from the river at a sixty-degree angle, stuck on a sandbar, riding up against the rock. The pressure of the water slammed us up against the rock and held us fast.

We climbed back onto the raft. Kevin instructed me to tie the oar down so that it wouldn't be swept into the river. I looked over at the waterfall to our left. The river cascaded downward ten or twelve feet. God, why hadn't I turned back with Karl and Marcus?

My legs quivered. If we could maneuver to the right, we would make it through. We tried to get the raft off the rock but were helpless against the current. We tried everything we could think of—pushing, pulling, rowing, prying the raft off with the poles—but the raft didn't budge.

Kevin quickly sized up the situation.

"I don't see much chance of the current getting us out of here. It's only six or seven yards to the right bank, while the waterfall is here on our left, and after that it's probably twenty yards to the left bank. The river is narrow, and the current is terrifically strong. You see what it means? The canyon must start here. We must be really close to the island. If we can just make it ashore, we can go on from here by foot and easily bypass the canyon overland to Curiplaya."

Kevin paused for a moment and looked around before he made up his mind.

"We don't have any choice. I'm going in. I'll try to reach the right bank. When I do, you throw me the machete. I'll climb up into the jungle and cut a vine. I'll throw the vine to you, and you'll pass the packs over to me on it. Then you tie yourself to the vine, and I'll pull you ashore."

"Don't go in, Kevin. It's much too dangerous. Wait a while," I called to him, but Kevin didn't hesitate. He took off his shoes and socks.

"I'll make it, Yossi," he shouted, and jumped into the river.

The current's tremendous force pulled him along. He disappeared for a moment but then bobbed up again. He was washed up against a rock about twenty-five yards downstream, grabbed onto it, and from there made it to the riverbank. I sighed with relief but then caught my breath. I felt the raft moving under me, slowly breaking free of the rock.

"Kevin! Kevin! The raft is moving, Kevin!"

It was slowly slipping away. Kevin ran swiftly toward me.

"Throw me my shoes, fast!"

I obeyed him automatically and threw his shoes as hard in his direction as I could. They landed on the rocky bank. The raft was almost free. It was headed toward the waterfall. I was trembling all over, looking at Kevin in terror, pleading. He was already hurriedly putting his shoes on.

"The machete! Throw me the machete!" he shouted.

The large blade whistled through the air and thudded to the ground. The raft had begun moving.

"You're leaving me, Kevin!" I shouted.

"Hang on as tight as you can, Yossi! Don't let go of the leather straps, no matter what! Don't let go! You're heading for the waterfall. You're going to go over it! Hang on tight!"

"Kevin, you're leaving me!"

"I'll catch up with you. Just hang on! Hang on!"

The raft came off the rock and edged vertically toward the waterfall. I could feel the surge of the river beneath me and held on to the leather straps for dear life. I was thrown into the air, raging water swallowing my screams; amidst the water I felt as helpless as a fallen leaf. The moment of terror lingered, then abruptly ended with a crash. The raft was pulled under the surface of the river, taking me with it. Darkness enveloped me. My lungs were bursting. I had no air.

Don't, don't let go of the raft! I told myself as the undertow dragged the raft along rapidly below the surface. The pressure on my lungs grew unbearable.

God, help me please.

I thought this was the end. Then I found myself above water, the raft floating again. I jerked my head around and saw Kevin, a hundred yards or more behind me, running in my direction. Relief washed over me.

"I'll wait for you wherever I manage to make shore!" I shouted, and waved at him.

Kevin couldn't hear me, but he waved back and kept running.

Suddenly I understood where I was: I had entered the canyon and was being swept swiftly toward the treacherous Mal Paso San Pedro. The raft bounced from wall to wall. It crashed into the rocks, tilted on its sides, was tossed over falls, and swept through foaming rapids. I held on desperately, closing my eyes and praying, *God, God.* Then the raft dove under again, taking me with it. I rammed into rocks so violently that I was twice thrown into the air, landing in the water, vulnerable to the torments of the river, sucked down to its depths. If I hit another rock, I would be smashed to pieces. I was running out of air. When I resurfaced, I saw the bound logs of the raft nearby. I managed to grab hold of them and climb aboard again.

The horrible dance of death went endlessly on. The current was incredibly swift. The raft was swept along like lightning. There was another small bend in the river, and then, still far away, I saw it: a mountain of rock in the middle of the river, almost blocking its entire breadth. The water pounded against it with a terrible roar. White foam sprayed in all directions, the white-capped maelstrom swirling at the foot of the terrifying crag, and I knew that I would never make it past.

I lay down on the raft facing the stern, not wanting to watch as death approached. I squeezed my eyes tightly shut and clutched at the straps for all I was worth. There was a crash. I felt nothing. I was simply flying through the air, then landing back in the water, my eyes still squeezed shut. I was sucked under the black waters for what seemed an eternity. I could feel the pressure in my ears, my nose, the sockets of my eyes. My chest was bursting. Then once more an invisible hand plucked me out of the current and, just in time, drew me to the surface. I lifted my head, gasped for air—a lot of air—before I would be pulled back under. Far behind me I could see the mountain of rock receding. I couldn't believe it. I had passed it. But how? I didn't feel any pain. No, I was uninjured. It was a miracle.

The raft was in front of me not far away. The logs had become loosened from one another. I managed to climb up onto what was left of it. The leather straps were torn, and I had nothing to cling to. I knew that I had to get to the life raft. I mustn't lose the life pack, I couldn't survive without it.

I jumped into the water, and two strokes brought me to the life raft. Again I crashed into the stone walls of the canyon; only now I no longer had a wide, solid raft to protect me. The life raft was small and narrow. Every blow lifted it half out of the water. Once again I rammed into a rock, injuring my knee, but much worse than that, the precious life pack came loose and fell into the water. I grabbed hold of it just as it was about to float away, but it was heavy, and I was afraid that it would drown me. I tied the waist belt to one of the logs and hoped that it would hold. But I was wrong. One more knock, one more dive over a fall, and the precious pack was bobbing behind me, out of my reach. I couldn't take my eyes off it.

I mustn't lose sight of it, I told myself. *I mustn't lose it, no matter what.*

I was fairly certain that I was already through the pass but still in a canyon. Steep stone walls rose on both sides, but the river was getting wider, the current milder, and I could have swum to the bank, but I couldn't abandon the pack. As long as I could see it bobbing behind me followed by the large raft, I didn't swim ashore.

The river turned a bend, and I waited in vain for the pack to make the bend behind me. It must have gotten caught on something. Nor did the raft appear. So, as the life raft neared the right bank, I took the chance to leap ashore, having no other choice but to abandon the big pack and raft.

I landed in the water close to the bank and, wonder of wonders, felt sand beneath my feet. I could actually stand up. I staggered out of the river, unbelieving. I had landed on a rocky strip of shore. Solid ground. I was alive!

It was a few moments before my breathing became regular. Then my thoughts returned to my present situation. The life pack was lost, nowhere to be seen, but maybe it would turn up. Couldn't the current knock it free?

And what about Kevin? Surely he would find me. I had seen him running in my direction. He would certainly make it this far today—or tomorrow at the latest. Yes, everything would be all right. I was sure. He would find me, and together we would walk to Curiplaya. How far could we be from each other? I didn't know. How long had I spent on the river? I didn't know. Maybe twenty minutes. The thought of the river made me shudder.

A steady rain had been falling and now grew stronger. There was no more point in waiting. It would be better to climb up into the jungle to find shelter for the night. I clawed my way up the stone wall. When I reached a height of about fifteen feet, I looked down and was overcome with joy. I could see the big raft. It was trapped between some rocks near the shore, bobbing and banging softly, maybe three hundred yards upstream. Now that I could see it, I could hear the sound that it made as it hit against the rocks. What luck! I thought that the pack was probably stuck there too.

I hurried down to the bank, but the bend in the river blocked my view, and except for the spot where I was standing, the river had no bank at all. I wouldn't be able to get any closer to the raft by foot. I waded into the river, very close to the bank, and tried to walk up-river, fighting the current. I progressed a few feet but then slipped and fell as if the bottom had been pulled out from under me. I was terror-stricken and scrambled back to shore.

Now what would I do? I was seething with anger and frustration. I desperately needed the pack. Maybe I could reach it by land, but scaling the stone walls could take hours. I choked back tears.

No, don't cry. Be strong. Don't give up. You're a man of action. Get on with it, do whatever must be done.

I knew I couldn't make it to the raft that day. It was already growing dark and still raining. I had to find some kind of shelter. I started climbing again, chanting to myself in a whisper, "Man of action, man of action." I could see the raft bobbing among the rocks.

Please stay there until tomorrow. Please stay put.

Improvising a shelter was no easy task. I uprooted small bushes, broke off branches, tore off leaves, and dragged it all back to a little alcove in the stony hillside. I scattered leaves about on the floor and piled branches in the opening until they formed some kind of barrier.

I was famished. I hadn't eaten since morning. A way down the hillside I saw a palmetto tree. I could eat the palm heart, as Karl had taught us. The tree was small, but its roots went deep into the rocky ground. I dug around them with my hands until I finally succeeded in uprooting it. The heart was at the very top. I took a large rock and smashed it against the trunk until I uncovered the soft, white heart. It was a small amount of nourishment, but I gathered every bit.

Suddenly I heard shouting.

It must be Kevin, I said to myself, and roared, "Kevin! Kevin! Kevin!" but there was no reply.

It must have been my imagination. No, I could hear something. A family of monkeys. I trembled with fear. Karl had told us that there were always jaguars in the vicinity of bands of monkeys.

God, let Kevin get here.

I was wearing a blue T-shirt that Marcus had given me, a brown flannel shirt, rough underwear, jeans, socks, walking shoes, and a large bandanna tied around my neck. I crawled into my camouflaged little niche. The stones cut into my back, but they weren't as bad as the cold. I was soaking wet and had no fire or anything with which to cover myself. I took the bandanna from around my neck and tied it over my face, and the warmth of my own breath gave me at least the illusion of comfort. Frightening thoughts filled my mind: wild animals, snakes. What if I didn't find the pack? What if Kevin didn't get here? I would either be devoured by wild beasts or die of starvation. I felt desperate, desolate, and I leapt out of the niche.

"Kevin! Kevin! Kevin!"

"Oha, oha," the cursed monkeys chattered.

I fled back to my alcove. I was choked with tears.

Don't cry. Don't break now. Be a man of action, I coaxed myself.

It was already dark. I replaced the bandanna over my face. I couldn't sleep, couldn't get the frightening thoughts out of my mind.

Karl, why didn't I listen to you? Marcus, why was I so cruel to you? Now I'm being punished.

I told myself that when morning came, I would find Kevin, and together we would make it out of this. When I found myself feeling hopeless, I whispered my mantra, "Man of action, man of action." I don't know where I had gotten the phrase. Perhaps I had picked it up from one of Carlos Castaneda's books. I repeated it over and over: a man of action does whatever he must, isn't afraid, and doesn't worry. But when I heard the rustle of branches outside, my motto wasn't all that encouraging. I held my breath and waited for the rustling to recede into the jungle.

I felt better in the morning. I pushed the branches aside and crawled outside. I roared Kevin's name a few times but then went back to being a man of action and sized up my situation. For starters I was absolutely certain that I was past the canyon. I remembered Karl's description well: the waterfalls, the rapids, the gigantic rock blocking the river. Yes, I was sure that that had been the mal paso, and Curiplaya was supposed to be not far from the pass, on the right bank, the bank I was standing on. There was a chance that I could make it there. There were cabins and equipment in Curiplaya. Karl had said that there was also a banana grove. And from Curiplaya it was four days' walk to San José de Uchupiamonas. There should even be a path cut through the jungle. I allowed myself to feel optimistic. I could do it. Not more than one day's walk to Curiplaya and from there on a path to San José. There might even be someone left in Curiplaya.

I hunted around for something for breakfast but found nothing. I decided to try to retrieve the pack once again. It would be worth investing an entire day looking for it as long as there was even the slightest chance of finding it. There was food in the pack, along with matches, a map, and a flashlight. If I could only find it, I'd be set.

It was no easy task. I started walking upriver. The route took me over jagged cliffs and smooth rock faces. I walked for two hours, climbing higher to progress and then back down to see if I could reach the shore. The stony walls were steep and smooth. I lost my footing a few times but luckily was caught by trees and bushes. Finally, from a cliff that towered fifty feet over the river, I spotted the raft in the water, still beating against the rocks. I was positive that the pack must be nearby.

At that point the bank of the river was a thin strip of land. I had no choice but to take the risk and started slowly climbing down, clawing at the sharp rocks. I took tiny steps, groping with my foot for a hold that would support my weight, my body covered with cold sweat. I said a silent prayer, *Don't slip. Don't fall.* If I broke an arm or leg, I didn't stand a chance. The last time I had gone rock climbing, I had fallen but had been saved by a miracle: Uncle Nissim's little book had been in my pocket. Now it was in the backpack. I should never have left it there.

It was still raining, hadn't let up at all since yesterday. The stones were damp and slick, but I kept climbing. My pants caught on a jagged edge and ripped. My knees were scratched, my fingers bloody. The strain on my legs was tremendous, terribly painful. I could tell that the rash was spreading over my wet feet again. When I was about ten feet above the ground, I turned and slid down the rock face on my rear end. My back was scraped, but I landed safely on the riverbank. I started searching, skipping over rocks until I reached the raft.

It was hard to believe, but the raft was still in one piece. All seven logs were still bound together. Yes, Don Jorge knew his business. Why hadn't we listened to his wife and stayed back there?

Before I began my search for the pack, I secured the raft well, just in case I met up with Kevin and the two of us might make use of it. I looked around among the rocks and crevices, and there, about ten yards away, in the cleft of a small rock, sat the precious pack, soaking wet but still afloat.

Thank you, God.

Words could not describe my happiness. I lay down on the rock and fished the pack out of the river and hurriedly opened it. I was saved! The contents were only slightly damp. The rubber bag had protected them well. There was everything: rice and beans, the flashlight and matches, the lighter, map, mosquito netting, red poncho, medicines, and most important, my wallet with Uncle Nissim's little book. Now I wouldn't die. I felt safe.

I opened the first-aid kit hoping to find some petroleum jelly for my feet. There was none. I found a bottle of pills, some of them unmarked, and a small box labeled "Speed." The pills might come in handy. There was also snakebite serum in the kit.

Thus equipped, I felt better.

Somebody up there likes me, I thought. *Just let Kevin find me.*

Up until now I had thought him the better off of the two of us—at least he had the machete—but now I was a wealthy man, and he, poor guy, had only the clothes on his back. Poor Kevin had nothing; he must need me. I had food and could start a fire. He just had to find me. Without me he didn't have a chance.

It was still pouring with rain, and I shivered with cold. I hurriedly closed the pack and set it down in a niche of the cliff. I kept only the poncho to protect me from the rain. Then it occurred to me that I should hang it up in some conspicuous place. It was bright red and might catch Kevin's eye. I saw a crag jutting prominently over the river. I climbed up to it and spread the poncho out over it, weighing it down with heavy stones so that it wouldn't blow away in the wind. Again I called out to Kevin, but I knew the shouts were pointless. The roar of the water was deafening, and there was no chance of anyone's hearing me.

On my way back to the pack I noticed a few yellow fruits lying on the shore and stopped to pick them up. Most of them were rotten, but I found one hard, fresh fruit and took a bite. It was delicious. I looked up and spotted the source: a tree laden with wild yellow plums at the edge of the stone wall.

Someone really is looking out for me, I thought.

I looked for a way up to the tree and found a slight hollow in the rock face where the rainwater ran off the mountain and down to the river. It was wet and slippery, but the incline was not so steep there. I had almost reached the tree—just a few more steps—when I saw a snake. It was green and coiled and just a few inches from my foot. I recognized it immediately as the deadly lora. Karl had told me they could blind their victims by spraying venom even from a distance.

I froze in my place. The snake, too, was motionless. Only its tongue flicked in and out of its mouth. It held the upper half of its body erect. I was afraid to move a muscle, but my fear and desperation soon turned to hatred. I took a step backward, picked up a huge rock, and flung it at the snake. Its body convulsed and then thickened, as if tied in knots. I picked up a flat, narrow rock, bent over, and started hitting the snake in a rage, over and over, until I'd sliced its head from its body. I was trembling, knowing that if the snake had bitten me, I would have died.

I picked up its green body and peeled its skin like a banana, revealing its pinkish flesh. I cleaned the internal organs out with one flick of my finger and was left holding the flesh. What should I do with it? Eat it or use it for bait? I threw it down to the riverbank. I would decide what to do with it after I got down.

I went over to the fruit tree, looking cautiously before every step. The lora was a tree climber, and I was afraid its mate might be nearby. I climbed up into the tree, eating ripe fruit as I went. The tree was heavily laden, but I had competition; tiny yellow ants swarmed on the trunk. I was all too familiar with them: fire ants. They stung me all over, but I didn't give in to them. I hurriedly picked as much fruit as I could, tossing it down to the riverbank. Then I climbed down and shook the cursed ants off. I felt as if I was on fire but was glad I hadn't let them drive me away. Now I would eat my fill.

Down on the riverbank I took one of the large tin cans that had been tied to the pack. It had two cups and a spoon inside. I drank from the river and then gathered up the fruit, filling the can with those I didn't eat.

I no longer had any desire to make a meal of the snake. I couldn't have started a fire anyway, because everything was still damp, and I certainly wasn't about to eat it raw. I found the fishing line in the pack, but the river was too rocky and the water too turbulent to fish.

I sat on the pack a while, leaning against the cliff, the rain still beating down on me. Kevin couldn't have continued walking along the riverbank, I reasoned, so he must be walking up on the ledge above the stone walls. There wasn't much chance of his seeing the poncho from there. I couldn't see any point in waiting by the river any longer. I might as well climb up to the ledge myself. I retrieved the poncho, folded it into the pack, put the pack on my back, and started scaling the wall back toward the plum tree.

Marching the length of the ledge, I searched for a cranny that would shelter me for the night and found an ideal place: a shallow niche cut into the stone wall about six feet above ground level. I climbed up to it. I would have liked to have started a fire now that I had matches and a lighter, but all the branches were wet, so I abandoned the idea.

In the second tin I discovered a large lump of salt, some spices, garlic cloves, and three lemons. I had a well-balanced supper: one lemon, three cloves of garlic, a pinch of salt, and a handful of plum-like fruit.

This night was kinder to me than the last one had been. I covered myself with the two mosquito nets, which, although damp, were comforting. I spread the poncho over them and covered my face with its hood. I breathed into the hood, and waves of warmth spread over my body.

What if Kevin doesn't make it here? I asked myself.

Tomorrow I will check the map, try to figure out approximately where I am and how far it is to San José. I'll spend tomorrow here waiting for Kevin, and if he doesn't show up, then I'll set out myself on the following day.

During the night I started hallucinating. Kevin was calling in desperation, *Help! Help! Yossi, save me. Wait for me. Don't leave, Yossi! Yossi! Help!*

I was sweating under my wet clothes.

I awoke stiff and hunched over, my body feeling the effects of my stone mattress. I came out of my hideout and sat studying the map. It was wet and torn, but I found the Tuichi and Ipurama rivers and the X that marked Curiplaya. I tried to use the map's scale to calculate the distance. A large river that fed into the Tuichi was shown on the map before Curiplaya. I hoped it would be passable.

It was raining again; the rainy season had begun in earnest. I knew the date; it was December 3. It was easy for me to remember that because I knew that the accident had occurred on the first and was careful to keep track of the date. I debated whether to begin walking toward Curiplaya or to wait for Kevin. Last night's hallucinations were still tormenting me. Kevin needed me and I needed him. We had to find each other. Together we could make it through anything. I decided to walk back toward him, hoping I would meet him on the way. Maybe we would at least come within hailing distance of each other.

I packed carefully and hoisted the pack onto my back. My feet were on fire, and I was afraid that I wouldn't be able to walk very far.

I took an upper out of the small box of pills in the first-aid kit and swallowed it. It did as promised. I trotted along hastily, skipping over rocks and hopping over fallen trees. I walked on without rest for hours, calling out, "Kevin, Kevin," every few minutes, but I was answered only by the roar of the river below. I felt no hunger, was unaware of the pain in my feet, didn't feel the weight of the pack or the irritating rain. At one place on the cliff I noticed a large hollow that formed a sort of giant cave, open on all sides, but roofed over by a protrusion of rock. Within it were piles of twigs, branches, and entire trees, all of them bone dry. Here I could get a fire started. Perhaps I should build a huge bonfire as a signal for Kevin. But I was too restless to stop; I had to go on.

Then I came to a dead end. The ledge I was walking along suddenly dropped off. Below me about two hundred feet flowed the Tuichi. The view was breathtaking. The silver river snaked through the thick jungle growth. I stood looking at the water for a long while, half expecting to see Kevin's body swept along by the current. I had to go on looking for him. He would die without me. He had nothing—no food, no matches—nothing. He didn't stand a chance if I didn't come to his aid.

Like one possessed, I scrambled up the rock face to reach the next ledge, hoping that I would be able to go on to the level above me. At a height of about two hundred and fifty feet I was trapped; I couldn't go any higher but couldn't go back down. I leapt across to a protruding nub of rock about a yard away. As I made it, the nub crumbled under my step and fell away from the wall. I fell backward, but fortunately my fall was broken by a tree. The pack on my back absorbed the impact of my fall, though the force of the blow bent the metal frame out of shape.

Once again I felt lost and hopeless. All of my walking had been for nothing. How could the mountain just drop off into nothing? And how would Kevin ever get here? I had no choice but to backtrack to the cave I had seen. There I would light a fire and make some nice rice-and-bean soup.

When I made it back to the cave, I collapsed. I lay there for a while and then, gathering my strength, got to my feet. I gathered dry twigs and branches. I arranged them properly, the smaller ones on the bottom and the larger on top. I had only a few matches, and the lighter had seen better days. Kevin's beloved book was in the pack. I tore out a few pages and shoved them under the twigs. It was easy to get a blaze going. In no time the larger branches caught fire as well. The fire provided both warmth and light.

Water was no problem. The whole cliff face was wet, and water trickled off it. I filled the tin can, set a big stone in the center of the fire, and put the can on top. The water came quickly to a boil. I was stricken with guilt; Kevin also would need nourishment, and the little food we had was all in my possession. I must use the provisions sparingly, for we might both need them. I carefully measured one spoonful of rice and one spoonful of beans into the boiling water. I peeled two cloves of garlic and added them and some salt and spices.

The tin can held about three quarts of water. The soup wasn't thick, but it was delicious. I drank a few cups, forcing myself to consume only the liquid and to leave the residue for morning. Then, my stomach full, I organized my belongings. The rice and beans were wet and moldy. So were the garlic and spices. I laid everything out on stones near the fire. I gathered more dry wood to keep the blaze going all night. I took the poncho and the mosquito nets out of the pack. I got everything else ready before I took my shoe off. That I put off to last, knowing that it would be far from pleasant.

The pain was excruciating. My socks reeked. They were covered with yellowish red stains. I gritted my teeth when I peeled them off. My feet were a horrible sight. Most of the skin had peeled off, and between my toes was a mess of inflamed flesh, blood, and pus. I was terrified that I wouldn't be able to walk. I knew that I had to dry my feet and put something on them. I dug around the first-aid kit again. In the absence of petroleum jelly I finally decided on the repellent cream and spray, which were slightly greasy. I spent the entire night holding my feet out to the fire and then pulling them back again. The pain was agonizing, sleep impossible.

When morning came, I realized just how weak I was. I crawled out on my hands and knees to gather more wood for the fire. I added water to yesterday's soup and heated it again. There were a few pieces of mushy fruit left. I didn't want to waste them and forced them down my throat. I sat there near the fire, the skin of my feet drying and beginning to heal. I tried to get the fire to smoke, reasoning that Kevin wouldn't see a fire in daylight, but he might notice the smoke, even if he was up above me on a higher ledge.

I was dizzy. I saw black circles everywhere and stretched my feet out close to the flame. My brow was feverish. Something came over me. Perhaps I fainted. I lost control of my bowels and filthied my underwear. I cursed angrily. After calming down, I removed my pants and underwear and crawled naked toward a jet of water streaming off the mountainside. I hung my underwear over a nub of the cliff so that the stream would flow over them. I went back to the fire and covered myself up with the mosquito netting, for the mosquitoes took advantage of every inch of bare flesh.

Bands of monkeys were gathering in the trees around me. There were two large groups, one of little black marimono monkeys, the other of larger brown howler monkeys, the kind that roar like tigers. At first I feared they had gotten together to get even with me for the monkeys we had killed earlier in our journey. Then I grew worried that they would make off with my precious supplies, so I gathered all of my belongings around me near the fire. I hobbled to the crag to retrieve my underwear, which the water had already cleansed.

The monkeys watched me curiously. Eventually they overcame their timidity and came within a few yards of me. They didn't seem to be up to anything sinister. It seemed more likely that it was the first time they had seen a monkey as funny-looking as me. All I could think about was how great it would be if I could trap one of them. I would let him smoke all night and have two weeks' supply of meat. I considered throwing stones at them but knew that would be pointless. They were too quick, and I was too weak. I watched them for hours as they performed acrobatics in the treetops above me, concentrating all my thoughts on the hope that one of them would miss a branch and fall on its head. I tried prayers and supplications—*Let him fall, just one lousy monkey. Please let him fall*—but that did no good. The monkeys went through their routines without a snag.

When it began to grow dark, I was overtaken with fear. I was completely unarmed, with nothing to protect myself apart from the fire. What if I fell asleep during the night and the fire went out? What if a jaguar was waiting nearby in ambush? What would I do? I looked for a long stick that I could use as a spear, but the branches were all dry and brittle. Feeling helpless and frightened, I gathered up more wood to feed the fire. Then I had a brilliant idea. I had once seen a movie in which a spray can was used as a flamethrower. I took the can of repellent and the lighter out of my pack. I held the lighter in my left hand, pushed down on the spray button with my right, and lit the lighter. It worked. The spray caught fire and gave off a large flame. I prepared my defenses: the spray, the lighter, the flashlight, and the snakebite serum.

That night I lay close to the fire.

Again I began hallucinating. Kevin crept up on me in the dark. He saw the fire and found me sleeping. He could tell I had eaten some of the rice and beans.

You should share, Yossi. You should always share, he whispered. *There isn't enough food for both of us. So you thought you were going to make it out of here without me?*

He smiled to himself, lifted the machete, and smashed it down against my skull.

No! No!

I came back to reality terrified, my heart pounding, drenched with sweat.

Kevin, Kevin, please come! Believe me, I haven't abandoned you. I'll wait for you. I won't eat any more of the food.

I trembled and whimpered. The fire cast menacing shadows. Beyond its light was only jungle and darkness, and I was afraid. "Man of action, man of action," I whispered to myself, and curled up in the mosquito net.

It was my fifth day alone in the jungle. I had never been so lonely, so completely cut off from human companionship. It was unbearable. For the first time in my life I realized how much I needed the company of other human beings. I remembered a book I had once read criticizing Barbara Streisand's singing about "people who need people." People have to learn to get along on their own, the author contended, be completely independent of others; our happiness and security must come from within. When I read the book, I agreed, but now I realized the truth expressed by the song. It was easy for a writer sitting in a penthouse to be cynical. I'd like to see him in my place now.

I had to be on my way. I was in better shape physically. My fever had gone down. My feet had gotten better. I enriched the soup with another spoonful of rice and one of beans and ate every drop that clung to the bottom on the pot.

I sat near the fire studying the map and estimated that Curiplaya could be no more than six or seven miles away. I hoped to make it in one day's walk. I would wait for Kevin to catch up with me. It seemed the logical thing to do. Kevin must be trying to get there too. He knew as well as I did that there would be food and shelter. Surely we would meet up in Curiplaya. If Kevin was still alive, that is.

I was beginning to lose all hope that he was still alive. Maybe he couldn't walk. Maybe he had drowned in the river or broken a bone. Even if he hadn't drowned, his clothes were still wet, and he couldn't have started a fire as I had. And what about his feet? I was sure that he must be suffering from the same problem that I was, but he had no medicine. And he had no food. He could die of starvation. The poor guy must be freezing at night. I felt awful.

For the first time my thoughts carried me far away. In my mind I had already been rescued from the jungle. I had made my way to a village, to La Paz, and from there by plane to Miami. From Miami I head for Oregon, where Kevin's family lives. I have already phoned them, telling them of his death, but still I owe them a personal explanation of what happened and how. Having to face his parents is the hard part.

I am going by Greyhound bus, and the trip from Miami to Oregon takes three days. Every few hours the bus pulls over for a rest stop and a snack at McDonald's, Burger King, or Jack-in-the-Box. I go into the restaurant just like all the other passengers, but when I get to the counter, I order four Big Macs and five fish sandwiches, six orders of fries, two large shakes, and three pieces of apple pie. The clerk thinks I am ordering for the group, but then I sit down at a table by myself. I bite into the hamburger, the melted cheese oozing out, the onion and pickle crunching; the milk shake goes down smooth and easy. The other passengers stare at me in amazement. They've never seen anyone eat like that.

Finally, I reach Kevin's parents' home.

"It wasn't my fault. Please believe me. I waited for him five days. I waited, but he never showed up. I saved food for him, I didn't eat it all by myself. I kept calling out to him. I waited and waited, and he never came. I had to go on. Believe me, I had no other choice."

Kevin's father and mother cry, and I cry with them. I look for the blame in their eyes, but they only ask me to tell them everything about the way it happened. I tell them how we set out on the trip, how close Kevin and I became, like brothers. I tell them how Kevin had told me all about his family and repeat the Santa Claus story for them and all his other stories about hunting and fishing in the forests of Oregon.

After an emotional farewell I feel better. They don't blame me. I get back on the Greyhound for the trip back to Miami. Once again I order gargantuan amounts of food at every stop.

I had this daydream hour after hour, lingering over every detail of the food I consumed until I was drooling with hunger and my stomach was howling. I drank another cup of the soup water and determined to stop torturing myself.

I still had some time before evening and planned my trek the next day to Curiplaya. Above me I could see the distant mountains, their crests forming a continuous, jagged line. I could climb to the crest, I thought, where the foliage must be sparse. I would only have to keep going straight and to make sure that the river was always on my left. I would be able to make faster progress.

I put my shoes on and hesitantly began to practice walking, mostly on the heels and sides of my feet, for the soles were very sore. I walked over to the cleft where the water ran. It trickled down slowly, drop by drop. I set a tin under the trickle of water and was about to turn back when I saw two snails clinging to the damp stone wall. I pounced upon the find and, when I got back to the fire, tossed them into the soup. From now on I would be more alert. There must be plenty of food to be had around here.

I removed my shoes and checked my feet. I thought that they could support my weight, but the skin was still open in a few places and I felt a strong burning.

There's no other choice, I repeated stubbornly to myself. *Tomorrow I start walking. If my feet give out or I come to another dead end, I'll go down to the riverbank and wait there for help.*

Karl had said that it was always best to wait on the bank; that was where help would come.

I took a small notebook and pen out of the pack, settled down into my regular position, my feet stretched out toward the fire, and started writing. I wrote down everything, beginning with the flight from La Paz until December 1, the day we were separated in Ipurama. I wrote about the relationships among the four of us and how we had all changed. I wrote about the upset on the river and how I had been spared from what should have been certain death. I described my isolation and ended with these words: "Thinking about Kevin is driving me crazy. Will he make it anywhere with only a machete? How could he dry his clothes? What kind of shape are his feet in? Can he get a fire going somehow? But he has the strength of three men. I pray for him and for myself. There's a wallet in the backpack, and in it is Uncle Nissim's little book."

That was the fifth of December.

CHAPTER 9

ALONE

At dawn my arsenal went back into the pack along with the rest of my things. I slipped my shoes on warily. Leaving the laces loosely tied. I tried hobbling about the campsite. It hurt, but I could walk. I slung my pack onto my back and set off. I was certain that I would make Curiplaya that day, and from there it was only a few days' walk to San José. There I would be able to organize a rescue party to search for Kevin.

I was still determined to follow a straight course along the crest of the range. After a few unsuccessful attempts I finally found a place where I could climb, but my pack kept pulling me over backward, and I was afraid of falling once more.

Just don't hurt yourself, Yossi. No matter what, you can't let yourself get hurt. All you need is a sprained ankle and you've had it.

I left my pack behind with the fishing line tied to it and continued up slowly, step by wary step, carefully testing each foothold, stone by stone. I trailed the fishing line behind me, letting out slack little by little. I inched my way higher up the face of the cliff, paused to heave a sigh of relief, and then dragged the backpack up after me. It wasn't particularly heavy, but still the fishing line sliced deeply across my palms.

I went on like that for several hours. The physical effort was draining, the humidity was high, and the heat was relentless. I was dripping with sweat. Worst of all, I was thirsty and had no water. It had been a serious mistake to leave the river.

Eventually I heard the distant rumbling of rushing water. Its roar was so loud that I was sure I was about to come upon a river at least as wide as the Tuichi. The sound grew louder, and I soon found myself standing next to a stream. It was narrow, but it flowed from a ledge high above and cascaded down in a tremendous waterfall at least one hundred feet high. Its sparkling waters struck the rock below in a deafening torrent. The rock face around it was overgrown with moss and green climbing vines. The view took my breath away. I was surprised that even in my present circumstances I could still appreciate natural beauty.

I lay down on my stomach and drank in some of the pure water and remained there resting in the shade for about half an hour. Wiser now, I filled the two tin cans I had with water. The water would mean another thirteen pounds to carry on my back, but at least I wouldn't find myself parched with thirst.

The climb became more treacherous. I proceeded cautiously and prayed that I would make it to the top in one piece. I could already see the crest from where I clung. It wasn't much farther, and this was the last rock face that I would have to scale.

Less than an hour later I dragged myself to the top. There was no shelter up there, and a strong wind was blowing. Now I had to keep going straight and make sure that the river was always on my left. But where was the river? Which way was I supposed to go? The view in every direction looked the same, and I couldn't recall in which direction the sun had set relative to the river the previous evening.

I was confused. Wherever I looked, I saw wooded slopes. Only now did I understand what a foolish mistake I had made. From a distance the mountains had appeared to be one continuous range, along the crest of which one could walk a straight course, but they were, in fact, individual peaks, and in order to progress, it would be necessary to descend to the foot of one and climb back up the next.

I felt suffocated with panic, a fist of fear tightened about my chest. I started running, refusing to resign myself to the error I had made. It took me a few minutes to get hold of myself and think things through. Tomorrow I would have to make the descent back to the river. If it was possible to walk along the bank, I would do so. Otherwise I would stay on the shore and wait. Perhaps help would arrive. Marcus and Karl would surely make it to La Paz by tomorrow or the next day, and on the fifteenth of the month Lisette would call the Israeli embassy. I could hold out until then.

It was growing dark, and I could find no shelter. There were no crags or cliffs, no caves or niches. Where could I spend the night? I had to choose a campsite quickly and get a fire going while there was still daylight. I chose a level area, cleared away the damp leaves, and replaced them with fresh, dry ones. I took out one of the mosquito nets and tied it down to four tree stumps with vines, so that it formed a long, narrow, translucent green pup tent. I looked for dry wood but didn't find any. I gathered a few branches and tried to break them and strip them away to the dry inner parts. It was impossible without a machete. My attempts at lighting a fire only wasted the fluid in the lighter and brought me to a state of despair. Reluctantly I crawled under the tent of mosquito netting and wrapped myself in the remaining net and red poncho. I took my arsenal out of the pack: the flashlight, the lighter, the mosquito repellent, and the snakebite serum. To these I added a tin can and a spoon. If any wild animal should approach me, I would make a horrendous clatter and scare it away. So I thought.

I tried to close my eyes, to escape into my fantasies, but I was too tense, uneasy. My stomach was growling with hunger, for I hadn't eaten anything all day. The fear, however, was harder to bear. I was in the heart of the jungle, totally vulnerable, with no means of protecting myself, no cave to hide myself in, no fire. I kept hearing animal calls, the cries of birds, and the buzz of insects. I secured the edges of the mosquito netting with rocks so that no snakes could come slithering in. The flashlight was near my knee. I kept hold of it for fear that I wouldn't be able to find it in the dark if I should need it. Off in the distance I could hear bloodcurdling screeches. A jaguar must have caught a monkey or some other prey.

A few hours went by; I was in total darkness. Suddenly I heard the snapping of branches, the stealthy thud of footsteps, something coming. Fear gripped me. It's only your imagination, I kept telling myself, only your imagination, but the rustle of the leaves and branches on the ground was so clear. I stuck my head out from under my covers, moved one of the rocks away from the mosquito net, and peered into the darkness. I turned on the flashlight. I couldn't see a thing. I sighed with relief but didn't really feel any better.

The fear weighed upon me; I had never been so terrified. I tried to lie back down and cover myself up, but I kept hearing sounds all around me, and my heart was pounding frantically.

God, just don't let a wild animal devour me.

I ran my fingers over my makeshift weapons, afraid that I might become hysterical. Again I heard rustling sounds around me. I sat up with a jolt, gripped the spoon, and started banging on the tin can. It made a dull sound, and I called out, "Shoo! Shoo! Go away! Shoo!" as if I were about to be set upon by a flock of chickens. I lay back down, my heart thumping. The sounds drew closer.

No, it's nothing. There's nothing out there. It's only your imagination. It's all in your mind.

I heard the rustle again, too close and too real to ignore. I clutched the flashlight, stuck my head out of the mosquito net, turned it on . . . and found myself face-to-face with a jaguar.

It was large, covered with black spots. One of its paws was raised off the ground, as if it had been about to take another step. When I turned the light on it, it put its foot down without stepping forward. It stood at a distance of about twelve feet. Just stood there looking at me. It wasn't blinded by the light, but it stopped and looked me over. It didn't appear particularly menacing; it wasn't roaring or licking its chops. Its eyes were neither ferocious nor meek. They were just great cat's eyes, staring at me. The jaguar stood perfectly still; only its tail waved slowly back and forth.

"Go away," I whined. "Get out of here. Beat it. Do you hear me? Get away."

I was trembling and started to scream loudly at the jaguar. "Get out of here, you son of a bitch! Go away! I'll burn you up! Get away!"

The flashlight had a chain to hang it from. I clamped it between my teeth in order to have both hands free. I felt around on the ground by my knees and found the repellent spray and the lighter. I held the lighter in my left hand and the spray in my right hand. Now I was calm. I didn't scream or tremble.

Maybe I shouldn't try it. I hesitated. *It might just make him mad, and then he might attack me.* But then I pushed down on the spray button and lit the lighter.

It worked. The spray caught fire and spewed an enormous blaze. I could smell the scorched hair on my left hand, and I was completely blinded. I held it for a few minutes, until the spray ran out and the flame of the lighter grew weaker. My makeshift flamethrower was exhausted.

My sight returned gradually, in concentric circles of fading darkness, and finally I could see the beam of the flashlight. The jaguar was gone. I shined the light around in fear, right and left, in back of me. The jaguar had vanished. I thought I could hear receding footsteps. Had it worked? Had I scared it off? I felt neither joy nor relief. I kept the flashlight on for a while but was afraid of running it down and turned it off.

I sat inside the mosquito net, wide awake, my heart jumping wildly at every sound until the merciful morning light. The sunlight gave me a tremendous sense of security, as if no danger could befall me. I packed up my gear while I murmured a hasty prayer of thanks and got out of there as fast as I could.

Now that the sun was shining, I remembered exactly in which direction the river should be and walked on rapidly. "Straight and to the left, straight and to the left." I sang out the rhythm of my steps as I made for the river along a diagonal course. Singing helped to keep my spirits up.

There was far less foliage on the higher ground, and I progressed quite rapidly. From time to time I came across a stream and stopped to drink. I felt I could safely empty the two big cans of water, and my shoulders were greatly relieved.

After a few hours' walk, however, I once again felt the dread of uncertainty. The sun was directly overhead, and I hadn't the slightest idea where I was. I feared that I might well be marching away from the river. I might end up on the other side of the mountain, lost forever where no one would find me. It was so easy to lose one's way and one's wits.

Nevertheless I knew that any source of water, however small, would lead me to the river, and before long I found a rivulet flowing in an irregular course. It trickled downward, and I followed it along. It descended the rock faces in leaps and bounds, cascading in waterfalls, and I was forced to leave it in search of a more moderate slope on which to make my own descent. I went on like that until I came to a waterfall that gushed downward from an immense height of one hundred and fifty feet, far higher than any other I had encountered. The sight of the water surging down from that height was awesome. For a moment I considered getting Kevin's camera out of the pack and taking a picture, but it would have been a difficult feat, and I changed my mind.

Down below, where the waters of the fall struck the earth, I could see another stream. I looked for a place where I could climb down, but by the time I found one, I could no longer hear the rush of water. The stream was not in sight. I didn't want to waste time and energy going back to look for it, so I decided to continue on my way down until I ran into another trickle, which I soon did. This time I was determined to stick with it no matter what.

I followed it down steep inclines and made my way around some small falls. I took great care not to get my feet wet. When I had to cross the stream, I did so by vaulting over it or tiptoeing across the larger rocks in its path. Once in a while I was helped over by fallen trees. Other streams joined the one I was following, and it widened.

I was walking along a river. The ground was flatter, but the undergrowth was quite dense, and without a machete to cut through it, the going was rough. I had no choice but to follow the natural lay of the land, which formed a sort of pathway, frequently obstructed. I scrambled over rocks and crawled under branches. Thorns tore at my clothes. I occasionally stuck my hand into a nettle and was stung. Once I disturbed the wrong branch and was attacked by a trail of fire ants, which dug their way into the back of my neck. The weather had given out as well, and it was pouring rain again. All my efforts to keep my feet from getting wet were wasted.

Since I was drenched anyway, it seemed like a good idea to wade in the river. It was quite shallow. The water came up to my knees or at times to my waist. Every now and then I lost my footing, alarmingly going under water for a moment. Although the pack was buoyant, it still made it difficult to surface. I was tense and listened attentively to the roar of the river, cautiously keeping an eye out for falls and rapids that might sweep me away. Helpless to do anything to prevent it, I could feel the painful rash spreading over my feet.

Was anyone up there looking down on me, aware of the fix I was in? One man, alone in the jungle, no other human beings around, at the mercy of heartless Mother Nature?

Please help me. At least make it stop raining. Let me be able to keep walking on my own two feet.

I couldn't tell exactly when darkness would fall. At times the sun would pass behind a cloud, and I would think that I had to hurry and set up camp. Then it would emerge, and I would go on marching, not wanting to waste the remaining hours of walking time. Finally, after a small bend in the river, I came upon a fabulous beach. Pure white sand, crystal-clear water, and a large bush laden with little red fruit. In the past two days I had eaten only a few cloves of garlic and a pinch of salt, and I pounced hungrily upon the sweet berries.

At first I picked the berries one by one and put them into my mouth, but I was soon gathering up handfuls and gulping them down. The sweetness was enthralling; the juices filled my howling belly. I didn't budge from the bush for at least twenty minutes, when my hands were red-stained with berry juice and I felt my hunger satisfied.

I lay down on my belly, thirstily lapping up water from the river and washing off my sweaty face. The river was quite wide at that point, wide as the Ipurama. It had to be the other river marked on the map, the Turliamos—there was no doubt about it—and Curiplaya was supposed to be only half a mile farther, on the bank of the Tuichi. Fantastic. I would be there by tomorrow. Tomorrow I would go on walking. Tomorrow, but now I was too exhausted and decided to set up my campsite there on the beach. At least I could count on a good breakfast.

I looked for some kind of shelter from the rain. I walked a little way downriver and spotted deer tracks on the sandy shore. The deer must have come down to drink. Probably jaguars would come as well. Still, I would be better off on the shore than in the dark, frightening jungle. A long, thick tree lay on the beach. It was enormous. The gnarls of the trunk left a space between it and the ground. The ground underneath was dry; the rain hadn't reached it. This is where I would spend the night.

I crawled under the tree trunk. I couldn't sit up; could only crouch on my elbows. I got the mosquito nets and poncho out and started getting ready for the night. Before I lay down, though, I went out to the berry bush to gorge myself once more. Afterward I lay under the tree, slowly chewing a garlic clove, and covered myself up. The sun went down, the moon came up, and it was an unbelievably beautiful sight. But a scenic view didn't do much to calm my fears. I counted the hours and minutes until morning would come.

At dawn I saw a doe and her fawn come down to drink from the river. They drew near the water, frisky and light-footed, and there the mother came upon my footprint. She paused for an instant and then fled, her fawn racing after her. If they had stayed to get a drink, and if I managed to injure the fawn, I certainly could have caught it. Its flesh would have been tender and delicious. As it was, I had to settle for a breakfast of berries, not venison. But I no longer relished them. I ate mechanically, forcing down a large quantity. I considered taking some along with me in the tin can, but it was rusty and reeked of garlic, and then I noticed that there were barely any edible berries left on the bush.

No matter, I thought. Somebody's looking out for me, I'll find something to eat today.

I started walking, toting my gear on my back. It was still raining. I waded along the river, trying to progress both rapidly and cautiously, pinning all my hopes on finding my way back to the Tuichi. The rain started coming down harder. My wet hair straggled into my eyes, and my ten-day-old moustache dripped water straight into my mouth. I was so cold and miserable that I didn't even notice that the roar of the river had increased in volume. Suddenly I fell. The river bottom had been swept from under my feet, and I found myself being carried downriver by the current. Now I was well aware of the river's roar. It was the familiar sound of water breaking over rocks. God, I was being swept over a waterfall!

I tried to make it back to the shore, but the pack was too big and bulky, bogged me down, and I almost drowned. I stayed under and slipped the shoulder straps off, leaving the pack secured to me only by its belt. I lifted my head out of the water to see the waterfall looming ahead. I swam frantically and finally managed to grasp a rock near the shore. The rock was smooth and covered with slippery moss, and I was about to be carried away again. I could see the waterfall, practically under me, about twenty-five feet high, cascading into a small pool cut into the rocks below. I slithered precariously up the rock I was clinging to. The weight of the pack tied to my waist kept pulling me back into the river. I let go of the rock with one hand and tried to get hold of the strap of the pack. I leaned over and fell backward into the river. My chest was crushed against the rock; I thought I was suffocating. My legs were caught in the current, but I held fast to the rock for dear life, digging my fingernails deep into the moss. I managed to pull myself out once again to sit on the rock. I rested for a moment, seized with fear, and then fished the pack out of the water and put it back on my shoulders.

"I won't abandon you, no matter how much trouble you give me," I said to the pack.

I tightened the shoulder straps and headed for the shore.

Not long afterward I was standing on a steep hill overlooking the river. Everything was soaking wet from the river and the eternal rain. Walking in the jungle had taken its toll on my clothing. My flannel shirt was in shreds. My underwear stuck out through my torn jeans. My feet were wet, and I could feel the horrible rash as it spread. The insides of my thighs were raw from walking for so long in wet clothing.

Just let me get back to the Tuichi, I thought, to cheer myself up, *then Curiplaya will only be a few hours away. I'll rest up and get myself back in shape. I might even find food and equipment. And isn't there a slim chance of finding people there too?*

I started picturing my arrival in Curiplaya. Little grass huts, a banana grove, and people sitting around a campfire roasting fish. I make my entrance, catching sight of them and shouting from afar. They hear my cries and come running toward me, carrying me into their camp. I am cared for, fed, and carried by stretcher to San José.

The shoreline leveled out again, and I walked in the river. I felt tremendous pressure on my chest, where I had slammed into the rock, and my feet were tormenting me. I walked at a steady pace, however, not stopping.

"I just have to make it to the Tuichi," I mumbled to myself, "I just have to make it to the Tuichi."

Alone, deep in the jungle, so small and insignificant, pitted against nature, still I sensed someone watching me. Or watching over me. Someone could see me, someone was providing for me.

It began to grow dark, but I marched on determinedly. No way did I want to set up still another campsite for a night in the jungle. I had to get to the Tuichi. After only a short while I could make out its distant, constant drone, the familiar sound of the great river. Like a horse who catches wind of its stable, I forged ahead with renewed energy. One more bend—and there it was.

The river that I had been following widened, expanding into a torrent sixty or seventy feet across. The Tuichi itself was more than three hundred feet across. A broad shore stretched about me, and the whole place was reminiscent of the mouth of the Ipurama, where Kevin and I had parted from Karl and Marcus.

I was overcome with relief and joy. Now at least I knew exactly where I was. From now on I would stick with the Tuichi. I would move on along its banks.

The gathering darkness made me ill at ease, an indefinable dread. Nothing was clearly visible; I was surrounded by long shadows. Suddenly the jungle had grown silent, magnifying the occasional rustle and cry. I found no place to take shelter, no boulder, tree trunk, niche, or cranny. Only the jungle provided such lairs, but I hadn't the slightest desire to venture back into the jungle. Where was I going to sleep?

I considered stretching out on the sandy shore. I took the pack off my back. My entire body ached, my feet burned, and my stomach growled with hunger. I spread the poncho out over the muddy ground, stretched out on it, shivering with cold, and tried to cover myself with the mosquito nets. They were soaking wet. The river and the rain had gotten into the pack and doused everything. I prayed that the food hadn't gotten wet. It was sealed up in waterproof bags. I would check tomorrow.

The last rays of the setting sun gave off no warmth, but one flat beam of light fell on the ground beside me and to my amazement drew my attention to the mouth of a cave just at the edge of the jungle. I crawled nearer and peeked inside but couldn't see anything. All was blackness inside.

Just don't let this be the den of a jaguar or some other wild beast.

I took out the flashlight and shined its beam inside. It was a cavern, round and deep, about seven feet long and four feet deep. Water had washed away the soil from an enormous gnarl of tree roots and left this hollow. I hurried in before total darkness settled in.

The cave was palatial. I was soaked from head to toe, but at least the wind wouldn't chill me here. I wrapped myself up in the mosquito nets as usual and put the hood of the poncho over my mouth, exhaling into it and warming myself with my breath. And once again I sensed, this time harboring not the slightest doubt, that someone had been watching over me.

It had stopped raining. The night grew bright, and through the crannies between the roots of the tree I could see brilliant stars sparkling in the night sky.

From the break of dawn I sensed that the day would be especially hot. The sun burned large and intense. I crept out of the damp cave with aching bones. By daylight the place looked even prettier. The shore was quite wide, caressed by the waters of both rivers: the Turliamos—so I had decided—and the Tuichi. A large tree stump had been washed up just where the two rivers met. I took off what was left of my flannel shirt and spread it out to dry. I noticed a pile of logs on the shore. They would soon be dry and make excellent firewood. A fire, some hot soup, a bath, laundry, and care for my sorry feet: I could to it all here. So I might as well spend the day. I liked the idea. The perfect spot for rest and recreation. After nine days alone I had earned that at least.

I scouted the area and found a berry bush on the bank of the Tuichi, but the fruit had not yet ripened; it was still green and sour. I looked around for a good place to fish. If I could only catch a dorado like the one we got in the Ipurama, it would last me for two weeks. The river rushed by rapidly, and I had doubts that I would be able to catch any fish. I clambered back over the rocks to my private beach. On the way I stepped on some kind of flat fruit, similar in shape to a carob. It was green with yellow splotches. When I peeled back the outer skin, I found black pits encased in a white, velvety pulp. I tried a bite. I thought it must be a wild variety of tamarind.

The fruit on the ground was rotten and infested with ants, I gazed up at the thick tree trunk, its towering branches laden with fruit, all out of my reach. The trunk of the tree was smooth and afforded no foothold. A machete would have saved me a lot of trouble. Machete-less, however, I decided to try knocking the fruit down by hurling rocks at it but soon concluded that this was both pointless and dangerous. I was blinded by the sun and couldn't see where the rocks were landing. One of them almost bashed my head in. I tried inching up the tree, hugging it tightly with my knees and digging my fingernails into its bark; but I fell back down into the mud. My failure infuriated me. I couldn't bear the thought that I might die of hunger while mountains of fruit hung over my head, out of my reach. It wasn't fair. Who was all the fruit for? My inside churned with frustration. Then I had another idea.

I rummaged in the pack for the fishing line. I tied it tightly around a rock and heaved it up at the tree. The line wrapped around a branch and caught. I tugged at the line, shaking the branch . . . and it worked! Fruit rained to the ground. I threw the line again and again, until the ground about me was covered with fruit and leaves. I hungrily broke a piece apart and put the pits into my mouth. There wasn't much flesh on each one, but I had an abundance. Now I could relax a bit.

I started gathering wood for a fire. There was no scarcity of kindling on the shore. I carefully chose the best. Karl had taught me what to look for. There are some branches that never soak up any water. Gray-colored, they are hard and heavy and burn for great lengths of time. At first I gathered up only wood of this quality. Then I selected thick logs to set near the fire to dry out. They would later catch fire and burn for hours. In the morning, after smoldering all through the night, they would still be red, and the fire would easily rekindle.

While I was gathering wood, I felt a sudden dizziness. Black circles swam before my eyes, the world was spinning, my legs gave out from under me, and I sank to the ground. I don't know how long I lay there unconscious, but it couldn't have been for long because when I came to, the sun hadn't yet changed its position. I staggered to the river, splashed water on my face, and drank thirstily. I went back to work, meticulously arranging firewood just at the mouth of my cave. The twigs ignited easily, but my lighter was about to run out of fluid. It would light once or twice more, and that was it. I owed my life to that cheap, disposable lighter. The twigs kindled the branches, which spread the blaze to the logs until I had a roaring fire going.

I dragged the pack and the mosquito nets out of the cave and spread them out around the fire. The bags of rice and beans were damp and moldy. I washed my socks out in the river and hung them up to dry. My feet were a pleasant surprise; they weren't as bad off as I had expected. They were covered with a light rash, but the skin wasn't peeling. There was no blood or pus.

I gingerly walked barefoot over the rocks with the fishing line and climbed up on a log that lay at the junction of the two rivers and set the line down there. First I had to catch a minnow, but even to catch a minnow I needed bait. The horseflies that were constantly droning would serve that purpose well enough. I lay in wait for them, letting them land on my bare legs and stroll about a bit looking for a choice, juicy spot, and just as they were getting ready to dig in, I took them by surprise. I squished one fly between two fingers, impaled it on a small hook with no float or sinker, and cast the line into the river. It floated on the surface at first, but after the fly got wet, it went under. I lost a few flies before I succeeded in catching a minnow.

The sun shone gently over me. Every now and then I put another ripe tamarind into my mouth and greedily sucked the sweet flesh from the pits. Wild beauty surrounded me: the two rivers, the mountains, and the never-ending jungle. And I alone in the heart of the wilderness along with whomever was watching over me. Before long I had four minnows. I went to try my luck with them in the mighty Tuichi.

I stuck a whole minnow on a larger hook, drew back, and cast it into the water. The current was swift, and the hook disappeared beneath the white waters. I waited a while, and when I tried to draw the line in, I felt that it had snagged on a rock. Nothing I did succeeded in loosening it. I let it go slack and then gave it a good yank and then another. I tried angling in various directions, waiting for the river itself to set the line free, but it remained firmly planted. The current was rapid and foamy, and it would be too dangerous to try to wade into the water. The thought of doing so made me dizzy with fear. I was not going to put myself at the mercy of the Tuichi again. I had no choice but to break the line. That meant losing one of the last two hooks I had left. The line itself was strong and resilient and hard to break. I wrapped it around my waist a few times and backed off, stretching the line tightly until it snapped to shore with a shrill whine.

I took my supply of minnows back to the fire and tossed some more wood on. I filled a tin with water and set it in the hottest part of the fire. I scraped the scales off the fish with my fingernails and gutted them using a spoon I had sharpened against a stone. I tossed the minnows into the boiling water and added some spices and salt. Three minnows and three quarts of water aren't exactly a recipe for the most delicious soup in the world. Watery, bland, and disgusting would be a more accurate description, but I drank it down to the last drop, even munching the crunchy bones. I was proud of myself for not having used up any of the rice or beans. I would keep them for an emergency. I no longer thought I was saving them for Kevin, though I did harbor some hopes of meeting up with him in Curiplaya.

The X that Karl had marked on the map appeared to be right on the bank of the Tuichi just past its junction with the Turliamos. I would surely make the camp the following day. I grew impatient. My clothes were completely dry, and the skin on my feet was healthy. Only the flies and mosquitoes pestered me. At the outset of our journey we had taken pills to ward off malaria, but they had long ago run out or been lost, and I hoped I wouldn't come down with the illness here. The mosquitoes sought out every bare patch of skin showing through my tattered clothing and attacked mercilessly. Since my encounter with the jaguar I was out of repellent and had no defense but swatting them with my hands. The mosquitoes were determined, however, and I gave up first. Then I had an idea. I would sew my clothes together, offering them fewer targets. I toiled a long while over my shirt, using the thin fishing line and a small hook. Then I repaired my trousers as well.

Proud of my resourcefulness and industry, I set about making my bed. I didn't surrender to laziness but put my shoes back on and went into the jungle to gather large leaves with which to feather my lair. I made a huge pile at the entrance and meticulously carpeted the damp ground. The leaves offered excellent protection from the cold and damp. I decided to put in central heating as well. I cautiously moved a few smoldering logs into the cave. I arranged them in a triangular shape and poked twigs and branches between them. After I blew on them a few times, they caught fire. I gathered the rest of my belongings into the cave in case of rain. Using the bags of rice and beans for my pillow, I covered myself as usual.

I was tempted to stay there on that shore and wait for rescue. Any plane that passed overhead would easily spot me, and there was a clearing large enough for a helicopter to land. Starvation was no threat here. The tamarind fruit could keep me alive for a month. I had the cave to sleep in as well. I could have done a bit of remodeling, stopped up the leaks, put in a chimney, brought more leaves for padding. It was an ideal spot, but I went on packing. I tied my shoes together by their laces and slung them around my neck. I would cross the Turliamos barefoot, dry my feet on the other side, and continue on my trek with dry shoes.

I was all set to cross the Turliamos when I noticed that my bandanna, the kerchief that Kevin had given me, had vanished. It had come in very handy. I had used it for a hat, a scarf, a bandage, a bedspread, and it reminded me of my friend, whom I missed so terribly. I went back into the cave and searched it thoroughly. I raked through the leaves, walked up the Tuichi, looked under the tamarind tree, went back into the jungle and found the spot where I had stooped to empty my bowels, but the bandanna wasn't anywhere. Greatly disappointed, I gave up the search and crossed the river.

For a while the Tuichi had a shoreline that I could walk along. Then the bank grew rocky. I crawled carefully over the boulders, taking care not to slip and fall into the river. The rocks kept getting larger, forming a low cliff parallel to the river. The jungle spread out above the cliff on an incline. There was no place suitable for walking. It might have been easier going had I climbed to the top of the ridge, but I was scared of getting lost again. Curiplaya had to be nearby. It was on the riverbank, and I mustn't miss it. Come what may, I was going to stick with the Tuichi.

The going was slow and hazardous. I was afraid of turning my ankle and falling straight into the frothy river. I walked along the rocks, climbed up to the jungle, and trod at its edge for a while, then descended once more to climb over the rocks and so on. I stopped for a break after a few hours. I drank, ate a few pieces of fruit, and plodded on. The slope flattened out. I gave up wending my way over the rocks and headed up to the jungle, never letting the river out of my sight.

A few more hours passed, and I thought that I surely must have gone more than half a mile. Doubt began to gnaw at me. What if I didn't find Curiplaya? How did I know that it even existed? Since it wasn't marked on the map, I had only Karl's word to go on. Maybe Karl had been mistaken or maybe he was lying. No, Karl would not have told an outright lie.

I remembered how concerned he had been for us. But he was a strange guy. And we had never seen the island and the little beachhead that were supposed to warn us that we were heading into the canyon. That could have cost us our lives; perhaps it had taken Kevin's. At first Karl had claimed that he had traveled the length of the river twice and then had contradicted himself when he said that he had never been down it. We hadn't been told about San Pedro Canyon until we were almost halfway there.

No, Karl wasn't particularly reliable. I remembered something else that was weird. Karl kept changing the date that he was supposed to return to La Paz. Looking back, the whole business about the truck he was to bring to his uncle's ranch seemed a bit fishy. Still I had seen the letter with my own eyes. I didn't know what to think. It was hard to figure Karl out.

If Karl had misled us about Curiplaya as well, if it didn't exist, what would I do then? I could go back to the Turliamos and wait there for a rescue party, which would surely arrive before long. Or I could try to go on, straight to San José. I was convinced that the camp did exist, however; it was marked so clearly on the map.

I was still trying to figure out what I should do when I noticed a fallen palm tree. It had been chopped down at an angle, undoubtedly by a machete. I cried out for joy—I had made it! There had been people here!

I ran ahead in search. I saw a great many machete marks on branches and tree trunks, and more palms that had been chopped down. Yes, the people in Curiplaya had been eating palm hearts. I ran on, following the machete gashes. I was overcome with joy that nourished a flickering hope. Maybe, just maybe, there would still be people there. In no time I stood on a hill overlooking a flat, rocky bank upon which four huts had been built. "Ya-ho-hoo!" I bellowed and slid down to the shore.

The place was obviously deserted, but at least I had made it to Curiplaya. I took off my pack and set it under one of the thatched huts. Signs of life abounded; flat, rusty tin cans, cardboard boxes, a circle of rocks around a burned-out campfire. The shelters were cleverly built: four sturdy trunks, on which a peaked roof rested, covered with palm fronds latticed in such a way that no rain could leak in. At the joints where the pilings of each hut met the roof there was a sort of ceiling and above it a kind of conical crawl space. A lot of equipment was stored up there in the first: panels of chonta wood and all kinds of poles, sticks, and large tins. I rummaged further, hoping to find more treasures, but the other huts contained nothing useful.

On the floors of the huts were V-shaped stakes. Between every pair of stakes lay a long, round piling, and the spaces between the pilings could be covered by the flat panels of chonta wood. They made a bed, raised a foot off of the ground. It was a clever idea.

I had everything I needed in the crawlspace, and I put a good, sturdy bed together for myself. Tonight I would sleep in a bed, with a roof over my head. Incredible.

Forgive me, Karl, for doubting you.

I stretched out on my bed to give it a try. The wood panels were hard but level. They felt like a featherbed to me. I noticed some rope ends straggling from the pilings and knew that these would serve to hang the mosquito netting. I took one net out and tied its corners to the dangling ropes. I now had an airy tent above my bed. I felt like royalty, the sacks of beans and rice under my head, my legs stretched out luxuriously, my body relishing the comfort.

Since it had stopped raining, I ventured out to check the area. In one of the huts I found a tube that still had a little repellent in it. In another I found a broken pole with a sharpened end; this would serve as a walking stick and a spear with which to protect myself. I scouted a wide circle around the camp but discovered no sign of a banana grove. I went back to my palace, stretched out on my canopied bed, and waited for the sunset.

Tonight I had nothing to fear. The fire in the hut was fantastic. I made some soup of rice and beans, one tablespoon of each. I sat on the bed in comfort and stretched my feet out toward the fire. The flies and mosquitoes barely troubled me. I gave myself over to physical pleasure and a sense of luxury, and it suddenly didn't matter to me that I was lost and alone. I was content with my lot: hot soup, fruit, shelter, a bed, and bedcovers. I felt good, safe, and optimistic.

Within a few days I will make it to San José, I told myself. There must surely be a trail from here. People come here from San José every year; the trail must be wide and clearly marked. I have nothing to worry about. I just have to stay on the trail and hope that it won't rain a lot so that I'll be able to get a fire going at night. Fantastic.

I was going to rescue myself. Now I hoped that no one was looking for me yet. It would be a great letdown if they found me just as I was about to make my own way out of the jungle. It was going to be so simple. I could make it on my own.

In the morning, while it drizzled outside, it was lovely lying in the warm, dry hut. It reminded me of rainy winter days, sitting inside a pleasantly heated home, with my nose up against the windowpane. I decided to spend the day there. I needed to rest before setting out on a long trek. I would get my feet thoroughly dried, get my strength back, eat my fill, and tomorrow . . . tomorrow maybe it wouldn't be raining. In any case, I would start out tomorrow.

I felt a little guilty about being so soft, spoiling myself this way, but it was so pleasant. I had no trouble appeasing my conscience.

Dreams crowded my mind, and I slipped easily into fantasy. Good daydreaming just takes practice. Once you get the hang of it, you cross oceans and continents at will. My knee suddenly itched. I scratched it and felt something round that didn't want to let go. I pulled hard and found myself holding a leech, about half an inch long and a quarter inch wide, gorged with blood. I heaved it into the fire with disgust and began checking myself over head to foot.

I panicked. I found about twenty leeches all over my body. They were everywhere: in my armpits, on the back of my neck, on my back, between my legs, between my buttocks even. All of them bloated and repulsive. Damn bloodsuckers! I squashed them one by one and threw them into the fire. I vowed to check myself each night before going to sleep to make sure that I wasn't covered with parasites.

The weather cleared up in the afternoon. I took advantage of the opportunity to gather more twigs and firewood. I found a huge grasshopper, about four inches long, among some twigs. I caught it to use as bait for fish. I tied my last hook to the line and stuck the grasshopper on it. The current was swift, and I couldn't understand why Karl had told us that this was a good, quiet place to fish. There wasn't much point in trying, and I was afraid of losing the hook. The grasshopper was still on the hook, but the current had mangled it, and it looked disgusting. I decided not to add it to the soup.

I once again sought the banana grove, the dried balsa logs, and the hidden tools but found nothing. I did, though, think that I had discovered the trail to San José. Tomorrow I would set out on it, and that would be that.

I saw an enormous fruit tree on my way back to the hut. A lot of big, heavy fruit lay on the ground. I happily split a piece of it open against a rock but found its pulp hard and green and oozing a white oily substance. I tried a bite anyway but spat it out with a grimace. It was inedible. I should have known better; fruit that wasn't rotten and ant-eaten probably wasn't edible. I still had tamarinds in the hut and ate a few to get the horrid taste out of my mouth.

I noticed a large stump in the center of the camp with the name *Pam* carved into it in large letters. Was that the name of a girl? Or perhaps the word for "women"? In another four days, when I got to San José, I would be able to ask someone. I would spend four more nights in the jungle, but then I would have a soft bed and people around me. How I longed to see people. I studied the map at length. It looked so close. Just a few inches.

I could do it.

CHAPTER 10

"I'M ON MY WAY TO SAN JOSÉ"

My hopes for clear weather were disappointed; it was pouring rain, but I didn't let that stop me. I packed up my things, slung my pack on my back, tightened the belt and shoulder straps, took up my newly acquired walking stick, and off I went.

Although the trail began wide and well marked, within a few minutes' walk it narrowed considerably, and I had to search for machete marks on the trees in order to follow it. It did run parallel to the Tuichi, however, and whenever I strayed from the trail, I simply had to progress along the bank until I picked it up again.

I got used to walking in the rain and was in a great mood. I thought I was keeping a steady pace and, barring any unforeseen setbacks, I would cover the distance to the village in four days. As I strode along, I composed a marching song, far from original or inspiring, but at least it kept time. I took a popular Israeli tune, "I'm on My Way to Beit Shean," changed the destination, and sang out loud,

> I'm on my way to San José
> On my way, yeah, yeah, my way
> I'm on my way to San José.

So I walked on through the lush jungle in good spirits.

The ground was fairly level. Every now and then a few hills rose up, but they weren't steep. The streams posed a greater obstacle. I passed over a great many that emptied into the Tuichi, forming basins too wide to be passable at the junction. I was forced to follow each one upstream into the jungle until I came upon a convenient fording place. The machete gashes were fantastic signposts. They led directly to the places where the streams were fordable. They sometimes took me far from the river, but I eventually discovered this to be a shortcut.

At one point I came upon a wide, sandy beach, just the kind of place for a picnic and a little romance. The sand was soft and clean and shaded by trees. Logs were piled up on the shore, deposited there by the current. I had an idea. Rescuers might come looking for me by airplane or by helicopter, so I should contrive some kind of signal that could be seen from the air. I started hauling logs and large rocks about, placing them in the shape of an arrow pointing downstream. Next to it I formed the letter *Y* for the first initial of my name, and after it I wrote "12" for the date. I was pleased with my ingenuity and sure the signal would be spotted from above. The truth is I still thought I would be disappointed if someone came to rescue me. I was convinced that I was so close that it would be a shame not to do it on my own.

Toward late afternoon I came upon a stream that flowed in a shallow defile. I quickly descended the rock wall, but the opposite side was an arduous climb, and the walking stick proved a hindrance. I hurled it to the top and, clutching at bushes and protruding rocks, struggled my way to the top. There I retrieved my walking stick and went on. Soon, on a fallen tree, I saw a nest holding four brown spotted eggs. They were only a little smaller than chicken eggs and still warm. The mother must have just left the nest. I was thankful to have happened upon nourishing food. I cracked open one of the eggs and was about to pour its contents into my mouth when I noticed the tiny baby curled up inside. Should I eat it or not? No, I couldn't bring myself to do it. I put the broken egg back in the nest with its brothers and sisters.

If someone above is watching over me, I thought, he'll surely provide me with other sustenance.

Not five minutes passed before I came upon a large fruit tree. The fruit, called *trestepita*, is round and yellow and, broken open, divides into three equal parts. Each contains about twenty pits, similar to the pits of a lemon but covered with a sweet, slippery membrane. The fruit doesn't provide a great deal of meat, but I savored the juice it contained.

I leaned up against the trunk of a fallen tree and took out the tins, emptied a few tamarinds out of one, and used it to gather up trestepitas. The tree was low, and by bending its branches, I could reach the fruit. I didn't leave a single one.

I continued on my way to San José with renewed vigor. This time the trail led me deep into the jungle. I was so far from the river that its roar was not even faintly audible. After walking for a very long time I found myself surrounded by towering trees. I had lost all sense of direction. I didn't know which way was north or where the river was. The trail looked strange. It was extremely narrow; I had to go very slowly for fear of losing it. It was often blocked by wild undergrowth or fallen trees. It didn't make any sense, for only a few months ago people should have been using it. I plodded on, still convinced that it would lead me back to the river at any moment, but two hours had passed, and it was growing dark. Then I finally heard the familiar rush of the river. I was extremely relieved to learn that I could rely on the trail.

I met back up with the river just where one of the springs emptied into it. It was a narrow spring that flowed down a narrow ravine. I stood there gaping; there was a large footprint in the mud. The sole of the shoe that had made it was just like mine. God, it must be Kevin! He was alive! Kevin had big feet and wore the same kind of shoes that I did. And who besides him could have left the print? I was overcome with joy. I stared again at the print in the mud. How was it that the rain hadn't washed it away?

The climb up the other side of the ravine was difficult. The wall was almost vertical. I had to throw the walking stick up ahead of me, but regardless of how tired I was after a day of walking I felt myself endowed with superhuman strength. Pushing with my knees and dragging myself up with my arms, I made it to the top. But something seemed funny. Five minutes later I came upon a fallen tree. Next to it lay heaps of tamarind and trestepita peels and pits. Then I knew. I collapsed, broken-spirited, to the ground and almost burst into tears. It wasn't Kevin. It was me. I had wasted more than three hours walking in a circle. The trail had led me back to where I had started.

Desperation began to gnaw at me. I considered giving up and heading back to Curiplaya. I was only two or three hours' walk from there. I could go back to my hut and my bed. But the thought of the village that must be nearby with food and people overcame my momentary weakness. So I had made a mistake. It wasn't the end of the world. I would learn from it. I would use the trail only when it followed the course of the river. If it wandered into the jungle, I would abandon it and make my own way until I met back up with it on the riverbank.

I was exhausted and famished and took the fruit out of my pack. It was a pathetic match for my appetite. A few fleshless pits remained. I gritted my teeth and strode back in the direction of the ravine. There I found what I was after. The mother must have abandoned the nest, for the eggs had grown cold. I broke them open one at a time and gulped down every last bit of the unborn birds. I expected them to make me nauseous, but they were quite tasty.

The sun had gone behind a cloud and now came out and shone brightly. I could still make some progress today. I had gone astray, but the entire day was not wasted; it wasn't so bad.

"It's no big deal. It's no big deal," I started to sing.

We used to sing a song like that in the Boy Scouts, and, silly as it sounds, it stuck in my mind:

> Oh, Mama, in what a fix am I.
> I'll have a baby by and by.
> Please tell me it's a lie.
> Please tell me I won't die.
> Please say it's no big deal.

I sang the tune over and over. Then I started dramatizing it, creating characters and a silly dialogue. *You're going to have a baby, and you think it's no big deal. All right, you won't die, but just you wait until your father gets his hands on him. You'll live, but tough luck for your boyfriend. Your father will kill him.*

I worked on a drama and lost awareness of my hardships and the passing time.

After that song I remembered another:

> Please say that you agree.
> He wants to marry me.
> If you say yea or you say nay,
> We're going to marry anyway.
> Please say that you agree.

I dramatized that one in my imagination as well, with a young boy, a young girl, and a nasty old aunt. I made up a silly story and wrote dialogue for them as well.

I was tired and drenched to the bone. I started looking for a campsite but saw no crags, boulders, or fallen trees to huddle under. Finally I selected a large tree whose roots protruded from the ground in every direction at irregular intervals. I chose a space between two roots that was just as wide as my body, cleared away the wet leaves on the ground, put my pack down, and went off with my walking stick to gather bedding.

There were bushes, trees, and plants of every kind. The foliage was astounding in its variety and beauty. I gathered up large leaves, similar to banana leaves, and spread them out between the sheltering tree roots. I also found a few palms. Without a machete the fronds were hard to remove. I cracked them close to the stump and then twisted them around and around until I could wrench them from the tree. I gathered about twenty large fronds that way and arranged them symmetrically over my sleeping place one on top of the other, all facing in the same direction and crawled under.

There was no way I could light a fire. My feet were damp. I took off my shoes and wrung the water out of my socks. I took the waterproof rubber bag out of the pack, put my feet inside it, and covered my legs up to the knees. Then I covered myself as usual with the mosquito nets and the poncho. Before I covered my head, I ate a few trestepitas.

I was troubled by thoughts of Kevin. I realized that there was no reason to assume that he was dead. Actually he stood a better chance than I did. Fire and food were my advantages, but I had spent many nights without a fire and had used but little of the rice and beans. There were eggs and fruit in the jungle, and Kevin had a machete. With it he could cut down fruit trees and find palm hearts. Even if that was all he ate, he wouldn't go hungry. I had them all around me and couldn't taste a bite. If I tried to get a palm heart, I would waste more energy than it would provide. Kevin was also stronger and tougher than I was. He was used to solitude, used to difficult walking; he had a weapon, and he wasn't carrying the weight of the pack on his back. Hell, he had a much better chance than I did. I wouldn't be surprised if he had already made his way to an inhabited area and been rescued. The more I thought about it, the more convinced I became that Kevin was alive. I just hoped that nothing had happened to him in the river.

The palm fronds made an impenetrable cover. The rain fell on them and ran off to the sides. I even managed to warm myself under their shelter. My feet were comfortable in the bag. My only source of discomfort was stones digging into my back, but I couldn't do anything about them. The walking stick lay at my side. At night it could serve as a weapon along with the tin can, the spoon, and the pitiful flashlight. I said a short prayer to God and asked forgiveness for eating the unborn birds. Then I gave myself over to fantasies until the break of dawn.

The pack was on my back, the staff was in my hand, and I was on my way. My feet were damp and raw, but there was no rash. The rain had cleared up and then started falling again. I didn't let it bother me and set straight out on my course. While I walked, I sang the same songs as the day before, and when I had gone through my entire repertoire, I had long conversations with the members of my family and daydreamed again.

Suddenly something jumped out, right from under my feet. My heart jumped with it, but I regained my composure as soon as I saw that it was only a wild chicken. Its wings were weak; it barely raised itself off the ground. It fled from me in skips and jumps. I started chasing after it through the underbrush, holding my spear in readiness. We ran around, me wearing an expression of grim concentration, the chicken crackling and screeching. I didn't catch it, of course, but it occurred to me that I might find a nest with eggs nearby. I went back to where I had first encountered the bird, and there on the ground behind a bush was a large nest and six lovely eggs. They were bigger than domestic hen's eggs and turquoise in color. They were still warm to the touch. I carefully cracked one open and poured the contents into my mouth. It tasted so good that I couldn't help polishing off three more. The two that remained I carefully padded with leaves and put into the tin with the fruit.

What a lucky guy I am! Six eggs! Thank you, God, thank you.

I also spotted fruit trees on my way. As usual the fruit was out of reach, but occasionally I found a piece that had just fallen and was not yet rotten or devoured by ants and worms. The monkeys were having a banquet in the treetops, stuffing themselves and then tossing down the scraps, peels, and pits, screeching and chattering as if they were making fun of me. I cursed them, hoping one would fall on its head. The curse worked—but on me, not them.

It was almost noon. I was descending a steep hill, and the grass underfoot was wet. I slipped and tumbled, landing on my backside right on a big, dry branch that lay on the ground. My weight snapped the branch in two, and its sharp, broken end penetrated my backside, cut through my underwear, up the anus, and deep inside. I was paralyzed by the pain. I screamed in agony and then raised myself up, groaning. The pain was excruciating. I lay back, writhing on the ground, my eyes brimming with tears. My underwear was drenched with blood. I screamed when I pulled the spear out, then felt around the wound, and tried to stop the bleeding. It was impossible to bandage. I lay there for another half hour, and after the bleeding stopped, I began walking slowly with clenched teeth in anguish and enraged.

I both scolded and consoled myself. *You hurt yourself, you idiot. You weren't careful enough, jerk. You're lucky you didn't break anything. That really would have been the end of you. Oh, Mama, if you could only see me now, how you would weep. Oh, Mama . . .*

The next time I stopped to rest, I ate the other two eggs, which miraculously hadn't been broken when I fell. I ate the remaining fruit. That was the last of my food, but I was sure that something would turn up before evening.

The trail turned away from the river once again, and I hesitated to follow it. Since the last time had led me astray, I had abandoned the trail whenever I noticed that it was taking me away from the river. I did so this time as well.

Without a cleared trail or even machete slashes to guide me, walking was not easy. I ran into many dead ends, impassable bushes and branches, an impenetrable thicket of bamboo, or a boulder blocking the way. My clothing was again in tatters, the improvised threads holding it together split apart one after another. I came to a thick clump of bushes and bent the branches down to clear my way, disturbing a hornet's nest. They swarmed upon me in frenzied attack. I was stung on my face countless times. I was stuck in the bushes and couldn't get away quickly. I could feel my lips puffing up and my eyes swelling shut. After a while I managed to blunder my way out in hysteria and ran, almost blinded, into more branches, stumbling, falling. I went down to the river, drank, and bathed my face. This wasn't my day. First my lousy ass and now my face. I went on my way, bitter and angry.

Then I picked up the trail again happily and followed it. Evening was gathering, and I suddenly noticed a group of animals not more that five yards ahead of me. I quickly hid behind a tree and peeked out at them. There were six wild boars, four adults and two shoats. They pranced about, wiggling their backsides, heading away from me.

"If only I had a gun, I would finish them off one by one," I muttered to myself.

I was safe as long as they didn't notice me, didn't pick up my scent. I watched them getting farther away, and then they stopped and started playing. They chased after one another and frolicked.

"Get lost, you idiots. I can't hang around here all day."

I took off my pack, got out the spoon, and started rapping it against the tin can. They heard the dull noise, pricked up their ears, and then ran off. I hoped I wouldn't find them waiting for me around the bend.

I stepped up my pace, anxious to get out of the boars' territory before nightfall. I found another wild chicken's nest with five turquoise eggs. I ate two of them and saved the rest for the next morning. I chose a nearby tree with protruding roots and made the same sleeping arrangements that I had had the night before: a mat of soft leaves on the ground and twenty palm fronds for cover.

I was glad to get into my bed, put my feet in the rubber sack, and give my tired body, my injured backside, and swollen face a rest. I had one medicine for it all, a magic potion: fantasy.

The night put me at ease. I was no longer frightened by wild animals, this due only to apathy, for I had no means of protecting myself other than the walking stick. I sometimes heard rustling and footsteps in the dark, but I paid no attention and went on with my dream. My cover of leaves warmed me in lieu of fire. I had no dry twigs or logs. In any case I wanted to save the few matches that I had left. I suffered most from the loneliness. It made me create imaginary friends who dropped in for chats. I often found myself talking aloud. When I caught myself doing so, I panicked and scolded myself, *That's far enough, Yossi. Don't go out of your mind.*

It was difficult to grasp that I had been in the jungle two weeks. Two weeks alone. I couldn't bear much more of it. I was physically weak and liable to lose my senses. Two days had already gone by since I had left Curiplaya. That meant I should be coming to San José the next day. Tomorrow I would be seeing people. I didn't want to delude myself. To make myself believe that and to count on it. What if I didn't make it tomorrow? I had been walking slowly, had lost my way, had wasted a lot of time. Anyway the Indians made the walk during the dry season. And they probably were better hikers than I. Maybe a four-day walk for them is like a seven- or eight-day walk for me. It made sense. I stopped thinking about the next day, but deep in my heart I fervently hoped that I would find the village. What a wonderful surprise that would be.

It had stopped raining, but the dampness of the last few days had taken its toll. The rash was beginning to spread over my feet, and my inner thighs were red and raw. There was an irritating inflammation between my buttocks as well, and I still suffered the tormenting pain of the deep gash in my backside.

I mustn't coddle myself, have to be tough. I have to ignore the pain and keep going, I reminded myself.

During breakfast, which consisted of two eggs, I swallowed an amphetamine. It was the second time I had taken one since the accident. It wasn't long before it took effect, and I sprinted through the jungle as if I had the devil on my tail, assaulting the overgrown trail, breaking through branches, skipping up hills, and hopping over fallen trees. I lost the trail again and stayed stubbornly near the river, always careful to keep it within sight or at least within hearing.

The first animal I met up with this day was a snake, a brown snake about six feet long but not particularly big around. It was slithering through the grass, and I only noticed it when it sped off at my approach. Without a second thought I grabbed a rock and chased after it like crazy, trying to get close enough to have a fair shot. But the snake was faster than I was and disappeared into the underbrush. I was sorry. If I had caught it, it would have been nourishing, even raw. I would have eaten it salted. For the past few days I had eaten only eggs and fruit.

Later I encountered a pair of tapirs, a mother and her young. They were massive, and the earth quaked under their tread. When the poor things noticed me, they ran off in fright.

I didn't actually see the third animal, but I knew it was there. It was before noon. I had emerged from the jungle and found myself standing on a lovely beach, the largest I had come upon since we had left Asriamas. The sand was so white, it was blinding. The river lapped pleasantly at the shore. The scorching sun was directly overhead. At long last some sunshine. I thought I would be able to dry out and heal the rawness of my skin. I bent over to remove my pack, and that's when I noticed the jaguar tracks on the shore, lots of tracks of different sizes. There was no doubt that this was not a solitary jaguar, but an entire pack.

I followed the paw prints in the sand. Under a shady tree I found small piles of feces, at least six separate piles. I stepped on one of them. Though no tracker or Indian guide, I knew enough to recognize that they were fresh; they were soft and didn't crumble. There had been a lot of jaguars on this shore. It seemed to serve as their meeting place, but I didn't want to leave, and the truth is that I wasn't really afraid. I just couldn't believe that I would be eaten by jaguars in broad daylight. I felt safe.

I made myself comfortable near the water and spread out all of my wet belongings on the warm sand. I gathered up a huge stack of kindling and used only two matches lighting a fire. I kept the fire well fed and placed a tin of water in it. I stripped off my wet clothing and spread it out near the poncho and the mosquito nets. I stretched out on the sand in my birthday suit, spreading my legs wide to expose my raw inner thighs to the sunlight. The flies and mosquitoes swarmed over me, and I was forced to cover myself with one of the nets. The sun shone through it, however, and gently caressed my body.

I lay there for about an hour and then got up to prepare soup. This time I put in two tablespoons each of rice and beans, intending to prepare them as solid food and take along on my way. I dipped the water out of the tin and drank it, until all that was left at the bottom of the tin was an oatmeal-like residue. The rice was all right, though it didn't smell fresh, but the beans had not cooked long enough. On top of that I had added too much salt. It tasted awful, but even so it was difficult to follow my resolve and save the bulk for later.

Since I had a good fire, I wanted to catch a fish and cook it. It looked like a good place for fishing. The river could have been as much as several hundred feet wide—from the bank it was hard to tell—and the current was not strong. I had no difficulty swatting a few big flies and tried to use them to catch a minnow. I stood on the riverbank, draped with the mosquito net, making sure the line had enough slack. The sun beat down on my head, and suddenly everything went black, and I lost consciousness. The cool water brought me to immediately. I leapt from the river, wet and frightened. I couldn't let that happen again. It was both terrifying and dangerous.

I stretched out again for a while, then donned my dry clothing and gingerly put my socks and wonderfully sturdy shoes back on. Before leaving this fabulous beach I invested a great deal of effort in marking it. There were heavy stumps lying about, and I laboriously pushed and rolled them until they formed an arrow pointing in the direction I was going. As before, I made a letter Y and the date: "14."

The map had also dried, and I studied it at length. The distance between Curiplaya and San José appeared to be twenty-five miles by river, or about thirty miles by the path alongside the river. I had been walking almost twelve hours a day. There was no reason to believe that I wouldn't arrive in San José within a day or two. Only one thing worried me. San José was on the left bank, the opposite side of the river. The only landmark before the village was a large river that emptied into the Tuichi from the left. Karl had told us that it was the village's source of water. He had said that San José lay not on the bank of the Tuichi but a few miles up that other river. On the right bank, the one I was on, there wasn't a single landmark to tell me where I was. So I couldn't depend entirely on the map. I was concerned that I might not notice the village and mistakenly pass it by. Then I would be lost. For good. Between San José and Rurrenabaque there were no other villages, and it would be impossible to walk the entire distance. The only really safe thing to do would be to cross the Tuichi and walk along the other side. That way I wouldn't miss the village. I went on, looking for a good place to cross.

Farther on I came to a dead end. A stream fed into the Tuichi in a deep, impassable wadi. I had to change course and march upstream into the jungle until the wadi flattened out and I found an easy place to cross it. This detour took several hours. I doubled back on the other side of the stream, straight and to the left, in the direction of the Tuichi. Another stream cut across my path, but this one I could ford easily, skipping from stone to stone, careful not to lose my balance and fall in. Beyond the stream was a field of thorns. There were no trees at all, only bushes and thistles as tall as I was. Having no other choice, I plodded into it, trying to clear a path.

I experienced a new kind of hell in the field of thorns. I lost my sense of direction, and my entire body was scratched and mauled. Scathing nettles stabbed into me, and I shook with pain and fear. At long last I made it back to the jungle and to the lost path. The trail here did not look as if it had been in use, however. It was unreliable and led me astray for a long while. It was frequently covered over completely with jungle foliage. It couldn't be that men marched over this path every year, I told myself, but no sooner had I done so than I suddenly heard, in the distance, human voices. There were speaking, and someone called out something. I started running and shouting, "Help! Hey, hey! Wait for me! *Espera! Espera!*"

I ran as if possessed. I shouted myself hoarse. I struck out at the branches that blocked my way. Then stopped to listen. Not the slightest whisper was to be heard. It must have been my imagination playing tricks on me.

My idiotic pride had long since worn thin. Now I prayed for someone to rescue me. Let people say that I was a wimp, that I should have been able to make it out of the jungle on my own. I just wanted to be saved.

It was now the fourteenth of December. Someone had to do something—Lisette, the embassy. Marcus must be back by now. Or Kevin perhaps. I was certain that I would soon hear the drone of a plane overhead. They couldn't help but see me. I had left unmistakable signs on two beaches. They would easily spot the markings. But maybe, just maybe, I would still make it on my own. I must be so very close to San José.

Toward evening I thought that I had found a good place to cross. The river was wide, but the current seemed mild. Furthermore, there were four substantial islands strung out between one bank and the other. I could go from island to island until I reached the other side. Still, I thought, it might not be as easy as it looked, and I decided to take some precautions.

I was loath to get my clothing wet again, especially my socks. I stripped, shoved my clothing into the rubber bag, and closed it inside the pack. I took out the fishing line and tied it to the shoulder straps. I set the pack in the river; it floated satisfactorily. I pulled it back in and set in on the edge of the shore. Then I jumped barefoot into the water, holding the line. The water was shallow. I could walk, wading farther out, slowly but surely.

The current was stronger than it had looked, and the sharp stones on the river bottom cut into the soles of my feet. Only the walking stick came to my aid. I leaned heavily upon it, taking one cautious step after another. As I went, I gradually let out the fishing line, until I made it to the first island, about seventy-five feet from the shore. Now I would pull the pack over and go on to the next island. That was my plan. But it didn't work out that way.

I gave the fishing line a yank, and the pack slipped into the river. The undertow sucked it beneath the surface, and though I tugged with all my might, I couldn't pull it to me. I decided to change plans and tied the end of the line to a small tree on the shore of the island. I would walk back across to the riverbank and carry the pack on my back, but first I wanted to check out the second island.

I walked quickly to the far side of the first island. As I walked, mosquitoes swarmed all over me. I was black with them. I swatted myriads of them with my hands, but they didn't leave me alone. I rushed to the water but discovered it to be deep. I couldn't touch bottom and almost lost my faithful walking stick to the current. I threw it up on the bank and tried swimming to the second island, but the current was so strong that I headed back to the first while I was still able.

I would never make it across the river, at least not with the weight of the pack on my back. Perhaps I should leave the pack behind? No, I still needed it. I returned to the bank of the Tuichi, picking up the pack on my way. I dried myself on a mosquito net as best I could and put my clothes back on. I was covered with mosquito bites and clawed at them in a frenzy. My only consolation that day was a new nest of wild chicken eggs. I gulped down four warm, delicious eggs and saved two for morning.

It was growing dark, and I had not yet set up camp. I didn't find a tree that offered any shelter. Either the roots didn't protrude far enough out of the earth, or the tree wasn't standing on level ground. The sun had almost set before I found a place to settle.

The rain started coming down again in the middle of the night, not a drizzle but a downpour, which seeped through my thatch of fronds. I shivered and curled up into a ball. I pulled the rubber bag high up over my knees and tucked the red poncho in all around me. I had three fantasies that by this time I had worked into long scenarios. Each was set in a different place. I put the hood over my face and went to visit Las Vegas, São Paulo, and my home in Israel, drifting from one to another all night long.

In the morning I ate the salty rice-and-bean paste together with two eggs. A real feast.

If anyone is looking down on me, he is absolutely heartless.

It was pouring rain, and all my efforts to keep my clothes dry were wasted. I was supposed to find San José today. Maybe I would spend this night in the company of other men. That thought drove me out of my mind. I didn't want to pin all my hopes on it. Well, if not today, then surely tomorrow, I thought, trying to convince myself.

Walking was difficult. I was soaking wet, heavy, and clumsy. I could feel the water in my shoes and knew only too well what it was likely to do to my feet. The ground was muddy and slippery, and the wind chilled me to the bone. The longer I spent here, the more likely I was to sink into despondency. Even marching songs were of no avail, so I decided to flee to São Paulo, Brazil, a city I had heard much about.

My uncle lives here, and I am visiting him. I like it here. Why not stay for a while? I make elaborate plans for putting down roots in the city. I meet a few people my own age, all of them students. I spend a lot of time with them and discreetly inquire which is the wealthiest family in town. Do they have a young daughter? They do, of course, and of course she is both intelligent and beautiful. But how can I meet her? How can I ask her out? I have to find a way. Maybe I should take my uncle's car and crash into hers. That sometimes works in the movies. Maybe I should just hang around waiting for her and win her over with sincerity? Maybe she won't be able to resist my charms? Finally I come up with a plan. I will get to the daughter through the mother. My first thought is to have her run me over, just a little, like in *Being There*, but that would be risky. Plan B is to save her from muggers. And that's what I do.

Hey, you, kid! Come over here a minute.

I'm no kid. You'd better watch it, or else . . .

He was a street urchin who always hung around the neighborhood.

Take it easy, pal. I didn't mean to insult you. I just wanted to know if you'd like to make a few bucks.

You bet, but it depends how.

This is going to sound weird, but . . . and I tell him my plan.

The kid drives a hard bargain, and I end up agreeing to pay him more than I had intended, but for this it's worth it. I just worry that he might double-cross me.

You'd better not keep on running. Don't try to con me.

You don't know us, señor. We never go back on our word.

The mother goes out to a large shopping center, wearing a fancy dress and carrying a fancy bag. She is elegant, aristocratic. She walks down the street like she owns it, oblivious to the admiring glances of everyone she passes. Then something happens: something that forces her down from Olympus. A short, dark-skinned boy brushes up against her, pushes her roughly, grabs her purse out of her hands, and runs off.

Thief! Thief! Stop him!

Now she turns to the crowd for help, but the dark-skinned boy knows his business; he has vanished into the crowd, quick as an eel.

This is where I come in. Around the corner the boy hands me the purse as we had agreed. I bend over and let him give me a punch in the nose before he takes off.

I return the fancy bag. She smothers me with gratitude and takes out a clean handkerchief to staunch the bleeding. Then she takes out a wad of bills and offers them to me. I look her straight in the eye and refuse to take her money. She begins questioning me.

Speak more slowly, señora. I don't speak the language that well.

We chat. I know I am making a good impression.

Perhaps you'd care to join us for dinner this evening, she says. My husband and daughter would be so pleased to meet you.

Well, I don't know. I . . .

Please do come.

The evening is unforgettable. I am introduced to her daughter. It's a special moment, charged with expectations of things to come. I know that she will someday be my wife.

We seat ourselves around the table. Liveried servants serve a magnificent repast: salads, soufflés, skewered meats, vegetables, baked potatoes. The table is laden with every kind of delicacy, and I do not pass up a single dish. I taste everything, trying to do so without a rude display of gluttony.

When it is time to take my leave, I have the nerve to invite the mother and daughter to visit me in the apartment I have rented in the city. On the appointed day, after poring over recipes, I decide to serve a pizza, the very best pizza ever prepared. I knead the dough and toss it into the air like a professional. I don't settle for tomato paste seasoned with oregano, but sauté onions in a deep skillet together with whole, peeled tomatoes. I add green peppers and numerous cloves of garlic. I spice the sauce and ladle it over the crust. I sprinkle aromatic grated cheese in a thick layer. The cheese melts even before I put the pizza into the oven.

Dinner is a great success. We drink a lot of wine. It doesn't take long from there to the wedding . . .

My belly was howling. Brazil had been swell, but I had gotten my digestive juices all worked up for nothing. No matter, one day the dream would come true. For now I had to find something to eat.

Walking was intolerably difficult. The rain poured down. The jungle was dark and gloomy, and I walked slowly. It wasn't much better on the path. It was often blocked and frequently left me abandoned, helpless, in the jungle. The little streams were brimming over and difficult to cross. Scaling the walls of the wadis and climbing steep hills was treacherous. My shoes were caked with mud, and I slipped often. I was exhausted. I leaned heavily on my walking stick. I was weak and famished but afraid to take another amphetamine. Fate mocked me: I came upon a fruit tree whose inaccessible branches were laden with manzanas de monte. The rain and wind had knocked a few of them down into the mud. I picked out and ate the best of them. Most already had fat worms crawling through them. If only I could climb the tree or chop it down, I would have enough food for two days.

You know, Kevin, if you were here with the machete, with your muscles that tree would have been down in less than an hour. And you know what else, Kevin? If you were here, you'd be the one carrying this cruddy pack, not me.

But I was alone, and the fruit was out of reach. The pack was burdensome, and the rain still poured down.

I no longer felt that someone was watching over me, but still I prayed. *Make the rain stop. Make me get to San José. May a plane come and find me. Do something.*

Nothing happened, and I kept walking mechanically forward, but I couldn't stand it anymore. I decided to hop a plane for Las Vegas.

I arrive at night. A hot desert wind is blowing. At the hotel I take a shower and freshen up, then go down to the casino, smooth-shaven and well dressed. I had last been here on my way back from Alaska and had left a contribution of a thousand dollars on the blackjack table. But Judgment Day is here; I have come for my revenge.

Lord, what cards I hold this evening! I am dealt blackjack on almost every round. I increase the amounts I bet and tip the dealer generously. I play recklessly, paying no attention to the dealer's cards. I have fourteen, and he has six showing.

Hit me, I tell him.

The other players at the table give me disapproving looks but are astounded when I am dealt a seven. What can I say?

Everyone gathers around to watch the big-time young card shark. I start betting two hands at once and wipe out every dealer in the place.

The pit boss comes to my table and watches anxiously. His face is blank, but I can read his thoughts. I could swear I hear him say, *Go on, sweetheart, keep playing. I know your type. You don't know when to get up and leave the table. You'll end up depositing all your money here.*

He's wrong, of course. My luck never runs out. The pot gets bigger and bigger, astronomical sums of money. They have to call the manager to raise the limit. The manager has been watching me through one-way mirrors in the ceiling. He signs the authorization, and the game goes on.

Waitresses showing a lot of cleavage try to ply me with drinks.

Not right now, honey, no thanks. Only coffee for me. Sure, you can put a little Grand Marnier in it, but just a little.

A gorgeous kitten materializes behind me, massaging my shoulders, brushing her breasts against my back.

I know why you're here, sweetie, I say to myself. It's not because of my charming smile, but it's all right with me. I'm no prude. Just a few more hands, and then we'll have a good time.

I get up from the table with $300,000 in chips. The manager signs the check personally. I have to admit that they are gracious losers. He shakes my hand and informs me that my luggage has already been moved to the VIP suite. He gives me a card entitling me to free use of all of the hotel's facilities. And this hotel has everything: floor shows, bars, restaurants, girls. You name it. They have it. I promise that I will be back tomorrow to triple my winnings. We are both happy.

Now I get down to business. I take my well-endowed bunny and go into the casino's fanciest restaurant. The credit card works wonders. The special treatment we receive is fantastic. Everyone has already heard about me. The table is surrounded by waiters.

Sweet-and-sour ribs, sir? Waldorf salad? Would you like to try a new kind of crepe? Wine? Fish in garlic and butter? A T-bone steak with french fries? What kind of dressing would you like on the chef's salad? Roquefort? Yes, sir, right away. A banana split or ice cream? Chocolate and strawberry ice cream? Yes, of course, sir. You know just what to order.

The flattery pays off for the waiter. I don't leave anyone out. They all ask me to return. If I was a big hit at the blackjack tables, that was nothing compared with the restaurant.

You can rest assured, my friends, that I'll be back very soon . . .

In the late afternoon I was surprised by another river cutting across my path. It was quite wide—one hundred feet at least—but most of it was a desiccated riverbed. Down in a relatively narrow channel a placid flow of water ran into the Tuichi. The Tuichi itself looked treacherous. Its waters were black with the mud it churned up. Logs, branches, and uprooted bushes were carried along by the current, which was extremely swift. I wouldn't have liked to have fallen into those waters.

I stood there frightened, staring helplessly at the two rivers. I was certain that the map hadn't indicated another river emptying into the Tuichi on this bank before San José. I knew the map by heart, and according to it, the next river on the right-hand bank was far beyond San José. Could I have passed the village without realizing it? San José was located up in the hills and was not visible from the Tuichi. I was supposed to have spotted it by the wide path and the balsa rafts on the shore. I might not have noticed and passed it when I was walking in the jungle, not along the bank.

Perhaps this river simply wasn't charted on the map. But how was that possible? The Ipurama and the Turliamos were marked, and they were no bigger than this river. The map wasn't dependable. Maybe this river had been overlooked because it was so shallow. I didn't know what to think, whether to backtrack and look for the landmarks on the opposite bank or go on, not knowing where I was. I finally decided to go on walking for one more day. Since I hadn't reached the village, I was bound to get there tomorrow. If not, then I would have no choice but to turn around and go back.

The remains of a path through the jungle lent credence to my assumption that I hadn't yet passed the village. The path continued, a narrow, difficult trail that took me about fifty yards from the Tuichi. What I found there surprised me and restored my hopes: traces of a campsite: two poles tied together with vines and a few palm fronds resting upon them. It was an old campsite. The vines were withered and dry, as were the fronds.

I couldn't have passed San José yet if there was a campsite here, I reassured myself. It also meant that San José couldn't be as close as I had assumed. Why would anyone bother setting up camp if it was only a few more hours' walk? I concluded that I must have at least another full day's hike ahead of me. It made sense. This was the path the villagers used on their way upriver to Curiplaya. It was reasonable to assume that they set out in the morning and set up camp after a day's walk. That put me a day from San José. I figured that this must be the first camp that they used on their way.

My spirits rose. I was sure it was the first camp; hadn't I been walking for four days already? So, I'd be there tomorrow.

You did it, Yossi. Congratulations. You made it. Tomorrow night you won't be sleeping alone in the jungle. You'll eat your fill. You won't be exposed to the rain and other dangers. One more day, Yossi, one more day.

It had stopped raining. The path led a little way past the camp and then dwindled and vanished altogether. I figured that this must be where the natives crossed the Tuichi. It was a convenient place to cross. The wadi was muddy. The stream ran through its center and was only about a foot deep. I crossed to the other side.

The land here was completely flat and well forested. There were no hills or steep inclines. The jungle was dense, and vines were draped from the trees amid bushes and reeds. I could neither go forward nor find traces of the path. I kept on looking for broken branches or machete strokes, with no luck. I returned to the riverbank, searching for signs of where the natives had resumed their march, where the path would be. Sudden claps of deafening thunder set the jungle quaking. Hell, it was going to start pouring again. I had better find shelter. I could use the remains of the camp back on the other side of the river. It would mean wasting the two hours of walking time I had left that day, but the rain slowed me down anyway. Tomorrow the weather would surely be more benign, and I would hurry on.

I crossed back to the camp. Thunder clapped, and lightning lit up the sky. The wind came up. It was going to be a terrible storm. I hurriedly set about reinforcing the remains of the camp. I replaced the vines with fresh ones and went into the jungle to look for palm fronds. It had already started raining. I had never seen such a downpour. The drops came down with a sharp sting. I tore off about twenty fronds. The effort wore me out, but I didn't give up. I arranged the fronds so that they were closely overlapping one another across the poles. I covered every crack through which the rain might seep. I knew that it would take a thick layer to keep the wet out. The jungle outside was well flooded over, as if the end of the world were approaching. From a distance the Tuichi looked turbulent and gloomy.

I hurried into my shelter. Water leaked through in several places, but I didn't dare go back outside. I tried to rearrange the fronds from inside. I got out my nighttime necessities: the rice-and-bean pillow, the rubber sack to cover my feet, the nets to use as blankets, and the poncho to wrap around everything else. I took off my shoes and wrung out my socks. Up until now I had managed to keep my feet in fair condition. I had only one more day to go. I prayed that they wouldn't let me down now.

Drops fell steadily through the leaks in the roof onto the poncho and dripped down to the ground. Outside I could hear the raging storm. In a very short time the ground became muddy, then soggy. I lay drenched in my shelter, miserable, trembling with both cold and fear. There was nothing I could do but pray to God.

The storm grew worse, and my shelter began to blow away, leaving open spaces through which the water streamed down upon me. I wanted to cry, to wail. I wanted away from this horror.

Why, why, did this have to happen to me? Please, God, help me. I'm afraid of dying.

Each minute seemed an eternity, and I had nowhere to flee. It required fierce concentration to immerse myself in fantasy. This time I went home.

I am married and have small children. My brother, Moshe, and I start a ranch on huge tracts of land we have bought in the Upper Galilee. We stock it with cattle I bought in Bolivia and Argentina of a quality not to be found in Israel. Most of Israel's meat is imported from Argentina, but we have a good climate and unused open spaces for grazing. Why shouldn't we raise our own cattle?

My brother and I work hard. The ranch prospers. We erect a huge house and all live together: my brother, his wife Miri, his daughter Lilach, and his other children, and of course me and my wife and our children.

We send our children to the regional school in a nearby kibbutz . . .

"Ahhh!" I came out of my fantasy with a scream. There was an earsplitting din, and the ground shuddered. The trees around me, their roots left with nothing to hold on to, were crashing down one after another. When a tree of that size falls, it takes a few other trees with it.

God, help me! Save me! God . . .

The uproar died down, and the ground under me grew still. I heard only the rain and the roar of the Tuichi. Drenched and clammy with sweat, I forced myself back to the Galilee.

My brother and I rise at six, have our coffee in large mugs with thick slabs of cake. We leave early for the range on horseback. We check the fencing, take a count of the herd, check on a pregnant cow. At nine we head back home. The kids have already eaten and gone to school, and now the cook devotes herself to us. She prepares omelets, salads, cheeses. Thick bread and butter, cream of wheat or rice pudding, hot chocolate, and her own special marmalade.

I don't know the source of our misfortune, but our fabulous cook leaves our employ. We place an ad in the newspaper: "Wanted: gourmet cook. Residence on ranch in Galilee. Good terms and pay."

We receive a great many applications and set up interviews. I am in charge. I sit in the office at the ranch and meet the prospective cooks. Each describes in detail the delicacies she or he knows how to prepare. I interview them one after another, listening to descriptions of every imaginable kind of food. This was my favorite among my fantasies since I could stretch it out and go into the minutest details of every dish and its preparation: Moroccan, European, hot and spicy, Polish dishes, Chinese food, and exotic concoctions. There is no end to the variety of food and no end to the line of applicants.

Outside it seemed that all the biblical prophecies of doom had been fulfilled, and there I was, by myself, the only human in this vast jungle. No other people, no settlements. Only San José, somewhere up there in the hills on the other side of the river, and I might at any instant be crushed to death by a falling tree. Yes, it could happen at any second, and it's the only thing that will pacify this jungle, let it settle peacefully back into its former calm. It wants to expel this arrogant interloper, this man who dared to think he could survive here alone.

I went on fantasizing until dawn. From time to time I was startled out of my daydreams in a panic, thinking my end had come, but despite everything someone was still watching over me.

The morning rays cast their light on nothing good. The rain still came down in torrents. The wind kept howling against my shelter, rattling its rickety poles, but they held fast. My breath under the poncho kept my wet body warm, and my fantasies kept my mind occupied, but I wanted to get up and start marching. I had to get out of the jungle, no matter what. Kneeling, I packed my things, slung the pack on my back, snatched up my walking stick, and dashed outside.

Good Lord! Rain flooded down. I turned to start in the direction of the river and stood rooted to the ground. The wadi was flooded. The entire riverbed was brimming with water, as deep as ten feet, I guessed. Incredible. A shallow stream, a wadi that had been almost dry, had overnight become a wide river, almost overflowing its banks. The Tuichi, which flowed by about fifty yards from where I stood, looked threatening. Its waters were black, and the current so swift it seemed that someone had filmed the river and was showing it at double speed. So many enormous trees floated downstream that the water itself was barely visible. The river had washed over its shores, gathering up all that booty. I assumed that the signposts that I had so laboriously erected, indicating my presence and the direction in which I was going, had also been washed away. I cursed the day.

How was I going to make it across the river? I started away from the Tuichi following the course of the unknown river upstream, but I didn't get far. There was no path nor hope of finding a place to cross. I had to go back to my shelter.

I was furious with myself. If I were to stay put, that meant spending another entire day in the jungle, and I wouldn't be sleeping in San José that night. I had had such high hopes of making it. There was nothing that I could do about it, however. There was no choice but to wait for the storm to blow over, for the river to recede so that I might cross it and be on my way.

I lay back down. My empty stomach was beyond grumbling or growling. I now felt the hunger with my entire body, a primordial need to eat, but all I had were the fruits of my imagination.

I suppose close to half an hour had passed when I became aware of water running down my back and shoulders. How could that be? I had a thick roof of leaves. Cold water reached my buttocks and feet. Then I grasped what had happened and had no time to spare. Both rivers were flooding, and I, fool that I was, hadn't seen it coming. The ground was level and flooded in a flash. I hurriedly knelt and shoved everything into my pack, including my socks and shoes. I didn't have time to close the rubber sack but rushed outside in my bare feet and began running. The water was already up to my ankles and would soon be knee deep. I ran in a panic but realized almost immediately that I had forgotten my walking stick in the shelter. I wasn't about to abandon my trusty walking stick. I set my pack down on a little rise and ran back.

By the time I had reclaimed the stick and had returned to the pack, the water was already past my waist, and the rise was flooded. The pack was floating, and I rushed toward it before it could be carried away. I put my arm through one of the shoulder straps and grabbed hold of a tree. I could feel the water tugging me toward the river. If I lost my hold on the tree, I would drown. I started swimming away, kicking hard, and succeeded in grabbing onto the next tree. All of my muscles ached, and I was afraid that they would give out on me, but the palpable fear of death lent me new, unfamiliar stores of energy. I pushed myself away from the tree with a great thrust, reaching from tree to tree. Once I missed my grasp and was swept away, but the jungle was dense, and I was rammed into trees until I caught hold of one of them. There was no chance of my climbing a tree and, anyway, I might have been stuck up there forever. I would be better off trying to make it to higher ground.

For once I was oblivious to pain. I was quite simply fighting for my life: pushing away, grabbing, pulling, snatching instants to catch my breath. I went on like that for half an hour until I came upon a hill that wasn't flooded. I stood there panting, water pouring out of the holes in my pack, my clothing drenched and torn, rain beating down upon me mercilessly.

I got my socks and shoes out and pulled them onto my battered feet. The red rash was spreading, and I knew only too well what was in store for me. I was bitter, despondent, and furiously angry that the whole world—all the mighty elements of nature—had ganged up on one solitary man.

On the other side of the hill the jungle had flooded only waist high. Walking was a torment. I sank into the mud, and each step was excruciating, for the mud had seeped into my shoes and socks and had begun to abrade the skin. Places I had passed so easily yesterday presented dangerous obstacles today. Every tiny wadi had become a stormy deluge. Every broad expanse was now a treacherous swamp. The area was suddenly overrun with frogs. Where had they all come from? Their croaking made a din, but, strangely, I didn't see a single one. The storm had left its traces everywhere. Broken trees lay like corpses on the ground, leaving gaping, flooded craters where they had been uprooted.

I went on as best I could, walking away from the Tuichi, fleeing to the hills. I went on for miles, hours passed, but nothing changed. I walked immersed in mud, without knowing where I was putting my feet. I got stuck in bushes and pulled myself free. I stepped on sharp rocks and bit back the pain. I was frequently forced to swim. When I had to haul myself back out of wadis, I slipped and slid, crawling on my hands and knees. When I tried to get a grip on a root or a bush, I fell backward, clutching the uprooted plant in my hand. I had no idea where I was or where I was going, I only wanted to find a resting place for my battered body. I wanted to get to someplace where I would be able to lie down and wait for the storm to pass. Finally I climbed a hill and looked for a tree with thick roots. I didn't want to lie down under a tree that was likely to fall over and crush me. Completely exhausted, I tore off a few palm fronds and lay down on the ground under what appeared to be a reliable tree.

The rain hadn't stopped but seemed to have abated somewhat. I took off my shoes and shoved my feet into the sack. They were so raw that I was afraid to take my socks off, fearful that I wouldn't be able to put them back on the next day. Both the mosquito nets and the poncho were dripping wet. I was shivering cold. The wind was still blowing, and I was afraid that I would come down with pneumonia. If I became sick, I would die.

I began praying. I prayed to God with all my heart. *Please forgive me for ever having doubted you and not putting all my faith in you.*

I know that you are always watching. Please don't let me get sick. Let me make it back to safety. Please God.

I considered taking a vow, promising something, but I didn't want God to think that I was haggling. I took out Uncle Nissim's book for moral support. The plastic bag had not kept it dry. I kissed the book and slipped it into my pocket.

It was the seventeenth morning of my solitude. The storm was over. I was in sad shape. I was far from my destination and doubted that I would be able to go on. My feet were infected. From now on walking would be torture. How could my body take any more? I was weak with hunger. I had eaten nothing for the past two days. Now how would I find eggs or fruit? The storm had washed everything away. Was I going to die of hunger or injury? Morbid thoughts filled my mind; there was no chance of my escaping into fantasy. I was distressed to the point of despondency. All my hopes of reaching San José faded away. I hadn't yesterday. I apparently wasn't going to today. Who knew if I ever would?

What an idiot I was. I should never have left Curiplaya. I could have waited there in my hut. I could have survived there for at least a month, and by then surely someone would have come looking for me. Someone would have done something.

Now what would I do? Where should I go? I no longer believe there was much chance of my reaching San José. I doubted that I would be able to cross the river. Though the storm had died away, the whole jungle was submerged. I was bitter and on the edge of absolute despair, almost ready to give up. I started back to Curiplaya.

Overcome by self-pity, I hobbled painfully on until I came to a trestepita tree. The tree was bent low, almost touching the ground. It still had fruit on it, and I eagerly sucked the sweet-sour pulp from the pits. The small quantity of nourishment tormented my aching belly, but it helped restore my hopes.

Someone is still watching over me. Uncle Nissim's book will protect me. I won't die as long as I have it in my pocket. I shouldn't underestimate its powers. I mustn't lose hope. I am stronger than I think I am. If I have been able to survive this far, I can go on.

I gave myself a good talking-to and turned toward San José once again. I was going on, no matter what. I trod through flood waters, swam across streams, climbed up wadi walls. I don't know where I got the energy. While I was wading through the mud, I made believe that I was one of the Zionist pioneers, draining the swamps. A long black snake passing near my foot startled me. I threw my walking stick at it but missed.

"Wait a minute," I called, chasing after it. "Wait a minute. I want to eat you."

My shirt caught on a branch and tore. The sharp branch slashed my upper arm down to the elbow. Blood spurted from the wound. I fought back tears of desperation.

It doesn't matter. I'll get over it. I'm going on.

I could neither see nor hear the river but followed the streams that cut in front of me. I knew that they would lead me to the Tuichi. It wasn't raining, but the wind was blowing, and it was very cold. The humidity formed a heavy mist.

Suddenly I heard a sputter, a drone, the sound of an engine. . . an airplane.

Don't be a fool, Yossi. It's only your imagination.

But the sound grew louder. It was an airplane!

They're looking for me! Hooray! I'm saved!

The sound grew louder, and I ran like a lunatic, ignoring my tattered feet. I had to get to Tuichi. I had to signal the plane. The sound was right overhead. I stopped, panting, and looked up. Between the treetops I saw a few gray clouds, and amid them, at a moderate altitude, a small white plane glided past.

"Hello, here I am! Help! I'm down here." I waved my arms frantically. "Don't go. Don't leave me here. Here I am."

The plane vanished from the sky, its drone fading away.

Now I became aware of my feet. The frantic running had torn the flesh from them, and I felt as if they were on fire. I collapsed to the earth, my face buried in the mud. I lay sprawled there and wanted to cry, but the tears wouldn't come.

I can't take any more. I can't budge another inch. That's it.

From the bottom of my heart I prayed, not for rescue, not even for survival. I prayed for death. *Please, good God, stop this suffering. Let me die.*

And then she appeared. I knew it was all in my mind, but there she lay, next to me. I didn't know who she was. I didn't know her name. I knew we'd never met, and yet I knew that we were in love. She was weeping despondently. Her fragile body trembled.

"There, there, stop crying," I tried to comfort her.

Take it easy. It's all right. Get up, Yossi, I urged myself, *you have to lead the way, keep her spirits up.*

I plucked myself up out of the mud and very gently helped her up. Tears still poured down her cheeks.

"The plane didn't see us. It just went by," she wailed.

"Don't worry, my love. It will surely be back this way. It didn't see us through the jungle trees. We can't be seen from the air. If we could get a fire going, the smoke might be spotted."

But everything was soaking wet.

When I heard the drone of the plane's engine once again, I knew we had no hope of being found that day.

I had made it back to the Tuichi, but there was no bank. I stood on the bluff, about twenty feet above the river, its rapids tumbling beneath me. I took out the poncho and waved it frantically, but I knew there was no chance of being spotted through the trees. The plane was flying too high and too fast. I watched it go past with longing eyes.

She looked up at me forlornly.

Don't worry. They'll be back tomorrow," I promised. "Look, we were almost saved today. I'm sure that that's Kevin up there. It has to be Kevin. I just know it is. He must have gone to my embassy for help."

I still did not recognize her: where she was from, why she was here. I just kept comforting her.

"They knew they'd have a hard time finding us today since the weather is so cloudy, but I'm sure they'll come back tomorrow and won't give up until they find us.

"You know, once in a while some guy gets lost in the Judeaen desert, and they call out the army and volunteers and trackers.

Sometimes they have to keep looking for a whole week before they find the guy, dead or alive. They never just stop looking.

"What we have to do is help them find us. We have to find a shore to stand on, so they'll be able to see us."

I remembered the beach where the jaguars had been. I had better head back there.

"Yes, that's a great idea. It's a huge beach."

I had marked it clearly, and while I assumed that the markings had all been washed away, the beach itself must still be there. It was so wide. I quickly figured the distance. I had first arrived at Jaguar Beach on the afternoon of the fourteenth. I had wasted the rest of that day trying unsuccessfully to ford the river. On the fifteenth, as well, I had stopped walking relatively early. That meant that a day's walk was between me and the beach. I could still get in a good few hours' walk today. Tomorrow I would start walking at dawn and perhaps make Jaguar Beach in the morning hours.

I explained my plan to her.

"Come on, love. Another day's walk, maybe less, and we'll be there," I said encouragingly. "There they will spot us easily. First the plane will go over and see us. The pilot will signal us with a tilt of the wings and go back to base. Within a few hours a helicopter will arrive, land on the beach, and pick us up. We'll be saved. It'll all happen tomorrow. We have to stick it out one more day. Come on, let's get going."

I changed direction for the third time that day. This time without hesitation. I knew that I was doing the right thing.

My feet barely obeyed my will, almost refusing to carry my weight. They couldn't stand much pressure. Every time I stepped on a rock or root, terrible pains pierced through me. When I had to climb a hill and descend the other side, it seemed an impossible effort. I had to get down and crawl, drag myself along with my elbows. But I kept my suffering to myself. She was with me. She was also injured, weak, and hungry. It was harder for her than for me. If I wasn't strong, she would break.

I have to push myself harder, hide my own feelings, and keep her morale up.

When we were climbing upward, I would bite my lip and plead with her, "Just a little farther, my love. Yes, I know how much it hurts. Here, I'll give you a hand. One more little push. That's all. You see? We made it. We're at the top. Now we have to get down. Sit like this and slide. Slowly, take it easy. Watch out. Be careful you don't slip."

Rocks and thorns sliced into my buttocks. I noticed with concern that the rash had spread to other parts of my body. Red dots had broken out under my armpits and around my elbows. The cut on my arm hadn't formed a scab. The edges were white. My fingers and the palms of my hands were also lily-white. I had been constantly wet for several days.

My body is rotting.

We walked until late evening. I didn't stop talking for a minute, chattering all day long, trying to keep her spirits up, trying to keep her from losing hope. When she stumbled or slowed down, I offered her my hand, caressing her sad face. I was so anxious to cover as much ground as possible that I didn't even notice that the sun had almost set. I had to hurry and find a place to rest our heads before darkness fell.

I tore off some palm fronds and spread them over some muddy tree roots. I didn't bother trying to get comfortable; my body was inured to discomfort. I covered myself with the wet nets and the poncho. Taking my shoes off had been agony. I didn't remove my socks. They would just have to remain wet and dirty with mud, blood, and pus. I pulled the sack over my feet very carefully, knowing how tormenting the slightest contact would be. I didn't change position all night long in order to give my feet a rest.

I believed with all my heart that tomorrow would be my last day of hardship. Tomorrow a plane would find me.

"Thank you, my love. Thank you for being here. Tomorrow you'll get the kid-glove treatment. Don't cry. Try to shut your eyes, to get some sleep. Tomorrow we still have a few more hours to walk. We have to get there early, before the plane comes.

"Good night, my love."

At the break of dawn a heavy rain began pouring down. My prayers and pleas were to no avail. She was awakened by the first drops.

"Today is the big day, the last day," I told her. "We aren't going to let a little rain stop us. Don't let it get you down. It's not so bad. When we get to Jaguar Beach, I'll build you a strong shelter. You'll be able to rest, to sleep, until the helicopter comes.

"You're hungry? Yes, I know you're hungry, but we don't have anything left for breakfast. Don't worry, I'll find something to eat in the jungle. You can count on me."

I couldn't stand. My feet were soft and mushy, as if a skinless mass of raw, bloody flesh had been poured into my shoes. I couldn't take a single step, but I knew that my only chance for survival was to walk. I had to get to the shore. If I stayed in the jungle, no one would ever find me. I stumbled forward like a zombie. I discovered traces of the path, but it vanished after a while.

Walking through the dense growth was like marching through hell. I tried to stay as much as possible on soft, muddy ground, to ease the pain of every step I took. I tried to keep my weight on my trusty walking stick and often pulled myself forward by clutching at bushes and branches. When I came to an incline, even a gentle slope, I got down on all fours and crawled, my face caked with mud, my clothes torn and weighing me down. I was weak and afraid of losing consciousness. All I had was water. Water had become the enemy. Other than water nothing had passed my lips. The girl was my only consolation.

We walked on together for a few hours, but Jaguar Beach was nowhere to be seen. I tried to locate it by looking for the four islands that had been strung across the river. I remembered them as being very close to the beach, but I saw only one solitary island in the river. I feared that the current had swept the islands away but found that hard to believe. The islands had been large and well forested. They couldn't have vanished without a trace.

I trudged on and on through the mud and finally came upon a fruit tree. It was tall, a species of palm. At its top were large clusters of dates. A family of monkeys were up there having a noisy feast. A few pieces of fruit were strewn on the ground. They were squashed into the mud and rotting. My body quivered, twitched with craving, an age-old primordial instinct. I was hungry like a wild beast. I pounced upon the dates in the mud. I didn't care if they were rotten. The worms did not disgust me. I put the fruit into my mouth, rolled it around with my tongue, cleaned it off with my saliva, spat it out into the palm of my hand, and then spat out the residue of mud in my mouth before putting the fruit back. Soon, however, I lost patience and swallowed the fruit together with the mud. I didn't leave a single piece on the ground. Even the worms were a source of protein. The monkeys started throwing half-eaten dates down at me. They laughed and tossed pits down on my head. I was grateful to them, for the monkeys didn't take more than one bite out of each piece and discarded a thick layer of edible pulp. I could see their teeth marks on the dates before I ate them.

I went on for several hours without stopping to rest. It required effort, a supreme and painful effort. Jaguar Beach was nowhere to be seen. I began to worry, though I didn't think that I could have missed it. It had been the widest strip of shore along the entire length of river. I must be moving more slowly than I thought. I was injured, and walking through the mud was slow and laborious. I can't give up. *I have to make it back there before the plane passes overhead again.*

Then I lost my head for a moment. It wasn't her fault. The hill was just too steep. I knew that I wouldn't make it to the top without a great deal of suffering and pain. Here I collapsed. She burst into tears and refused to go on. I was sick of speaking to her kindly and lovingly.

What the hell does she think? I wondered, enraged. *That I'm having a picnic?*

"Stop coddling yourself," I shouted. "I'm sick of you and your whining, do you hear? Who needs you anyway? I don't have enough problems without schlepping a crybaby along? You don't help with anything. All you do is cry. Would you like to trade places with me for a while and carry this lousy pack on your back? I've had it with your bawling. You can cry your eyes out, for all I care, but you'd better not stop walking, because I'm not going to wait for you anymore."

I behaved cruelly but felt relieved to have let off steam. Afterward I felt ashamed of myself. I went over to her, gave her a hug, stroked her hair gently, and told her that I was sorry for having lost my temper and hadn't really meant any of it. I told here that I loved her, that I would protect her and bring her back to safety, but she had to make the effort and walk.

I had by now grown faint and dizzy, become weaker and weaker. When I came across a fallen tree that blocked my path, I had to walk around it. I couldn't lift my legs over it.

I have to make it to Jaguar Beach. Have to, have to, have to!

I could hear the plane's engine in the distance. I waited as it drew near. I knew that the plane wouldn't be able to see me, but I at least wanted to see it. The sound was dull and distant, then faded altogether. Had I imagined it? Maybe they were looking for me somewhere else. But Kevin was there, I was sure of that, and he knew where I was.

Toward evening I came to an area where a puddle of water floated on the mud. I walked on, oblivious, and before I had a chance to comprehend what was happening, the earth swallowed me up. I sank swiftly. Shocked and in a panic. I found myself up to my waist in bog. I went into a frenzy, like a trapped animal, screaming, trying to get out, but the mud was thick and sticky, and I couldn't move. My walking stick cut through it like a hot knife through butter and was of no help at all. I reached out to some reeds and bushes, stretching my body and arms in their direction. I tried pulling myself out by them, but they came loose in my hands. I continued sinking slowly.

I came out of my convulsive throes and calmed down. I tried to act rationally. I stuck my hands down deep into the mud, wrapped them around one knee and tried to force one leg up out of the mud. I pulled with all my might, but to no avail. It was as if I had been set in concrete. I couldn't budge. I wanted to cry again but felt only a thick lump in my throat.

So this is it, death. I end my life in this bog.

I was resigned. I knew that I didn't have the strength to get myself out, and no power in the world would reach down and pluck me out of the swamp.

It would be a slow, horrible death. The mud was already up to my belly button. The pack rested on the mud, and I was relieved of its weight. Suddenly I had a brilliant idea. I would commit suicide. I took the pack from my shoulders and rummaged through it hurriedly until I found the first-aid kit. There were about twenty amphetamines and perhaps thirty other, unidentified pills. That was it. I would take all of them. I was sure they would kill me or at least make everything good and hazy before I drowned. First I opened the tin of speed. I held a few of them in the palm of my hand.

You're being selfish, Yossi, really egotistical. It's easy enough for you to die, just swallow the pills, and you're off to paradise. But what about your parents? Your mother: what will this do to her?

You can't die like this. Not after all you've already been through. It wouldn't be so bad it you had died on the first day in a sudden accident. But now, after all this suffering? It isn't fair to just give up now.

I put the pills back in the tin. I strained forward, leaning my torso out across the mud and moved my arms forward as if I were swimming. I moved my arms back and forth, pulling and wriggling in the mud. I kicked my legs in fluttering movements. I fought with every ounce of strength. Fought for my life.

It took about half an hour, maybe more. As soon as I got my legs free of the mud, I crept forward without sinking. I left neither the pack not the walking stick behind. After I'd advanced another six feet, I was out of the quagmire.

My entire body was caked with a thick layer of black, sticky mud. I cleared it out of my nostrils, wiped my eyes, and spat it out of my mouth.

To live. I want to live. I'll suffer any torment, but I'll go on. I'll make it to Jaguar Beach, no matter what.

CHAPTER 11

RESCUE

It was growing darker and darker, and I stopped walking. I left my pack resting against a tree trunk and went to look for palm fronds. I hobbled slowly and finally sank to my knees, crawling on all fours like a wounded beast. I faltered back to the spot I had selected, dragging a few fronds behind me.

"These will have to do for tonight. This is the very last night that we'll be spending in the jungle, and anyway we don't need so many fronds, we'll cuddle up together and keep each other warm."

I started clearing an area for the two of us to stretch out, the girl and me. It had to be wider than usual, for I wouldn't be sleeping alone. I cleared away all of the wet leaves and broken branches.

"Come, lie down over here by me. Lie down and hold me tightly . . ."

I suddenly realized that I had actually prepared a sleeping place for two.

"You're alone, idiot, alone."

I had taken leave of my senses. I was delirious. I had to get hold of myself. If I didn't bring myself back to reality, I would go mad.

I am alone. I am alone, I am alone.

I moved the fronds and my belongings to a smaller niche between protruding tree roots and lay down upon the cold ground. It wasn't raining, but heavy drops still dripped from the towering trees. I peeled my shoes from my feet. My socks were caked with mud, but I didn't dare remove them. Even if I were able to get them off, I would never have been able to put them back on, so I just left them on my feet, mud and all. I emptied out the rubber bag and cautiously, gently, inched it over my feet, up to my knees. I spread one of the mosquito nets out upon the fronds, wrapped myself with it, and pulled the other over me, tucking the edges in under my body. I arranged the poncho so that it covered me from head to toe, protecting myself from both the wet, muddy earth beneath me and the water dripping from above. I put the hood over my face as usual. My hands were wet, my body covered with wounds, scratches, rawness, and rash. I tucked my hands in the pits of my arms, where there was a little warmth.

I wanted to keep my mind occupied. I longed to speak with her, but I controlled myself.

I tried to go back to my standard daydreams—Las Vegas, Brazil, the ranch in the Galilee—but I couldn't keep my mind on them. The fantasies wouldn't come.

Only one longing stuck in my mind: to arise from a good, long sleep in my soft bed at the old-folks' home in La Paz, take a shower, and get breakfast ready. I diced onions and fried them in a well-greased skillet. They sizzled in the pan, spattering oil until they were golden brown. I sprinkled grated cheese over them, inhaling the delicious aroma of the quickly melting cheese. Then I scrambled a few eggs in the skillet and made a juicy omelet, which I gobbled down greedily.

I couldn't get the picture out of my mind. My belly ached. My whole body cried out for nourishment. Food. I had nothing. The beans were as hard as rocks. The rice was wet and foul smelling; the mud was more appetizing. If only I could get a fire going. I would tomorrow. Tomorrow I would be at Jaguar Beach. There was no doubt about it. Even if I had been hobbling at a snail's pace, I had still covered a great distance. Jaguar Beach couldn't be far.

Time dragged slowly by. I fought to get the smell of the omelet out of my mind. Suddenly I felt that my bladder was full. I usually relieved myself before I lay down and covered myself with the nets and the poncho, then waited until morning to relieve myself again, but on this night I simply couldn't wait. Getting up would involve a great deal of pain and bother: taking my feet out of the bag, unraveling the layers of covers, getting out from under the palm fronds, trying to get the buckle and the rusty zipper of my jeans open, and then wrapping myself back up again. I would never be able to manage all that and get back in place as I now was. My body had found its repose and was beginning to warm up. So why not just piss in my pants?

What's the matter with you? Have you lost every scrap of self-respect? If you piss in your pants, you will be foul-smelling, and it will irritate the rawness of your thighs. Make the effort, Yossi, get up.

No, I can't. I just can't.

I lacked the resolve and lay there motionless and peed on myself. The warm urine was pleasant, spreading out over my legs and up toward my belly, soaking into my pants and the nets. I could smell it. Later I peed twice more and actually enjoyed it; the feeling of warmth was so good.

Another hour passed, the night must have been half gone, but I couldn't fall asleep. I tried to grasp some thought to occupy my mind until the morning light. I wanted to think about something pleasant: people, being rescued, a plane, a helicopter, food. My shriveled belly churned.

"Ow!"

Something pinched hard into my thigh. Startled and frightened, I took my hand out of my armpit and reached down to feel the spot. Something had dug itself into my flesh and wouldn't let go. It wasn't a leech, but some kind of bug, almost an inch long, and I couldn't get it off my thigh. I pulled hard, and it dug its pincers into my thumb. A powerful body writhed between my fingers. It was a gigantic ant, incredibly strong. I squeezed off its head with my fingernails, and the contorted body finally grew still. I let it fall between my legs and dug the head out from where it clung to my thumb. The little son of a bitch! It must have crawled in while I was getting my bed ready.

Then another bite, more pincers. One near my knee and another by my waist. I hastily reached out for them. The ants dug in deeply. I tore their bodies apart, happily listening to the crunch they made.

"How are you getting in, you little mothers? I'll kill you!"

I was wrapped up in several layers, airtight, in two mosquito nets and a poncho. There was no way for them to crawl in. Perhaps there had been a few of them on the palm fronds, and they had dropped down on me. But what had they been waiting for? Why had they only now started biting?

I didn't have long to spend pondering that question, for I was immediately subject to still another attack and panicked. The ants bit, pinched in several places at once, and it hurt like hell. These ants didn't burn like fire ants but were bigger and stronger and sliced into my body with their pincers.

I fought them like a madman, dismembering one after another. I wanted to get up and run away, but where would I go? It was dark, and I was barefoot. Where could I run? I would never find another shelter. I couldn't leave this one but had to stay and fight. The ants were coming at me from every direction, one after another, and I fought them off furiously. I didn't have anywhere else to throw them, and a great pile of their corpses heaped up between my thighs.

It went on the whole night long. I can't find words to describe the horror of it. The ants came at me from all sides and began biting my face, the back of my neck, my chest, waist, and thighs. One ant bit into the sole of my foot, and I couldn't get at it, down inside the rubber bag, out of my reach. It took a big bite, tearing into the bloody flesh, took another bite, and another.

"Come a little higher up. Come on, just a little closer, and I'll rip you apart!"

I had begun collecting a few ants at a time, rubbing them together between the palms of my hands, letting the pulp fall between my legs. I didn't have a moment's rest. I had forgotten about my hunger and my aching feet. I was in a fury, filled with loathing and vengeance. I pulled them off my eyelids, out of my ears, out of my hair, from my arms and legs. The pile of bodies was enormous, and I had to spread my legs farther apart to make room for them all. I had gotten used to the stinging pain of their bite and killed them by the dozens, but the horror was never-ending.

With the first rays of morning light I pulled myself to a sitting position with a feeling of great relief. I shoved the palm fronds aside and just sat there stunned, staring. The earth around me was alive and teeming. The mosquito nets were red all over as was the trunk of the tree above me and my pack, all covered with swarming insects. My shoes crawled with them. The ground about me for a radius of at least ten feet teemed with an army, not of ants, but of termites, millions of them. My entire body was covered with clusters of them.

I was in shock but soon realized what had happened; the termites had made short order of the nets and poncho, simply eating their way through the nylon, leaving gaping holes through which they had swarmed.

Horrified, I leapt to my feet, oblivious of the pain, and fled, crunching insects under my feet. I stopped about twenty yards from the spot where I had been lying and destroyed the last of the creatures that still clung to me. My body was like a sieve, drops of blood seeping through the pores of every patch of bare skin. The tree I had been lying under was a horrifying sight, and the reddish-brown termites were eating into all my belongings. I took a few steps closer to them, stopped to get my nerve up, ran into their midst, threw my pack as far as I could, and dashed away. The pack already had quite a few holes in it. I shook it off and killed the termites that clung to it, repeating the motion a few times. I ran back and pitched from among the swarming insects one shoe, and then the other, followed by the sacks of food, the nets, poncho, and my walking stick. I heaved it all as far as I could from the terrifying circle of bugs.

I carefully scrutinized each item, squeezing the insects between my fingers and stamping on them. The nylon bags that held the food were full of holes, and streams of insects busily gnawed at the leather of my shoes. I shook them off and crushed them beneath my feet. It was a great relief finally to put my shoes back on, and I went on ridding my possessions of termites.

It became evident from the stench emanating from me and from the nets what had happened. What a fool I was! Why hadn't I thought of it before? The urine. It was because of the urine. Karl had told us that urine attracts insects. There must have been a nest of termites somewhere nearby, and the smell of fresh urine had attracted them for a salty, late-night snack. I looked over at the teeming circle, and my skin crawled. What a horror. How had I survived it? Where had I gotten the strength? I put my pack on my back and got out of there as fast as I could.

My feet felt as if I were walking barefoot over hot coals, each step a piercing pain. I kept my head bowed, leaned on my walking stick, and trod mechanically on.

Just let me get to the beach.

I would lie there, rest, and wait for rescue. If someone came looking for me, I would be saved. If not, at least I would die there in peace.

I suppose that it was a nice enough day, but that no longer made any difference to me. I walked along apathetically, falling on all fours whenever I came to an incline. My elbows and knees were raw and bloody, but the thick layer of mud that clung to my body covered my wounds. I dragged myself forward, clutching at roots and bushes, and for a moment lay perfectly still, sprawled on the earth. I could hear the river, but I couldn't see it.

I have to go on. I can't give up.

I saw a cluster of nettles nearby and dragged myself over to them, touching them with both hands. Their sharp sting helped me forget the agony of my feet. I came upon a tree whose lower boughs were swarming with the familiar little ants, fire ants. I must have been nearly delirious. I shook the branches and let the ants shower down on my head, crawl along the nape of my neck, my back, and into my pants. I walked on with the bite of ants burning into my body and derived a strange pleasure from the pain. Anything was better than thinking about my feet.

I was weak and famished. From time to time I would fall forward to lap up a little water from a brook that crossed my path. Toward noon I lost all awareness of where I was setting my feet and fell into another bog. I sank swiftly up to my knees and then up to my waist. Again I tried forcing my legs out, and almost got one foot out of my shoe, but not out of the mud.

I no longer thought of my family but simply longed for death. Then, once again, I changed my mind. I fought on and on and found myself inexplicably out of the bog. Some unseen hand had freed me. I myself hadn't the strength. I was convinced that a miracle had taken place.

I came to a steep wadi, about ten feet deep. It seemed familiar, but I couldn't recall why. I fell while climbing down the wall, plunging to the water, scraped and bruised by rocks on the way. Climbing back up the other side was easier. I found myself crawling past the wadi and got up to walk. I was certain that Jaguar Beach couldn't be far away, probably just around the bend. Distracted by that thought, I almost stepped on a large turtle. It took a quick glance at me and then pulled its head inside its shell. It was a tortoise and must have weighed ten pounds. I was starved and stood there staring at it. Now and again it poked its head out of its shell to see if I was still there and then drew back inside. I considered tying it to my pack and carrying it with me to the beach, but it was too heavy. Perhaps I could hit it with a large rock, break its armor and eat it raw. The turtle stuck its head out again, meeting my gaze with eyes that struck me as sad. I recalled how my own life had only a short while ago been miraculously saved.

"You'll live, turtle," I pronounced magnanimously, and continued on my way.

Around the next bend I did come upon a beach, but it wasn't Jaguar Beach. It was quite wide and rocky with a single hut in the center of it. The hut was leaning to one side as if about to fall over. Other than that there was nothing but a few pilings lying about. A strange feeling overcame me. The beach offered shelter, which meant that there had been people here. What kind of place was it? How was it that I hadn't noticed it the first time I had passed by here?

I didn't waste time trying to figure out where I was. I hobbled over to the thatched roof, leaned my pack against one of its pilings, and lay down on the ground for about an hour. I thanked God for having led me to some kind of shelter. I spread the poncho out in the middle of the beach. It was full of holes from the termites. I set a few rocks on it to hold it down and then dragged myself to the river. I stuck my feet in the water and washed the mud from my shoes. Then I filled the tin with water and started back toward the hut. I was almost there when I picked up my head to see how much farther I had to go, and there, beyond the thatched roof, carved on a thick log was the word *Pam*.

I couldn't believe my eyes. Now I understood that funny feeling that had come over me. I was back in Curiplaya.

Suddenly it dawned on me. The storm had washed away the other three huts and almost destroyed this one as well, which was why I hadn't recognized the place immediately. The floodwaters must have also swept away the four islands by which I had hoped to find Jaguar Beach. The beach must have been washed out, or else it was still under water, and I, in my desperation to reach a resting place, had trekked all the long way back to Curiplaya. Now I understood why Kevin and I hadn't seen the beach and the island that were supposed to mark the entrance to the canyon. They had probably both been washed out by a flood the year before, only Karl hadn't been aware of that.

I found the panels of chonta wood and, propping myself up on my walking stick, put together a bed. I lay down on the hard planks that were so kind to my back and didn't budge until evening, other than to cover myself with one of the nets. The urine had dried, but the net still stank and was full of gaping holes, souvenirs of the night before. However, it did keep the flies and mosquitoes off me. I knew that there was still something else that I had to do, a difficult task. I was frightened, as if about to undergo surgery without benefit of anaesthesia. I had to take my socks off. I kept putting if off, trying to get my nerve up.

I sat on the wooden panels. First I removed my shoes, which in itself was agony. Then, little by little, slowly, painfully, I peeled the sock from one foot. It was incredibly painful, torture of a degree that I had never before experienced. The sight of what had been inside was more horrible still: red, raw flesh. There wasn't a shred of skin left on my foot, and that wasn't the worst of it. My toes were plastered together in a stinking pulp of blood, pus, and mud. My bare foot was so sensitive that the slightest breeze passing over it was like a thousand tiny needles stabbing into my festering flesh. It was a good thing that I hadn't removed my socks on the way; if I had seen what condition my feet were in, I probably never would have had the fortitude to go on.

I rested for a short while and then clenched my teeth and took the other sock off. That foot was just as bad. I threw both socks into the tin of water to clean the pus and mud from them. I bunched the second net into a wad and rested the heels of my feet on it. I couldn't cover my feet with a net; even its light touch was unbearable. Fortunately it had grown dark, and the mosquitoes had ceased pestering me.

I lay there watching the lingering rays of the sun. The light on the Tuichi changed from a blinding glitter to a dull silver to a waver of shadow and finally succumbed to the gathering darkness. All told, I was quite pleased with my situation, having made it to the shore. There had been no plane overhead that day, however. Had they given up looking? If they had, I would surely die here. I hadn't eaten for almost a week. I was injured and exhausted.

I'm going to die . . .

I hastily drove the thought from my mind. People don't just lie down and die, just like that. I actually stood a fair chance of survival. If it didn't rain tomorrow, I would be able to crawl about and gather up some twigs to get a fire started. I still had rice and beans; I would eat, dry my pitiful feet in the sun, and everything would be all right. Anyway, I was sure that they wouldn't give up looking for me that quickly. Kevin wouldn't let them, and neither would the embassy just abandon me. An Israeli citizen is an Israeli citizen after all. This was the nineteenth day since the accident, that is, the nineteenth day of December. I hurriedly calculated that today must be a Saturday. No wonder there had been no plane. The pilot had his own family, children. The embassy was closed, and even if it stayed open, whom could they pressure into looking for me? All of the generals were surely holed up in their own homes. The offices were all closed. There would be no one to call. That meant they wouldn't look for me tomorrow either, for tomorrow would be Sunday. But on Monday, on Monday they would certainly start looking again. I had no doubt.

There was a hard, round, swollen lump on my forehead. I couldn't remember how I had gotten it, but it caused me to tremble with pain from time to time.

Just don't let me get sick. I have to make it through another two days.

A gentle breeze pricked at the soles of my feet but dried them as well. I was very cold, having covered myself with only one net. The poncho was spread out on the rocks, and I had no palm fronds for shelter. I laid the rubber bag over my face but still shivered with cold. I slipped into fantasy and was particularly tormented by one dream: a cheese-and-onion omelet in the old-folks' home in La Paz. I couldn't get that sizzling skillet out of my mind, and my empty belly howled for food.

I was so immersed in my daydreaming that I didn't notice that the sun had come up. I shook myself with a start, but it wasn't the light that commanded my attention but the sound of helicopters. I could hear the roar of the propellers. My heart in my mouth, I sat up, excited and expectant, waiting for the noise to grow louder and for the helicopters to appear, but I soon realized that it was all in my feverish imagination. I sank back down on the plank, bitterly disappointed. It was Sunday, the twentieth of December. I had been alone in the jungle almost three weeks. Tomorrow help would arrive, tomorrow, the twenty-first of December. They would have to come looking tomorrow, and if not tomorrow, then the next day, Tuesday, or maybe Wednesday. But Thursday would be the twenty-fourth, the day before Christmas, followed by a long weekend, so that meant that if they didn't find me by the twenty-fourth, they wouldn't look anymore after that. In another week I would have been alone in the jungle an entire month, and no one would believe that I was still alive. I myself didn't believe that I could survive until then. My brother, Moshe, was the only one who might still come to rescue me after Christmas, but I had written him not to take any action until the beginning of January, and it would take him a while to figure out what had happened and to come to Bolivia. I would surely be dead by then.

I tried to overcome my fears, to think positively. I was afraid that they would give up looking, and then I myself would give up and lose my will to survive. I tried to think of some other course of action, some other way to keep myself going. First I considered walking through the jungle once more, trying to make it to San José, but I immediately rejected that option. Even if my feet were to heal before I started out, they were certain to be afflicted once more. The rainy season would last another three months, and I would have no shelter from the pouring rain. Then I wondered if I should try my luck on the river. I could hitch two or three logs together and tie myself to them. I realized, however, that such a plan was out of the question, that it would be suicidal to hazard the river on my own. My memories of being swept through white-water rapids, bashed against rocks, and pulled under the gloomy waters were too vivid for me even to consider attempting it. The only way I would go back to the river was if I knew I was dying. Then I would throw myself into the water. As long as I was still alive, even if I held out for another six months, I wouldn't hazard the river. Six months in the jungle? Was there a chance of living through the rainy season? Of waiting for the miners to come back to their camp?

My mind raced feverishly, evaluating new ideas as they cropped up, restoring my hopes. I spent hours devising intricate plans; the greater the detail, the better I felt. The excitement kept my mind off the sizzling skillet, my suffering feet, my howling belly, and the irritating lump on my forehead.

First of all, I would stay right where I was, waiting for a plane until Christmas. During that time I would try to get a fire going and take care of my feet. I would dry out the rice and beans and make soup and get my strength back. On the twenty-fourth of December I would empty out my pack. I knew exactly where I was: just a few hours upriver was the Turliamos with its lovely beach, cave, and tamarind tree. I would walk there, stuff my pack with as much fruit as I could, and then walk back to Curiplaya. I could live on the fruit for two weeks, going back for more when necessary. I would save as much of the rice and beans as I could, using them only when I couldn't find anything else in the jungle. I would build myself a shelter on the hillside, where I would store all my belongings in case of a flood. If necessary, I could easily flee up there myself. At the same time I would reinforce the hut down here, perhaps put up some walls to keep the wind out. Inside I would gather a large reserve of firewood, light the fire once, and never let it go out. It would burn perpetually, day and night.

I would be a Robinson Crusoe of the Bolivian jungle, living here by myself, rising to the task of each new day, which would be simply to live through that day, to find enough food to sustain myself for another twenty-four hours. I was certain that it would not be difficult. I would gradually get to know the jungle: where the fruit trees were, where the rabbits lived, where the deer came to drink. I would get a sturdy stick, make some stone tools, just like the cavemen. One day I would kill a snake and the next a turtle or a frog. I would surely find birds' eggs up in the hills.

I had a brilliant idea. I would seek out wild chickens' nests, which usually hold five or six eggs apiece, but I wouldn't touch the eggs. Instead I would mark the location of each nest and check on them every few days. Five or six nests would mean thirty eggs. The eggs would hatch into chicks within a few weeks. I would let them mature a bit and then one day come armed with one of the mosquito nets and the fishing line. The net would serve as a trap, spread out over the nest and propped up by a stick. I would tie the line to the stick and hide. When the hen came back to her chicks, I would give the line a tug, the stick would fall, and all of them would be trapped. I would rig up a bamboo coop near my camp and keep them caged in it, feeding them with worms and fruit. They would grow up and lay more eggs, and I would have all the omelets I could eat. Better yet, once a week, on Shabbat (the sabbath), I would roast a chicken, just like Señor Levinstein at the old-folks' home. I would become a chicken farmer.

My life wouldn't be boring. Each day I would have something different to do: hunting, farming, fishing. I still had the fishing line and one hook left. I would put together a slingshot. I could dig holes and cover them with brush. Perhaps I would trap a wild boar, a tapir, or even a jaguar. If I did get a jaguar, I would skin it and have a nice, warm fur coat.

I would be the king of the jungle, like Tarzan. I would live alone, but I wouldn't go out of my mind. I wouldn't let the loneliness drive me mad. I would dream my dreams, tell myself stories, let my mind wander endlessly, and never give up hope. Then summer would come, and the rains would stop, and I would once again be among other humans. I would be a celebrity. The modern-day Robinson Crusoe would be world famous. Someone would write a book about me, and it would be made into a movie, and I would get rich. I would build a big house, have my own ranch and a cook and everything else I could possibly desire.

But for the time being . . . if I could only have that omelet, even without the onions, without the cheese. I had been dreaming for hours, weaving fantastic plans, when the longing for that damned omelet struck again. My whole body shook with pain, and the hunger bored into me. My forehead was burning with fever. The pain was strange, as if something was eating away at me from within. The cool breeze that came up again stung my feet, and my spirits fell. The hell with being famous, with getting rich. I didn't want to be a hero, I just wanted out of there. If only they would come tomorrow.

The sun was setting, and I braced myself for another long night of pain. I considered crawling over for the poncho, but it seemed so far away. I tried to make myself comfortable. My bones stuck out all over and scraped against the hard wooden planks. Then I got a terrible pain in my stomach. I hadn't had a bowel movement for the past ten days, and the pain pierced my gut. I rolled down off the bed and crawled on my knees, holding my feet as high off the ground as I could. I sat on a fallen log and tried to empty my bowels, but I was constipated. My attempts caused a strain on the rectum, and the deep cut, which had healed over, opened up again, and I started bleeding. I tried to stop the bleeding with my fingers, and that stimulation helped me to gradually empty my intestines of waste, which was dark green, almost black, and rock hard. I crawled back to my pallet and lay down in relief.

The sunlight faded, and dusk began to envelop me when I became aware of a distant drone. A plane, I thought, but forced myself to stop. It was almost nightfall, and I was fed up with imaginary airplanes and helicopters. But the drone grew louder.

It wasn't a plane. In fact, it sounded more like a bee, and it got louder and louder. I covered myself up with the mosquito net, but the buzz was so loud, I thought a bee had gotten through a hole in the net and was inside, right by my ear. Please, no, anything but to get stung on my face. I had enough problems without that. The noise engulfed me, and I got up with a start. I threw the net aside, but there wasn't any bee. The noise was loud and real. I looked out over to the river and gasped.

My God, dear God, there are people out there!

I dimly made out four figures disembarking from a canoe. I raced toward the water's edge, not feeling any pain, my chest bursting with joy and excitement.

"Hello! Hello!" I tried to call, but nothing came out.

A tall, curly-haired fellow was standing next to the canoe. He looked up at me, gaped, stunned for a moment, and then called out, "Don't move, Yossi! Stay where you are. I'm coming!" It was Kevin. He ran frantically to me and threw his arms about me. We stood there for a long while, embracing each other, murmuring unintelligibly.

For the first time I wept. Nothing could have held back the flood of large, warm tears that streamed down my cheeks. I was holding on to Kevin—this was not a dream. I was safe now; someone did watch over me after all. The tears kept pouring down. Kevin was also in tears. We held each other tightly, almost unable to let go.

CHAPTER 12

KEVIN'S TALE

hree other men had come in the canoe with Kevin. Two stood a short distance away, staring at me curiously, obviously moved. The third, a short, stocky fellow, approached us.

"Are you all right, young man?" he inquired.

I nodded my head.

"I don't suppose you're hungry?" he asked with a smile, and took a sack containing three bread rolls out of his pocket and handed it to me. I devoured them ravenously, scarcely bothering to chew.

"Take it easy, young fellow. There's more where that came from."

The man took a can of tuna fish out of his other pocket and opened it. It took me only a few seconds to finish it off.

"Get the bananas," he instructed one of the others.

I tossed down five sweet bananas and still contemplated him hungrily.

"We'd better get going now, before dark. This isn't a good place to beach the canoe."

Kevin carried me over to the narrow craft and gently sat me down inside it. Then he ran back to gather up my belongings. He shoved them into the pack, which he tossed into the canoe.

"Wait a minute, Kevin. I left the poncho over there on the rocks. I want it."

Kevin came running back with the poncho, and then we were on our way.

My eyes were still brimming with tears as we progressed down-river. I couldn't stop weeping quietly, offering prayers of thanks to God. I couldn't bring myself to believe that it was really happening, that it was all over. I hadn't been expecting it, hadn't even dreamed of being saved today. It had never occurred to me that anyone would come for me by river. He had saved my life. Kevin had saved my life. I wept with joy.

The river was turbulent, and Tico, the owner of the canoe, wouldn't let us sit side by side, so I sat behind Kevin, wrapped in an army blanket. A dead fawn lay on the bottom of the canoe.

Tico found a good place to beach the canoe and with his companions set up camp. It wasn't necessary to erect a shelter. They simply spread sheets of nylon on the ground. It wouldn't rain tonight.

Kevin lay me down on the beach and propped my head against a log. He gently washed and dried my feet and then with the tender hands of a skilled nurse rubbed them with an oily, white cream. That done, he carefully put a pair of clean socks on them while I bit my lip in pain.

"I had the same thing," he told me. "The doctor told me it's some kind of fungus. This cream works wonders. Your feet will be all right in just a few days."

They cleaned the fawn and skewered pieces of it. A large pot of rice was already simmering over the fire. Tico came over holding a cup. He had made some lemonade for me. I drank it down gratefully. Then he and his crew went into the jungle to hunt. Kevin covered me with a blanket and then lay down next to me. We stared up at the sky and smoked. He listened attentively while I told him what I had been through.

"I knew that you'd make it. I just knew that you would hold out," he said. "I was positive that as long as nothing had happened to you in the river, I would surely find you. That's what I told your embassy too. They didn't believe me. No one did, but I just knew. There's one thing that I don't understand, though. How come almost all of the rice and beans are left? It looks like you ate hardly any at all."

"It's hard to explain," I answered. "It was raining most of the time, so I couldn't light a fire. Anyway, I thought I should save it. I didn't know how long I'd be stuck here. Now you tell me what happened to you."

Kevin agreed to telling me his story only after he had heard every detail of what I had been through.

"Compared to you, I was on a Boy Scout field trip." Then he began his tale.

"I'll start from the moment I jumped off the raft into the river. The undertow was much stronger than I had expected, and I was completely helpless. Luckily for me, the current swept me over to the right bank. I climbed out of the water and immediately noticed that the raft was about to slip back into the river. All I could think was, *Good Lord, here I am barefoot*, so I called to you to throw me my shoes and then the machete. You yelled something like, 'Don't leave me,' and I thought, 'What the hell? Who's leaving who?' And then you went over the falls. I thanked God when I saw you bob up a long way downriver, still clinging to the raft. I quickly put my shoes on, picked up the machete, and started walking along the rocky shore. I was sure that I'd catch up with you that day or the day after.

"You know how hard it is to walk along the riverbank, and I had no choice but to see if the going would be any better on the other side, where the bank didn't look as steep. That river is a real bitch, but I finally managed to swim across.

"I was very worried about you and didn't know what to think. The river was so treacherous—white water, jagged rocks, sharp bends—and you had no experience and were on your own. You might have fallen into the water and drowned or broken a bone.

"The next day I walked along the river, and when I ran out of bank, I slipped into the water, after stuffing my shirt full of dry wood to help make me buoyant. I had taken off my shoes and filled them with wood chips and tied them to my belt. The river was extremely hazardous, and whenever I came to a section where it was possible to walk on dry ground, I got the hell out of it.

"After a few hours I came to a place where the sides of the river were sheer rock faces and the water was frothy. It looked terribly dangerous, so I decided to climb. I had spent about two hours working my way up the cliff when I came upon a heap of feathers next to a large dead parrot. I touched it; it was still warm. It had been killed just that moment, and I wondered if I could bring myself to eat it raw. I tied it to my belt and started walking. Suddenly an enormous falcon rose up off a nearby boulder and took flight. We looked right at each other. It was angry that I had stolen its prey.

"'Thanks for the meal, pal. I may be a thief, but I need it more than you do.'

"Every time I came to a brook that trickled down to the river, I followed it to see if there was any sign of you. Then I had another surprise: four dry balsa logs. I still hadn't seen the island and the little shore that Karl had told us about, however, so I didn't think there was any point in building a raft, since I must still be upriver from the mal paso.

"I stopped for lunch at noon. I chopped off the parrot's head with the machete, tore its beak out, and took a bite. I cracked its skull open and sucked out its brains, knowing that they contained a great deal of protein.

"I kept on walking, though my feet were damp and my shoes were full of holes. They were full of sand and pebbles, too, which tore the skin off my feet. It was terribly painful, but I was sure that I wasn't far from Curiplaya.

"On the third day after losing you, Yossi, I awoke at dawn, painfully aware of my feet. I knew that if I went on walking, they would only get worse, but like I said, I was sure that I wasn't far from Curiplaya. I cut a branch from one of the trees to use as a walking stick. I put all of my weight on it as I walked. I kept looking for the landmarks Karl had described but saw no sign of them. Suddenly I realized that I didn't have the machete with me. I wondered how I would get along without it. I remember that when I had broken off my walking stick, I had stuck it in the mud. I must have forgotten it there. I decided not to go back for it. My feet hurt so badly that retracing my own footsteps for hours seemed absurd.

"On the fourth day I couldn't stand on my feet anyway, so I just lay where I was. I got to wondering if I was ever going to see you again. I was certain that if you were alive, you would be waiting for me in Curiplaya. Then I remembered Marcus and the way I had been treating him lately. I felt guilty for having made light of the pain he was in and not believing how much agony his feet were causing him. Now I was getting what I had coming to me,

I thought. When I got back to La Paz, I would have to apologize to him.

"I rested all that day and night. Once, I awoke to the sound of an approaching animal. I had no flashlight or machete. What could I do? I gripped my walking stick and went back to sleep.

"The next morning I felt a little better. My feet had dried and scabbed over, but when I tried to stand up, I discovered that they were worse than they appeared to be, and the sores split open. I couldn't take a single step. It was horrible. I slid along on my backside and the heels of my feet, inching toward the river. My mind was made up, though: I was going into the water, even though Curiplaya must be near. The cool water felt good.

"I looked around for a log to hang on to and found only a small stump, about three feet long. I drifted in the river for about twenty minutes, clinging to the log. The current swept me along swiftly, and my main concern was what might await me around each bend. But it wasn't so bad. After a short while I noticed that steep cliffs loomed on both sides of the river, and I thought that I must be approaching the pass. I let go of the log and swam frantically for the right bank, where I climbed up the cliff. I was surprised that my feet no longer hurt as much as they had before and I walked for more than half an hour. Finally I climbed back down to the water's edge at a place where there was a small shore with a lot of logs scattered about. The water was placid, and I decided that this couldn't be the pass after all.

"The sight of all those logs made me think about putting a raft together. I set about that task quickly and just as swiftly gave up on it. The logs were so big and heavy that I couldn't budge them. Some of them were stuck deep in the sand, and others were rotten. Only one big, sturdy one was of any use. I dragged it into the water and straddled it with both legs.

"The current carried me downriver. Once, the river broadened and became so shallow that my feet stubbed against the rocks on the bottom, and another time I was washed up against a rock and took a good hard knock. Another time I got caught in a whirlpool, but finally the log got free, taking me with it.

"I floated on with the log, and after a few hours I saw a shore with two thatched huts on it. I started calling out, 'Yossi! Yossi! Yossi!' but there wasn't any answer. The place looked deserted, and I knew that it must be Curiplaya, and that the village of San José must be only thirty miles farther on. I didn't expect to find you on my way; I thought that you must already be there.

"The river grew quite calm. I drifted along. I may even have dozed. I dipped my face in the water, struggling to stay awake. Then suddenly I noticed two men walking through a stream that fed into the right bank of the river. I called out frantically, '¡Ayuda! Ayuda (help)! I can't walk. I'm lost.' The current was strong, and I couldn't make it out of the river. To my great relief, they heard me. They gestured, 'Downriver. Go farther downriver,' and I could see a small beach downstream. I let go of the log and swam to shore.

"I waited there for almost an hour, wondering what was taking them so long. Maybe they had no intention of coming after me. Maybe they had meant to tell me that there were other people farther downriver. Then I saw them coming on a balsa raft and knew that I was saved.

"I told them what had happened and asked if they had seen any sign of you or the raft, but they hadn't seen a thing. They were hunters and had been deep in the jungle for five days. 'You're a lucky guy,' they told me. They only came hunting that far upriver twice a year, so I really had been incredibly lucky. Somehow, deep inside, I was sure that it had been more than simple luck or circumstance.

"Four hours later we arrived on the outskirts of San José, where Fausto, the hunter, and his son lived. They brought me to their ranch on the riverbank and lay me down under a thatched roof. They promised that the next day they would send someone on horseback to take me up to the village, which was still nearly an hour and a half away up the river.

"Late the next morning a guy named Pablo turned up and took me to San José on horseback. I asked him how I could get to Rurrenabaque, and he told me I had two choices. One was to make a six-hour ride and then a three-hour walk to the town of Tumupasa, and from there go on by truck. I wrote off that possibility: I couldn't walk. The other way was to take a balsa raft downriver.

"Pablo took me to a man who was the mayor of the village. I told him my story and asked him to arrange for a raft that could take me to Rurrenabaque, and he promised to see to it.

"From there Pablo took me back to Fausto's. I lay there on a hammock, and one of the women treated my feet. She smeared an oily cream over them, which took the burn out of the sores, and I felt much better. A few of the villagers came over for a curious peek at me. They tried to console me but said they hadn't heard a thing about you and that 'the river is bad, very bad. It's hard to believe that your friend could still be alive.'

"Around eight the next morning the mayor showed up with the raftsmen. This was the seventh day since I'd lost you. He promised that the raft would soon be ready to go. I arranged to send payment for his expenses by way of the priest from La Paz, and he took my word for it. At two that afternoon he came back and said that they wanted to wait until the next day to set out, as it was raining. That day one of the village babies died from a stomach disorder, and everyone was sad and gloomy. I, on the other hand, was thinking about how lucky I was to have been saved. I was still alive, but what about Yossi? You might have drowned. You might have broken a leg or a rib. I didn't want to think about it. You hadn't drowned. You had certainly been swept along with the raft and made it to Rurrenabaque.

"We left in the morning of the eighth day on a trip that the raftsmen said would take a day and a half. It was pouring rain and very cold on the raft. The balseros decided to pull over to the side and look for some kind of shelter from the rain, though we were drenched anyway.

"'Let's go on,' I begged them.

"'We won't get any farther than Santa Rosa today in any case and will spend the night there. So there's no reason to be in such a big hurry,' one of them replied.

"We did finally set out again and arrived in Santa Rosa that afternoon. There was a group of thirteen young men there, who were very kind and friendly and got my spirits up. They were maintenance men, getting a summer camp ready for French tourists. We decided to spend the night there.

"The next morning I counted off the ninth day. The two balseros and I were once again on the river. By now I no longer deluded myself that I would find you in Rurrenabaque. My two raftsmen, who were experienced professionals, had a difficult time maneuvering the raft through the treacherous passes. It was obvious that you wouldn't have been able to do it on your own.

"Rurrenabaque is on the banks of the Beni River. We reached it that afternoon. The Beni is much wider than the Tuichi and looked mild and placid, but the balseros told me that it is dangerous too. I clambered ashore and headed straight for the navy base. The CO was in a meeting with his senior officers, so I had no choice but to try to tell his secretary in my broken Spanish what had happened to me. She didn't understand a word. Two Swiss priests who served in the area came over when they heard that a man had been saved from the jungle. They had another Swiss, who spoke English, with them. He translated what I said into German, and the priest then translated into Spanish, and that was the way my tale was told to the secretary.

"I asked her to place an urgent call to the Israeli embassy in La Paz, but she couldn't do so as there were no direct lines, and I had to wait for the commandante to get out of his meeting.

"The priests took me to their parish. For the first time in weeks I had a good hot shower. They gave me clean clothes and fed me. The nuns tried to console me for your loss. They told me that the Tuichi was known as a particularly dangerous river.

"'Your friend surely drowned, and even if he did make it out of the river alive, his chances of surviving in the jungle were slight.'

"No one in the entire town offered me any hope of finding you alive, but I just wouldn't believe it.

"On the tenth day a plane from La Paz was supposed to come in at eight in the morning, and I went to the terminal to wait for it to land. The priest, Father Fernando, had filled out official-looking papers, testifying to what had happened and allowing me to fly without a passport. I waited until five-thirty, but no plane ever showed up. I was upset, for I wanted to get to the Israeli embassy in La Paz. The navy office in Rurrenabaque hadn't even sent the embassy a telegram as they had promised me they would. I was raging. I had wasted an entire precious day doing nothing.

"The following morning one of the nuns awakened me excitedly. A plane was about to land at any moment. She had a truck standing by. By quarter to nine I was airborne.

"When I arrived in La Paz, I headed straight for the American embassy. I knew that I had to hurry to the Israeli embassy, but I needed some kind of identification. The consul listened apathetically to my tale. He simply remarked that I was lucky to be alive and offered his consolations on the death of my friend.

"'But he's not dead,' I insisted.

"'Of course he is. How could he possibly have survived alone in the jungle? Just thank God that you're alive, and get yourself home to spend Christmas with your family,' the consul replied.

"'And what if I was lost in the jungle? What would you do? Wouldn't you even send a party out to look for me?' I yelled.

"'We would notify this country's foreign office and your family,' he answered.

"'And what if it was your son or brother out there in need of help?'

"He didn't reply. Before I stormed out of his office, I asked him to prepare a new passport for me and to notify the Israeli embassy that I was on my way over. Afterward I found out that he never even bothered to make that simple phone call.

"I arrived at the Israeli embassy. I spoke into the microphone at the entrance, explaining in broken Spanish that I had just come from the jungle and that an Israeli friend of mine was still lost back there. I was aware that I was being observed on closed-circuit television. A door finally opened, leading to an inner room. A security man scrutinized me from behind a plate of bulletproof glass. Then he took from me, through a slot in a window, the documents that the navy office and Father Fernando had given me, and finally I was allowed to enter.

"The consul listened carefully to my story. I kept emphasizing how urgent it was to get a helicopter and start looking right away. Then I spoke with the ambassador and went through it all again. I told him that my brother had a white-water business in Oregon, and I asked him to call your parents in Israel and get them to help pay the expenses of bringing my brother, together with the necessary equipment, to Bolivia in order to go looking for you. The ambassador promised to do all he could and asked me to call him back that afternoon.

"At two that afternoon I placed my call to the Israeli embassy and was informed that on Monday morning they would have a meeting with the Bolivian air force and that I should come to the embassy then.

"I went straight to the Rosario Hotel, and the desk clerk there told me that Marcus hadn't been back yet. I didn't yet think much of that, for I had never agreed with Karl's estimate of how long it would take them.

"I went over to the Jewish old-folks' home to try to find some Israelis who would be willing to come help me look for you, but the place was empty. No one but Grandma was there, so I just left a note.

"So the twelfth day passed and the thirteenth. Monday finally arrived, the fourteenth day. A Bolivian officer was waiting for me at the Israeli embassy, and he took me to La Paz air force headquarters. We wasted long, precious hours there going over the accident in detail, exactly where it had happened and the events that had led up to it. They listened to my less-than-fluent Spanish and promised that they would do everything that they could, but I had no faith in them at all.

"The Bolivian officer then took me to navy headquarters, and we went through the whole business again.

"When I got back to the Israeli embassy, the consul informed my that he had gotten hold of a plane and that the search would begin the next day. Thank God.

"I went to the Swiss embassy and notified the ambassador that Marcus and Karl were missing and asked him to put in a call to Apolo to find out if they were there. I myself didn't yet think there was any reason to worry about them, but later at the Austrian embassy the consul gave me a great reason to worry.

"The mention of the name Karl Ruchprecter caught their attention. The clerk asked me to wait and then showed me into the consul's office. He was a heavyset, red-faced man, smoking a pipe.

"'Have a seat, my young friend,' he said. 'Tell me what you know about Karl Ruchprecter.'

"I told him briefly about Karl, what he had told us about himself, and how he had talked us into going along with him on an expedition into the jungle. I told him how he had changed plans because of his uncle.

"'Uncle?' the consul asked. 'What uncle?'

"'He told us he had an uncle named Josef Ruchprecter, who owns a big cattle ranch in Reyes Province. Karl was supposed to bring him a truck from Chile next month.'

"I told him the story that Karl had told you, Yossi, that his uncle was a Nazi war criminal and that that was the reason he lived in Bolivia.

"'Interesting, very interesting,' the consul kept repeating.

"I told him about the Indian village that we had been supposed to visit, how it had turned out to be farther away then we had thought, so we had to turn around and go back, and I told him how we had rafted down the river, how we had split up from Karl and Marcus, and about the accident that you and I had had on the river. I told him that I had come to report Karl's disappearance and perhaps to organize a rescue party if no one heard anything from him within the next day or two.

"I was amazed when the consul laughed. 'That's a good one: help you look for Karl Ruchprecter,' he said. 'We'd much rather help him get lost.' And he laughed some more. 'An uncle who raises beef cattle? A fugitive Nazi? Karl has such a vivid imagination.'

"He noticed the stunned look on my face, and this is what he told me: 'Karl Ruchprecter is quite well-known to us, but he doesn't have an uncle in Bolivia. Karl himself is the escaped fugitive. He is wanted by both the Austrian government and Interpol. He's a professional troublemaker, an instigator. He was involved with radical leftist groups in Europe about ten years ago. He and his friends stirred up a lot of trouble, and the Austrian police were looking for him. He was either lucky or well connected enough to make his way here. Someone must have provided him with a false passport.

"'We know that he is here, but there's nothing we can do about it in Bolivia. Now you've brought me some really good news: he's out there in a dangerous jungle without proper food or equipment. It would be nice if he never came back. We certainly aren't going to help look for him,' the consul told me with a good chuckle.

"I was angry of course.

"'And what about the Swiss guy he's got with him?' I demanded, but the consul just shrugged his shoulders.

"I was anxious and confused when I went back to the Israeli embassy. The same Bolivian officer helped me to clarify a few details. First he looked on maps and aerial photographs for the Indian village that we were supposed to visit and then made a few phone calls, but he always got the same answer: there is no Indian village, civilized or otherwise, in that entire region.

"I learned that Karl had the reputation of being a dangerous bastard. A few years ago he talked a young German guy into going into the jungle with him, promising him exciting adventures. The German became sick and weak after a few days and pleaded with Karl to take him back, but Karl refused and just abandoned him. The poor guy managed to make it to a little ranch, where they saved his life."

A chill ran up my spine. Could it really be true? Karl had seemed like a good guy to me. Marcus had taken to calling him Poppa. Could it be that Karl was a threat to Marcus's life? I couldn't bring myself to believe that. Karl had been fond of Marcus; he would never harm him.

"On the morning of the sixteenth day the flight they had promised me took off at nine in the morning and landed in Trinidad, a town in the interior, an hour later. I waited there until the afternoon, when the pilot of the rescue plane informed me that the weather was horrible and he couldn't take off. I was asked to come back the next morning.

"I was at the air force headquarters early the next day, but the unpaved runway at the airport was still wet from the previous night's rain. The plane still couldn't take off through all the puddles. The pilot kept telling me there was simply no way anyone could survive seventeen days in the jungle. Especially not in this kind of weather. And especially not a gringo. He didn't come right out and say, 'Your friend is dead,' but he might as well have.

"Once we were finally up in the air, the pilot told me that an order is an order, so he would fly over the river as he had been told to, but that there was absolutely no point to it, that it was all a dreadful waste of fuel.

"At first we flew at a reasonable altitude over the river and followed its course, but the mountains soon forced us to go higher. From up there we couldn't see anything but trees, and the pilot was not careful to follow the crooked path of the river. He flew a straight course over it, and I realized that there was no hope of spotting you, unless you managed to set the whole jungle ablaze.

"I was more depressed than ever. The pilot made it clear that this was the last search flight he would take me on.

"I went to the navy headquarters in Rurrenabaque. It was evident that no effort was being made to find you despite all the promises I had received. The commandante was nice enough, polite, full of good intentions, but he explained to me that the navy could not possibly organize a search party, as it was against regulations to take a boat up the Tuichi. The only other option I had, he said, was to find someone who would accept payment for taking me up the river.

"'Do you know of anyone who might be willing?' I asked.

"'Come with me,' he said, 'quickly.'

"After a five-minute motorcycle ride we were at the house of Tico, the king of the river.

"'Would you take me to San José?' I asked him.

"'Sure, I was going there tomorrow anyway,' he told me, 'with Father Diego.'

"I explained to him what had happened. 'Would you take me on to Curiplaya?'

"'I can take you even farther than Curiplaya,' he declared.

"'Up to San Pedro Canyon?'

"'Yes, almost. But that's as far as I can go.'

"On the morning of the eighteenth day it was pouring rain, and we had to put off leaving for another day. The next day we traveled upriver until evening and set up camp on a pleasant beach. We were back on the river by six thirty the next morning.

"Tico really is a pro at river navigation. He maneuvered through the dangerous passes, and when we came to shallows, one of the crew stood up in the prow and hit at the river bottom with a stick, indicating to Tico how deep it was.

"We arrived at San José at ten thirty, and Father Diego set off up the path to the village. Now we could start searching. Tico told me that he had to be back in Rurrenabaque two days later, so he intended to go upriver until we came to a beach called Progreso and then turn around and head back to Rurrenabaque.

"'If your friend is still alive,' he said, 'then he is most probably near the river, and it is reasonable to assume that we will spot him.'

"We traveled upriver—Tico, two crewmen, and I—into a stretch of the Tuichi that Tico was less familiar with, and he was very cautious. We went on without stopping, looking right and left. We saw no trace of a campsite or fire. The storm had left its mark everywhere. Once in a while we encountered a flock of large birds swarming around a carcass on the shore. Tico and I exchanged glances. I didn't want to stop. I didn't want to check. I had never in my life been so depressed.

"Hours passed, and I was beginning to resign myself to the fact that we weren't going to find you alive. Yes, Yossi, it was very sad. I was already thinking of heading back to La Paz. I thought that I would probably find your brother there, and together we would be able to organize another, more effective search party.

"The crewmen stopped the canoe; they had spotted some game and wanted to go into the jungle to do some hunting.

"'I'm paying, and you're not going to stop. We're going on!' I insisted.

"The crewmen looked angry, but Tico understood me, though I don't think that he harbored any hopes of finding you. Half an hour later they stopped again. They had spotted a fawn that had come down to the river for a drink. Tico took aim and fired, and the fawn dropped to the riverbank.

"Around five thirty it started to get dark. The canoe was slowing down. I looked desperately at Tico. He shook his head with sorrow and said, 'We'll have to stop at the next shore and turn the boat back. That's it. I'm really sorry, Kevin.'

"Then I saw the shore and I knew it was over; tears were choking my throat. 'Yossi, how will I lead my life knowing I've lost you?'

"The men were turning the boat 180 degrees when suddenly I looked over at the shore and saw a rickety thatched hut, leaning over on one side. All of a sudden someone came out of it. *No, it can't be Yossi. It doesn't look anything like Yossi. Yes, it is. It is Yossi!*

"Dear God, there you were, after twenty days, and nobody had believed that you might still be alive. Thank God, thank God, Yossi, my dear friend."

CHAPTER 13

GOING HOME

I hung on every word of Kevin's tale, awed by his persistence. How would I ever be able to repay him for saving my life?

I was bewildered by the information about Karl. Could it be that the man had fooled us all along? Nevertheless I was eager to see him and Marcus, especially Marcus. I particularly wanted to apologize to him, to be his friend again.

I was in for another unpleasant surprise when Kevin informed me that my parents were aware of my disappearance. Why had they been told? My mother and father must have been going through hell.

The fact that I had been in Progreso rather than Curiplaya was another surprise, which left me completely confused. What kind of a place was Progreso, and where was Curiplaya? If I hadn't reached Curiplaya, where had I been walking for fifteen days? Had I come close to San José? Had I stood even the slightest chance of making it? Tico answered all my questions.

Progreso was very near the Mal Paso San Pedro. It had been established ten years earlier on rumors of gold to be found in the vicinity. Miners had set out from San José, but the results had been disappointing. The camp they had built had been deserted since then, which explained the impassable state of the trail and the fact that I had encountered no signs of life on my way.

One other thing also became evident: the horrible storm I had lived through was the worst the area had suffered in a decade. Indeed, only because of the heavy rains had Tico and Kevin been able to come this far upriver; the water simply flooded a great number of obstacles that normally would have blocked their way.

The encampment was about thirty miles upstream from Curiplaya. By boat it was a short distance but could take a week to cover on foot. Tico had no explanation to offer as to why Karl had failed to mention Progreso to us. It seemed that he had intentionally lied about the location of Curiplaya.

Tico didn't believe that I could have reached San José on my own. The natives did cover that distance in a few days but only during the dry season, when streams could be crossed. During the rainy season, and with my meager provisions and equipment, it was hard to believe that I would ever have arrived in San José. That I had survived at all for so many days was cause enough for wonder.

The sun shone down on a lovely day, but it was damp in the canoe, and a chilly breeze blew against us. All along the riverbank I saw flocks of vultures swarming over the carcasses of animals, victims of the flood.

We made rapid progress, and Kevin pointed out Curiplaya as we passed. We made only one stop, to buy dried venison from some hunters. Kevin and I chewed on it all the way, and he remarked that dried meat was fabulous when you had some good beer to wash it down.

We came to the junction of the Tuichi and Beni rivers in the late afternoon. The Beni is one of the three principal tributaries of the Amazon, and the sight of it was impressive. A short while later we reached Rurrenabaque, a maze of wooden houses tucked amid the foliage. The houses closest to the river were raised up on sturdy pilings.

Tico bade us a brief goodbye near the Hotel Berlin, a wooden building with a spacious courtyard. Kevin carried me up to the hotel and set me down on a lounge in the yard. A crowd of curious townspeople gathered around me. "*El desaparecido* (the lost one)," they murmured. All of them had seen the sad-looking gringo who had come to search for his poor, lost friend. They stared at me as if they were seeing a ghost, and in truth I did look like some kind of ghost: emaciated, unshaven, dirty, and dressed in tatters.

A crowd followed us to navy headquarters. Kevin carried me into the office. I asked to telephone my parents as soon as possible, but the commandante wasn't in any hurry. He insisted upon hearing what had happened to me, and as he listened, he filled in forms with my name and passport number. He was about forty years old, pleasant looking, and kind, wearing blue work clothes, void of the formality and arrogance that characterizes many South American military men. He referred me to his unit's doctor and promised to call the Israeli embassy in La Paz in the meantime.

The doctor, a cheerful, bespectacled man, informed me that he couldn't possibly examine me until I had had a thorough scrubbing. The shower, behind a partition in the patio, wasn't really a shower at all. A conscript ran to a faucet to fill a pail with water, set the pail down next to me, lathered my body, and poured bowlfuls of water over me until the pail was empty, and then went back for another pail.

The doctor checked my blood pressure and took my pulse. He checked my hair for lice and with a pair of tweezers pulled off the remaining leeches. He said my feet were in horrible condition and gave me a cream to use. He advised that I rest and eat well and promised that I would soon be back in good health. I told him that I suffered from painful headaches, and he gave me some pills.

The doctor and the nurse who assisted him insisted that I tell them what had happened to me, and I was forced to repeat, in brief, all that I had been through. The nurse brought tea and rolls, and she and doctor listened attentively to my story. I changed the subject only once.

"Doctor," I asked, "would you mind if I ate your roll?"

They burst out laughing.

"Of course not. Bring him some more rolls," he instructed the nurse.

Kevin was waiting for me in the office of the commandante. They had notified the Israeli embassy that I had been found. I felt a lot better knowing that they would inform my parents and put their minds at peace.

We went back to the hotel. I was wearing the snow-white dress uniform of the Bolivian navy but was barefoot. In all of Rurrenabaque, in all of Bolivia, there wasn't a single pair of shoes to be found in my size, 12 1/2.

We settled into our spacious room. Kevin draped the mosquito nets that the hotel provided over our beds. We sat up all night talking, weighing various hypotheses concerning the failure of Karl and Marcus to turn up in La Paz. We couldn't wait to unmask Karl. He had taken us into the jungle, feeding us a lot of lies, conjuring up an Indian village. If Marcus hadn't insisted so stubbornly that we turn back, we certainly would have gone on and run out of food. Karl had also misled us regarding the river, his false information almost costing us our lives. And if that didn't suffice, we now knew that he was a wanted criminal as well.

But what had he wanted from us? Why had he bothered making up a cock-and-bull story about a Nazi uncle? Why had he lied about the ranch and the truck? What had been the point of it all? It hadn't been for money: he spent more than we paid him. We hoped that we would be able to get some answers once we were back in La Paz.

Afterward we grew silent, each lost in his own thoughts under our mosquito netting. Kevin dozed off, but every hour or two I would startle him out of his sleep, screaming, "Hurry, Kevin, fast!"

He knew the problem without being told and leapt up, heaved me over his shoulder, and ran for the bathroom. The enormous amounts of food that I had consumed had upset my digestive system, and I had a terrible case of diarrhea.

The weather the next day was terrible, and we knew that there would be no plane, but I wasn't disappointed. It was probably the happiest day of my life. I felt like I was in paradise: the town, the people, the general atmosphere, the lousy weather—just being alive.

I spent the morning sitting with Kevin in the hotel coffee shop. People came from all over town to see us. They had heard about us and came to offer us their best wishes and enjoy the happy ending to our story. Each one brought some small gift: cakes, candies, fruit, souvenir postcards, or a simple, warm handshake. All kinds of characters turned up: farmers, businessmen, army officers, and even a young Swiss, a mochilero like ourselves, who had drifted into Rurrenabaque and decided to settle down. He had bought a plot of land a little way up the Beni River. Every day he rowed himself up there in a small boat to till his cornfield.

We ordered cakes and coffee from the hotel restaurant for our numerous guests. The hotel owner herself scarcely left our table and never stopped talking.

Toward noon Tico passed by on his way to the river, and we joined him, poor Kevin toting me on his back. Kevin took pictures and asked one of Tico's crewmen to take one of us together with his employer.

A strange phenomenon bedeviled both Kevin and me; I had a funny-looking lump on my forehead, and Kevin had one on his throat. I was occasionally seized by a severe pain, as if someone or something were pinching at me from within. Tico noticed it and knew immediately what the trouble was.

"That's the *boro*," he said.

"What's the *boro?*" we asked, and Tico explained that it results from the bite of a mosquito whose sting deposits an egg under the skin. In time the egg hatches into a worm, and the worm begins crawling around inside the body.

"You must be joking," I said, terrified.

"No, I'm not joking. Everyone around here gets it once in a while, and it's not particularly dangerous. Let's take care of it now."

I was first. Tico sat me down on the sandy riverbank near the canoe. He and his cheerful brother, Lulo, both lit cigarettes and began blowing smoke right onto the boil-like swelling. It felt peculiar, like something really was moving around inside.

"The nicotine draws them out," Tico explained. "In just a minute you'll see."

Kevin and Lulo clenched my head, and Tico squeezed the boil between his thumbs. I bit my lip against the pain. Tico squeezed harder and . . . *plop*, the worm popped out of my forehead. Kevin looked disgusted. One more squeeze, and I, too, could see the worm, resting in the palm of Tico's hand. It was fat and white with a few black spots, and it was still alive.

Kevin was next, but he was tougher than I had been, and no one had to hold him. They again exhaled smoke onto the boil, and Tico commenced pushing and squeezing. The worm that wriggled slowly out of Kevin's neck was even larger than the one that had come out of me. It was a repulsive sight, like a long, white strip of fat. The thought that live worms had been eating away at us . . .

A few weeks later a dozen more worms were pulled from my body, this time by a doctor in São Paulo, who used a knife and a needle.

The next morning the commandante came by early to inform us that the plane to La Paz would be taking off at eleven o'clock. We packed our few belongings and said our goodbyes to the hotel owner, who refused to accept payment for the time we had spent there and charged us only half the bill that we had run up in the coffee shop. A friendly neighbor brought us a bag of mangoes. There is no more delicious fruit in the world than the mangoes of Rurrenabaque.

Tico came to say goodbye, tough as always. I couldn't find the words to express what I felt for him and promised myself that I would someday come back to visit him. An army truck took us to the airport. The terminal consisted of a single building outside town and a long, unpaved airstrip.

The terminal was crowded. Everyone who held tickets for the previous day's flight and everyone who had a ticket for today's was gathered, and since it was obvious that they couldn't all fit on one plane, a lot of arguments broke out. The next day was Christmas, and they were eager to get home to their families. When the plane made its approach, everyone started shouting and shoving. The commandante led us through the crowd to the door of the plane and bade us farewell. The pilot gestured us aboard.

"Goodbye, Commandante. Goodbye, Rurrenabaque. I'll never forget you."

In La Paz we flagged a cab for the Rosario Hotel. We couldn't wait to see Marcus. He would go out of his mind when he heard what had happened to us, and he must have a tale of his own to tell. And Karl? We were dying to confront him.

Kevin dashed into the hotel but came out just a few minutes later wearing a grave expression. Karl and Marcus hadn't arrived at the hotel yet.

"I can't believe that all flights from Apolo have been grounded because of the rain," he said. "We flew in from Rurrenabaque, and it's just as rainy there."

What the hell had happened to them? They hadn't taken a dangerous route, they had been well fitted out with a shotgun, ammunition, a knife, and a tent. What could possibly have happened?

I tottered into the Israeli embassy on my own two feet and received an emotional welcome: hugs, kisses, tears of joy. Everyone was at a loss for words.

"First of all, call home," the consul instructed me.

The secretary got a line for me, and soon I heard my father's voice.

"Dad, it's me, Yossi. I'm all right. I'm safe now."

My father's feelings came over the phone with his voice. "Don't you ever do anything like that again," he said sternly, and then my mother was on the line. She was crying. "I can't stand it any longer. I want to see you. Come home. Yossi, come right home."

"Everything's all right, Mom. I'll be home soon. There's nothing for you to worry about now."

We all calmed down a bit, and I swore that I wasn't lying.

"Honest, I'm not injured, and I'm not sick. Everything is just fine. I'm sure that you had a worse time of it than I did."

The old-folks' home was practically deserted. The consul had given Kevin permission to stay there. Grandma looked over our papers and showed us to a room.

"You don't have to go through your spiel, Grandma. I know the rules."

She obviously didn't recognize me.

A letter had arrived by express mail. It filled in my story as experienced on the other side of the ocean.

Ramat Gan
December 23

. . . The consular section of the Foreign Office notified Mom and Dad that you had been involved in an accident with a raft on a river somewhere in the jungle. They said that your American friend reported the incident to the embassy only eleven days after it had occurred, so we assumed that you had been missing for about twelve days. I tried to cheer Mom and Dad up. I know that you are an excellent swimmer and don't lose your head in an emergency. I tried to get Mom and Dad thinking that way too.

The next day we placed a phone call to the Israeli embassy in La Paz, and that was when we found out that the accident had taken place on the first of the month and that you had been missing for eighteen days. That came as a great shock to us. Dad broke down and cried incessantly. Mom decided to put up a front to help Dad keep himself together, but she would also go off by herself to cry all the time.

Ever since we got the bad news, the house has been full of people trying to keep our spirits up. Mom had been a real trooper, serving coffee and cakes. She wouldn't allow any crying or carrying on. She didn't want it to look as if we had given up hope, like we were already mourning.

I tried to hide my feelings, but every time people came over, they asked me to read your letter again, and I couldn't take it anymore and would get all choked up. It was terribly hard on Mom and Dad, on me, on the whole family, and on our friends.

The worst part of it all was feeling so helpless. We wanted to help you, to help look for you, to do something, but there was nothing we could do. Dad called friends with contacts in Bolivia. They even got in touch with the Mossad. The Israeli police commissioner personally called both Interpol and the Bolivian police.

I considered flying to La Paz to make sure the search parties kept looking and perhaps join them myself, but Dad was afraid of losing another son.

The more time passed, the more difficult it became for Mom and Dad. He lost hope, and she also began to have doubts. I believed that you were still alive, but I could imagine what kind of shape you must be in. Dad's friends said that it would be impossible for anyone to find you by searching the area, that you yourself would have to make your way back to civilization. It was almost Hanukkah, and all we could do was pray for a miracle.

The miracle happened on Monday. We got the good news on the second day of candle lighting. It was the twenty-first of December. The Israeli embassy in La Paz called at twelve thirty at night to tell us that you had been found.

Yossi, you've never seen such happiness! So much crying! Everyone was in tears, offering one toast after another. We called up half the country to let everyone know, and we've had guests all week, tons of food, drinks, and mountains of *sufganiot* [doughnuts]. Mom spent the whole day making them, hundreds of them. Dad stayed drunk for three straight days.

As I'm writing this, I am reminded of what we went through and get the shivers. But all's well that ends well, and that's the main thing.

Your brother,
Moshe

Kevin was already involved with preparations for a second search party. He was determined to go looking for traces of Karl and Marcus. This time he decided to go properly equipped: a shotgun, ammunition, suitable clothing, medicines, and people to help him. He got the five hundred dollars that Marcus had left with his friend Roger.

I was torn with indecision. I was terribly eager to go along with Kevin, but I wasn't sure that I was capable of it, especially since my feet were not entirely healed.

The consul became furious when he heard that I was even considering going back into the jungle.

"I'll shoot you myself before I'll let you do it," he said in a rage. "What's the matter with you? Have you no consideration? If you don't care about us, at least think about your parents."

Kevin gave me another good scolding and didn't want to hear about me going along. Some Israeli friends volunteered to go with him instead. I was so thin and weak that I would have been more of a burden than a help. I accompanied them to the airport, and saying goodbye was one of the most difficult things that I had ever done. We planned to meet in Brazil as soon as we could. Neither Kevin nor I had given up on completing our travels in South America.

I couldn't stop thinking about Kevin on my way back from the airport. The cab pulled out onto the highway and then wove through the maze of city streets. Passing cabs honked, and buses filled beyond capacity sped by, leaving a trail of black exhaust. The sidewalks were crowded with people: ragged beggars alongside elegantly suited men, loudmouthed vendors, and filthy street urchins. A stench rose from the sewage that ran down the gutters. A big city, overcrowded, noisy. People, thousands of them—good people, lovely people.

Tears ran down my cheeks. The cab driver noticed and gave me a worried glance. I tugged at my nose once or twice and throatily commented, *"La vida es bonita. ¿No es,* señor?*"*

"Si, señor," he agreed, "life is beautiful," though he was probably thinking, "I swear, these gringos are absolutely *locos.*"

EPILOGUE

Kevin's second rescue mission was both arduous and disappointing. Only one of the Israelis stuck with him to the end, and their two Bolivian guides often called on *them* for help.

They started out from the village of Ipurama, which had been Karl and Marcus's destination. They progressed along the Ipurama River, searching its banks for signs of them. Within a few days they had made it down to where the Ipurama flows into the Tuichi, the place where our party had split up. From there they started back, painstakingly searching both banks of the river.

They never found a single trace, any sign at all that Karl and Marcus had passed that way: no campfires, shreds of clothing, broken branches, feces, or footprints. Nothing. It was as if the two of them had vanished into the jungle air.

I later met up with Kevin in Brazil, in Salvador, the capital of Bahia. I had been cared for solicitously by my uncle in São Paulo. My feet were almost entirely healed, and the enormous quantity of steaks that I had downed had gotten my weight back up and cured my anemia. We went to Rio de Janeiro together for Carnaval. Then Kevin returned to the United States, and I went home to Israel.

A few months later I flew to Oregon, where I met Kevin's wonderful family. Then I went to visit Marcus's family in Schaffhausen, Switzerland. It was a difficult meeting. They wanted to know every detail of our trip and Marcus's disappearance. I told them the whole truth, keeping nothing back. We cried together.

As a final gesture Marcus's father held a sort of rite of absolution. He thanked me for coming to see them and for telling them all I could about their son. He ordered me to stop feeling guilty and asked me to pass that message on to Kevin too.

While it seemed that Marcus's father had given up hope, his mother, a devoted spiritualist, harbored not the slightest doubt that her younger son was alive: if he were dead, she maintained, he would have contacted her from the other side; he would have found a way to tell her goodbye. I knew what she referred to, as I remembered Marcus had told me once about the telepathic communication he'd had his entire life with his mother.

Her faith never diminished. A year later she financed a group of Seventh-day Adventists, who agreed to form a search party. They came back empty-handed, battered, and bitten.

Rainer, Marcus's brother, believed that Karl had planned for us to separate from the beginning. He suggested that Karl could have hidden food and equipment earlier at the junction of the Ipurama and Tuichi rivers, then engineered our split. Karl could have led Kevin and me to believe that he was heading up the Ipurama in the direction of the village, but in fact, gone off in the opposite direction, toward the Peruvian border. Karl had done so, in Rainer's opinion, so that it would appear as if something had happened to them, that they had perished in the jungle. Then Karl could have easily assumed a new identity.

Kevin, while still in Bolivia, met a charming Israeli girl at the old-folks' home. Orna joined him on his search for Marcus and Karl. As if that drama wasn't enough for him, Kevin was also falling in love. About a year later Kevin arrived in Israel for a re-union with Orna, and soon after they married. They live happily near Tel Aviv with their two beautiful sons, Eyal and Yuval. Kevin and I are close friends to this very day. I love him like my brother. I owe him my life, for which I will be eternally indebted to him. I admire him for the person he is, a giant of a man. Karl used to call him "strong like three men," referring not only to his body, but also his special spirit. Kevin will always be a role model for me, for he is one of those rare people of continuously high morals; he never hesitated when immediate decisions or action were needed. Kevin, from the bottom of my heart, thank you, my brother, my friend, forever.

Six years after coming back from Tuichi, I was contacted by an Israeli magazine with an offer to write several articles about South America. This was my first opportunity to return to Rurrenabaque. I found that it had changed. The town was bigger, busier. Settlers from the altiplano had flocked there by the thousands. Convoys of trucks, arriving empty, left creaking under loads of mahogany. Saloons had materialized and with them loud music and the stench of urine.

Tico seemed happy to see me and delighted to take me up the Tuichi in his motorboat. The river was as magnificent and wild as before. We set out for San José, still the only settlement on the river, and continued to Progreso, where I had been rescued. It was a less emotional journey than I had expected. In fact, I was surprised how much I enjoyed myself. There was no animosity between me and the rainforest. On the contrary, I felt a strong attraction and was determined to make the jungle a part of my life.

Back in Rurrenabaque I was introduced to an old Hungarian, a refugee from World War II, and though he was drunk when we met, I found what he told beyond compelling. He began by claiming to know Karl well. He hadn't seen him for some time, but just a few months earlier in Cochabamba a Swiss priest had mentioned that Karl had visited not long before.

Excited, I flew to Cochabamba and found the priest, Father Erich, at a mission just outside town. Both he and Sister Ingrid, a nun who also lived at the mission, confirmed that Karl was alive, living nearby in the town of Santa Cruz. They showed me a photo they said was recent and told me stories of troubles he had caused them. I left bewildered: I wanted to believe, and I didn't want to believe. In no time I was in Santa Cruz and spent a week doing the best detective work I could but found not a single bit of corroborating evidence.

I had maintained contact with Marcus's mother and knew that she had never accepted her son's death. About two years after my return from Rurrenabaque I flew at her request to Schaffhausen to meet with her. She insisted that she had new information to share, information, it turned out, she had received from a clairvoyant renowned for his success in finding lost relatives.

"Marcus is still alive," she told me. "That is certain. He lives in Peru on a high plateau with Indians who found him nearly dead and nursed him back to health. He has lost his memory, which prevents his coming home." On a map of Peru she had marked a remote Andean community. She gave me the map and asked me to go there to look for him. I agreed.

Cuzco, the ancient Inca capital, is one of my favorite South American cities. I have a friend there, José Ugarte, who happens to be a mountain guide. Looking at the map together, we determined one thing was sure: the clairvoyant couldn't have picked a better spot. Huanacaran was one of the most dangerous places on the continent, a zone controlled by Shining Path guerrillas. The night before our departure my friend came to my hotel room and, with his eyes fixed on the tile floor, told me he couldn't go. I didn't blame him, though it was too late to find another guide.

I remember that night so clearly. Marcus's mother had made just one request before I left: have faith in her conviction. But I lacked her confidence. The story she told was too far-fetched. That night in Cuzco, however, I knew I had to believe as she did, otherwise it was better not to go. I thought of Marcus, and suddenly I was back in the jungle, where one discovers the darkness in one's heart. How frightening that can be. *Marcus, your mother can still hear your heartbeat; she can hear your voice singing. Wherever you are, I am coming to take you home, my brother. You know you'll always live in my heart. Wait for me there, Marcus, I am walking toward you.*

There were three of us at the train station: a cook who spoke Quechua, a helper from Lima too broke to say no, and me. The journey was full of surprises. At the first station José Ugarte appeared. He had spent a sleepless night, repenting his decision not to go. Farther down the line, representatives of the military climbed aboard. They briefly checked our documents and destination, then trouble started. The cook was dragged away in handcuffs. At the point of submachine guns the rest of us were taken off the train for interrogation. A gringo escorted by a suspicious-looking little band, well equipped for mountain survival, claiming to be looking for a friend lost years ago in Bolivia! They weren't buying that. But I guess the calls they made to the contacts I gave them convinced them of my story, since they let us go and even provided a letter of introduction to the mayor of Azángaro, near our destination.

We reached Azángaro and found the station all but deserted. Once a prosperous city, Azángaro had been largely abandoned. Suspicion clouded the faces of those who remained. We couldn't help but laugh at the derelict municipal palace, where we went to present our letter and seek the mayor's assistance. No guards, no staff, an empty antechamber leading to a short, echoing hallway. We knocked and opened the door of the mayor's office, and the man lost not a second jumping out the window at the sight of us. The night before, three officials had been murdered in Asilio, less than fifty miles away. So much for assistance.

We couldn't find a driver who would carry us to our destination but caught a bus that still made the run partway. José didn't know the region, but he knew mountains. The second day we reached the point marked on our map. Its pastoral tranquillity belied the terror of the Azángaro locals. Marcus could have lived there, but he never had. No one recognized the man in the photo that I carried. Ultimately we traveled through ten similar communities. Never had a gringo lived in any of them.

Back in Azángaro I sought out the local priest, who ministers to all sixty-eight communities in the province of Azángaro. He had never encountered a foreigner in residence nor heard of hermits living alone in the mountains.

Karl and Marcus's disappearance remains a mystery. It is difficult to imagine what could have become of them. Karl was tough and strong and knew how to take care of himself in the jungle. He could have survived even without food and equipment. He had had a shotgun, which made it almost unthinkable that they had fallen prey to jaguars or wild boars. The village of Ipurama was only four days' walk from the point where they'd set out. Kevin had been back and forth over the route without finding a trace of them. What had become of them?

I can think of two possibilities. One is that Karl might have been seriously injured, perhaps in a fall. Marcus, who had been ill, thin, and downhearted, would never have made it out of the jungle on his own. The other possibility is falling trees. On rainy nights, as I had seen, trees uproot themselves and topple over, taking other trees with them. A tree could have fallen on their campsite, crushing them as they slept. To this day the mystery remains . . .

The rainforest has ever since been a major part of my life. While visiting San José on the Tuichi River, I found out that the situation in the village was desperate; the small, isolated community was struggling for survival, forced to destroy their ancestral lands with their own hands. They had no options for income other than slash-and-burn agriculture, hunting, or working as cheap labor for the loggers and miners, who are in the process of overtaking the region. I met with the community leaders and heard their fears about the steady elimination of the rainforest villages, since the youth are lacking employment and thus forced to leave for the big city. So together, we initiated the Chalalan Project.

The Chalalan valley lies not far from the Tuichi banks, about an hour downriver from San José. It is the most amazing rainforest scenery I've ever seen in my life: monkeys hanging from palm trees and a lake surrounded by precious, undisturbed hills. The beauty of the place makes one's heart sing. So we obtained from the government an official concession of this land to the local indigenous people, and the community of San José declared it a protected area for conservation of nature and development of alternative economic routes for the forest dwellers. A group of volunteers, together with the indigenous community, worked with scientists and designers and engineers to build an "eco-village." Our goal was to prove that the forest could provide its inhabitants with all their needs and even make them prosper, if only it were treated with respect and that the sustainable use of renewable resources would be far more lucrative than the destructive exploitation of the nonrenewable resources.

In July 1998, the Chalalan project finally became reality. It was officially inaugurated as one of the most celebrated ecotourism locations in the entire Amazon. I passionately invested all my faculties and facilities in Chalalan and completely immersed myself in the project.

It was the involvement of the Inter-American Development Bank and Conservation International, both out of Washington

D.C., which made it possible. The bank granted us an amazing one and a quarter million U.S. dollars, and Conservation International agreed to take on the execution and provide their technical expertise and much-needed ongoing supervision.

Through my humble role in this project, I had the opportunity to experience moments of grace in the mightiest of all forests. I shared unforgettable times with exceptional people, some of whom became the best of friends. I served a purpose that was bigger than I, and together with a few others, I made a small difference. I feel fortunate, blessed, and grateful for that experience.

The nomadic life that I had adopted kept me constantly on the move. For a while, I settled in California until I was approached by an international company that was implementing a new technology they had developed for curing opiate addiction. They recruited me to help expand their role in the international marketplace. So I had to become an expert in a new, exciting field, learning everything I could about addictions to heroin and methadone.

Through my work I met thousands of people who were living in hell and desperate for help. I named my vocation "the field of agony." Like an emissary I kept traveling the world lecturing about opiate dependency. I helped in establishing seven treatment centers, moving from Mexico to Europe and back to the United States. I worked in Thailand and China, finally settling in Australia, where I established my own clinic of treatment and research of addiction. In Australia I also initiated the Alma Libre Foundation, which promotes abstinence-based treatment for opiate-dependent individuals and invites society as a whole to revisit the unjust prejudice and discrimination toward thousands of people suffering from a disease that is a sign of our times.

In the last few years I have changed my work and moved to "the field of joy," working in the capacity of inspirational keynote speaker and seminar leader. I have also developed a training program called The Manifestation of Vision.

I speak mainly in corporate environments, traveling the world as a guest of companies and organizations to support their conferences with an opening or closing keynote presentation. This has been an amazing personal growth opportunity for me, for I am challenged to keep a tight tension between my talk and my walk.

Having lived a rich life since my adventure in the Amazon, I feel it is time to share my experiences and insights in a humble effort to contribute to the spread of harmony on this planet. The release of my upcoming books, *Laws of the Jungle* and *Glimpses*, will mark the beginning of this new endeavor.

I now live with my family in the depths of the Australian rainforest where I am surrounded by the purity and lushness of the natural world. The remoteness from civilization, complete immersion in natural surroundings, breathtaking mountains covered with forest, fresh water springs, and rich flora and fauna inspire me every moment I am there. I feel part of it; moreover, when I step out of my house at night I clearly discern that I am standing on a living planet, turning and moving in its course under the brilliance of the Milky Way. I realize just by looking up to the sky that I am part of something infinite, and I feel infinitely grateful for life.

UNCHARTED DOMAINS

Since my experience in the jungle, I've discovered that sometimes the extraordinary can be seen by the naked eye, allowing a quick glimpse into the miraculous. Not that the hand behind the veil is sloppy in any way, but due to urgencies and circumstances, the work of miracles is sometimes exposed. When this happens, the world as we thought we knew it ceases to exist; it is uncharted from that point forward. Overwhelmed and puzzled, the mind rushes in like a fool, desperately trying to make sense of it all. But how can we understand what cannot be grasped by the senses?

I lived through my jungle adventure at a young age many years ago. And though I had encountered the forces of creation, felt the hand of providence caressing my skin, and seen the work of miracles, I was too young to comprehend it all.

And when we cannot fully understand the significance of something, when we cannot validate the total experience with the senses—can't see, can't taste, can't smell, can't touch, can't hear, and cannot conceive—we are left with a choice: to deny or to believe.

I have experienced miracles firsthand, and tried time and again to use reasonable explanations to deny or believe until my mind tired. Now, no explanations are needed. I do not deny and I do not believe; I simply know miracles to be part of the world I live in.

There's an old myth about a young king lost in a forest for days. He finally finds a camp, but to his dismay, it is deserted. In the remains of a campfire, on the shimmering coals, he finds a piece of salmon. Famished, he quickly shoves it in his mouth only to find that it is scalding hot. He burns himself so badly, in fact, that he is too wounded to live—but not wounded enough to die. He becomes the Fisher King, and, tortured, he awaits redemption in his castle.

The legend continues and tells about a young knight who ventures out into the world aspiring to be its savior. He rides like all other knights: to defend good values while searching for the king and his castle. But this young knight is particularly naive—in fact, most think he is a fool. On his first venture he finds the Fisher King, but young and innocent as the knight is, he fails to bring redemption or an end to suffering. Instead, his visit brings only heartbreak and strife; he is simply too young to carry such responsibility. Now innocence is lost, and the young knight is back on his horse searching for the king and his castle and defending good values. It takes decades for the castle to appear again, but by then he is mature and ready.

I have identified myself as a dreamer fool just like the knight in the legend. If you are just a dreamer without being a fool, you will never leave home and risk losing everything you own—your assets, your ideals, your image. And what if it is all in vain and there is nothing to find? Only the fool can take such risk. I was that fool, for the dream was bigger than everything I risked. And I've lost it all time and again, and through those experiences, I have found what I truly own, for all that can be taken from me is not mine to begin with. I have found home now; there is no longer a need to search.

May you find the courage to walk your own path. May you dare to venture into the uncharted domains of your own heart. Here is my advice to you, the adventurers—fear will show you the way; walk steadily toward it, for otherwise you will always be running. Have trust and faith to guide you like a torch piercing darkness. Do not believe and do not deny, but find out for yourself—for there is no truth but the one you have earned in your own experience.

Quandong
Mount Jerusalem National Park
2005